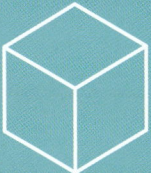

ART

ROB COLSON

First published in Great Britain
in 2020 by Wayland
Copyright © Hodder and Stoughton, 2020
All rights reserved

Series editor: Amy Pimperton
Produced by Tall Tree Ltd
Editor: Lara Murphy
Designer: Gary Hyde

HB ISBN: 978 1 5263 1304 1
PB ISBN: 978 1 5263 1305 8

Wayland
An imprint of Hachette Children's Group
Part of Hodder and Stoughton
Carmelite House
50 Victoria Embankment
London EC4Y 0DZ

An Hachette UK Company
www.hachette.co.uk
www.hachettechildrens.co.uk

Printed and bound in China

Picture Credits

FSC
www.fsc.org

MIX
Paper from
responsible sources
FSC® C104740

Contents

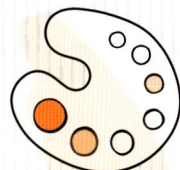

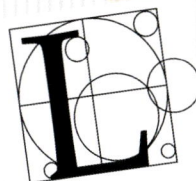

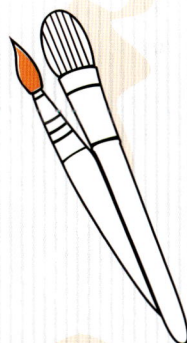

Top art jobs

Is art your favourite subject at school? Do you spend your free time doodling designs? You can put that creativity to use in a wide range of exciting jobs, creating stylish looks for the world we live in. You might become a designer, making the clothes we wear, the furniture we use or the posters we see. Or you might use your art skills to create animated films or TV shows. Artists make their mark in lots of different ways.

ANCIENT ARTISTS

As an artist, you are doing something that people have done for tens of thousands of years. Ancient designers created clothing and jewellery from materials they found around them – brightly coloured stones or the skins of the animals they hunted. Ancient painters created images of animals and people on cave walls. Art brings pleasure to people's lives, and with today's technology, there are more ways for us to express ourselves than ever before.

.... Ancient artists used natural materials, such as soot, to create cave paintings.

PRACTICAL SKILLS

Making art requires lots of practical skills. Today, many artists and designers work mostly on computers, while others use traditional skills, such as carpentry or glassmaking, to craft objects. You'll need to pay close attention to the details and put in hours of practice to perfect your skills. You will also need knowledge from other STEAM subjects to create your art, such as maths and science.

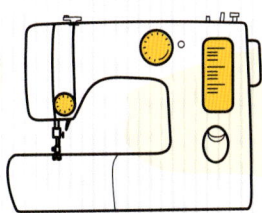

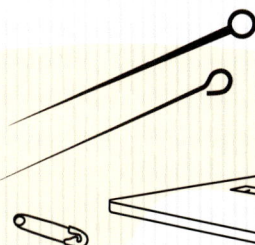

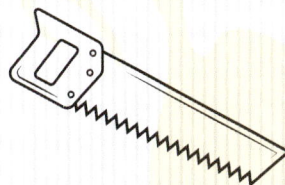

ART COLLEGE

Often, the first step to a career in the visual arts is a degree at art college. You'll get to try your hand at lots of different kinds of art, from painting and sculpture to film-making and graphic design. You will also learn the theory and history of art and design and study subjects such as colour theory – how to combine colours to best effect. At the end of your course, you get to display your work to the public at a degree show.

Animator

Are you a big fan of comic books and storytelling? Animators tell stories with moving pictures. They create animations and visual effects for everything from film and TV to video games and mobile phone apps. You will work closely with writers, directors and actors to develop characters and storylines that bring your ideas to life.

STORYBOARDS

Storyboard artists work with directors to turn the words in a script into images. A storyboard is a series of comic-strip images that tell a visual story. Once finished, the artist presents the storyboard to a creative team and talks them through each image. This is the stage where any problems with the script can be fixed before the film or game is made. Storyboard artists also play an important role in developing the final look and feel of the animation.

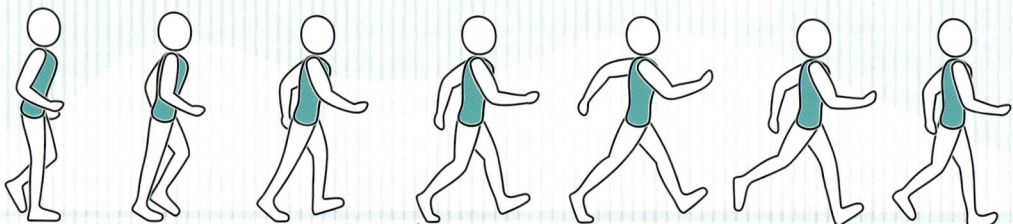

Japanese animator and director Hayao Miyazaki has made a series of award-winning animated feature films, including the Oscar-winning *Spirited Away*, about a young girl who enters a world of ghosts to free her parents from a wicked witch. Miyazaki uses a mix of hand-drawn images and computer animation to create a rich visual style for his films, which are often set in fantasy worlds.

3D MODELLING

Most animation today is made using computers. 3D modellers create animated creatures that look solid. Often these creatures will interact with live actors in the finished film. To bring your creatures to life, you'll need a great understanding of biomechanics – the study of the way bodies move. Often 3D modellers copy the actions of real creatures to make their creations more believable and sometimes as scary as possible!

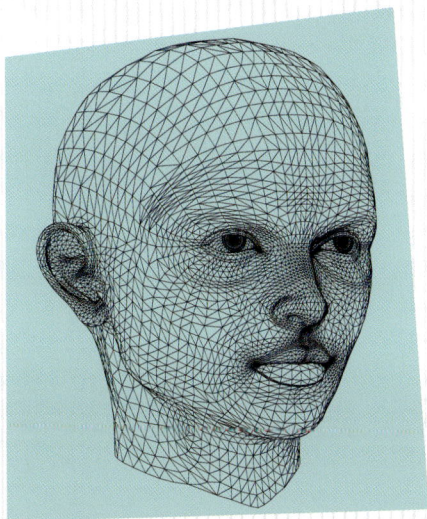

↑
.... A 3D computer model of a human head

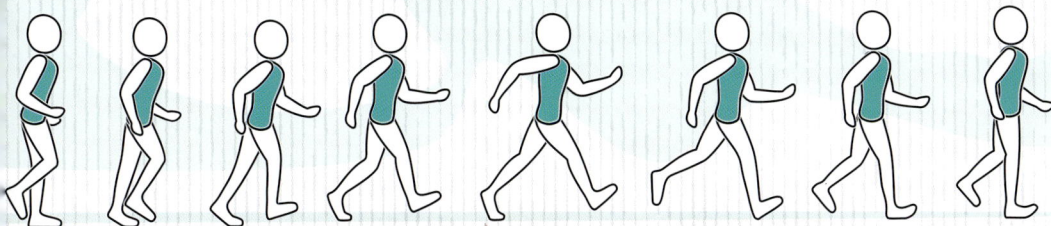

Set designer

Do you enjoy working with your hands and making things? Set designers plan and build the sets for film, TV and the theatre. Working closely with the director, the set designer is responsible for creating the look and atmosphere of the production. You'll need to be highly imaginative to come up with exciting solutions on a tight budget and be prepared to work to tight deadlines.

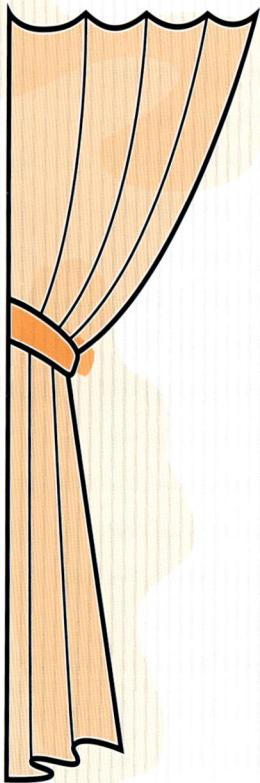

THEATRE SETS

Theatre designers are in charge of the sets and costumes for plays and musicals. Each play may need very different sets, for example creating the impression of an intimate room or a vast landscape on stage. Designers produce drawings and models of their ideas before making the full-sized set. They also need to be on hand during rehearsals for any changes that the director wants to make.

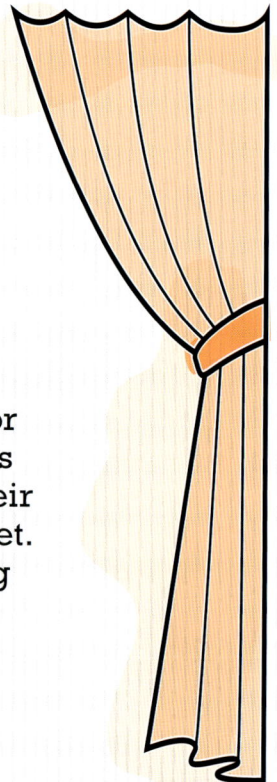

HEIDI ETTINGER
(1951–)

American theatre designer Heidi Ettinger made her name designing the sets for a series of hit shows on Broadway in New York. Ettinger is known for creating sets in many different styles, including an award-winning design for *Big River*, a musical based on the Mark Twain novel *Adventures of Huckleberry Finn*.

SCENIC ARTIST

Scenic artists put the painting and sculpture skills that they learned in art college to use by building the props for sets. One week you may be painting an abstract landscape to go at the back of a theatre set. The next week, you may be building a realistic landscape in an animal enclosure for a zoo! Scenic artists need to be practical and flexible to help their clients to realise their visions.

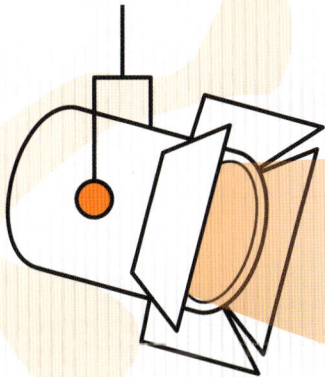

Special effects artist

Do you spend hours designing ghoulish outfits and make-up for Halloween? You might love creating special effects for films. Working on set doing specialist make-up on actors, or on computer screens long after a film has been shot, special effects artists let their creativity run wild to create weird and wonderful scenes.

COMPUTER EFFECTS

For today's big-budget films, artists create most of the special effects using computer-generated imagery (CGI). These are effects, such as explosions, that are added to the film after it has been shot. In many films, the action is shot in front of blank green screens and the background is added later using CGI. Artists working in CGI combine great computer and technical skills with flair and imagination.

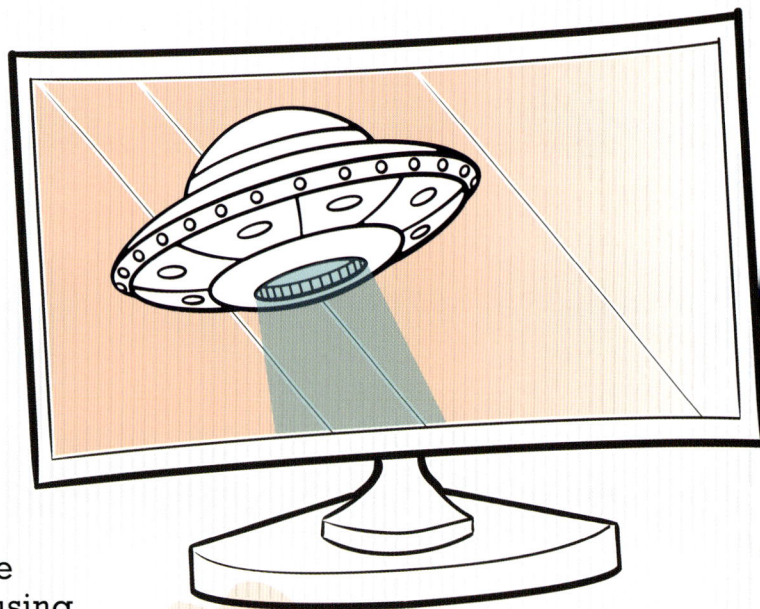

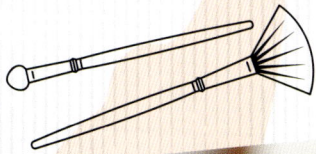

PROSTHETIC MAKE-UP

Make-up artists transform actors into a variety of monsters using prosthetics. These are masks or artificial body parts that have been sculpted out of materials such as latex. Prosthetic make-up can turn an actor into anything from an ape to a zombie. In modern films, prosthetic make-up is often combined with CGI to create truly outlandish fiends.

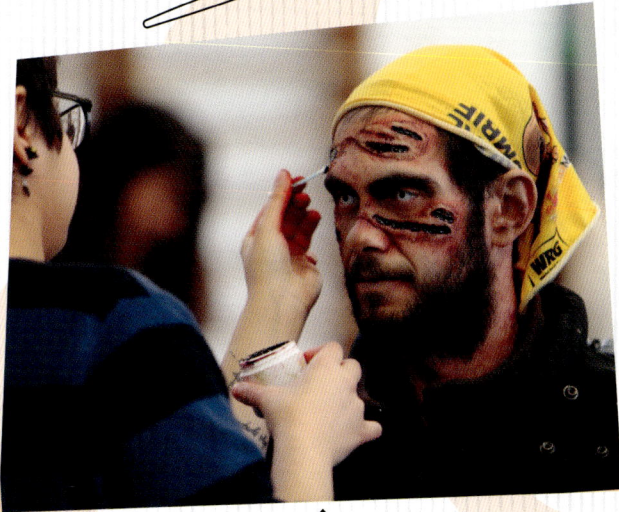

A make-up artist reapplies make-up to an actor on set.

STEAM STAR: RICK BAKER
(1950–)

American make-up artist Rick Baker made gory effects for horror and sci-fi films, such as *Men in Black* and *Planet of the Apes*. He specialised in using prosthetic make-up to create ghouls, memorably turning pop star Michael Jackson into a werewolf for the music video *Thriller*. In a 50-year career, Baker won a record seven Best Make-up Oscars before retiring in 2017.

11

Behind the scenes:
Film set

On set, a team of artists and craftspeople form a film's art department, which is responsible for creating the fictional worlds the films are set in. These might be magical fantasy worlds or accurate reconstructions of historical settings. On big-budget productions, an art department may employ hundreds of people, working in a wide variety of roles.

ART DIRECTOR

Art directors are in overall charge of the art department. They are project managers, liaising with directors and production designers during filming, who in turn will instruct their teams. Art directors need to make sure that the right teams are in place and that they are doing exactly what the director wants them to do – mistakes cause delays, and delays in filming can cost thousands of pounds a day.

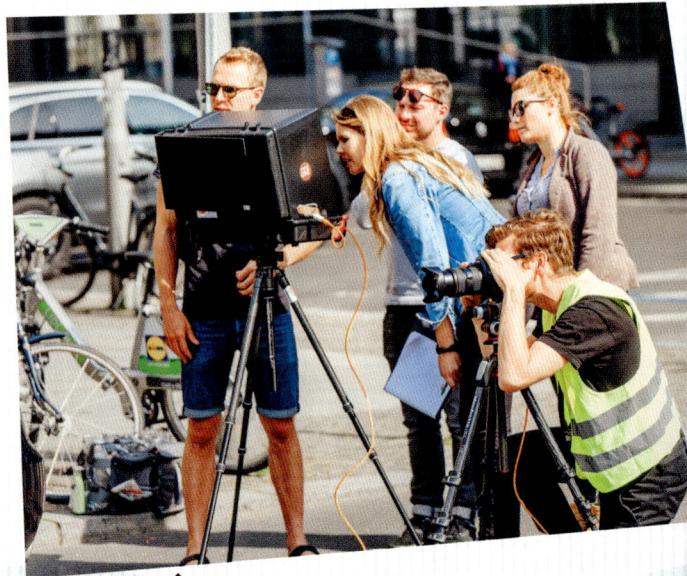

Film crews can include a large number of people.

BUILDING SETS

Construction crews are responsible for building sets. They include scenic artists and prop-makers, working alongside carpenters, electricians, plasterers and painters. The construction crews work closely with the camera and lighting crews to achieve the right overall atmosphere for the film – for instance, the director may have asked for a dark, menacing street or a colourful landscape.

LOCATIONS AND PROPS

As well as building sets, members of the art department need to check out locations for filming. These might be grand mansions, city streets or remote mountains. The team needs to negotiate a price and permission to film. Production buyers source props for the films, scouring shops and markets for just the right pieces. Anything that can't be bought will need to be made from scratch. Artists in the art department provide craftspeople with detailed instructions and drawings to guide them in making each prop.

The set of a *Star Wars* film in Tunisia

Interior designer

Do you insist on having the decor in your bedroom exactly how you want it? Interior designers have strong opinions on how rooms look. They model rooms and other indoor spaces, including private houses, workplaces and public spaces. They decide on colour schemes, furniture and lighting. You'll need a flair for colour combinations and to know how to get the most out of any space.

HEALTHY SPACES

Large companies employ interior designers to create happy and productive workplaces. Having technical know-how in other areas, such as building regulations, psychology and ergonomics – the study of how people work – would be a real advantage. The goal is to produce beautiful, healthy, eco-friendly environments for people to work in, and to do it all within a strict budget!

EXHIBITION SPACES

As well as shaping living and working environments, interior designers are employed by museums and galleries to design exhibition spaces. They arrange the exhibits to give visitors a pleasurable and easy path around the space. Interior designers work closely with curators and researchers to understand the needs of an exhibition, sketching out their ideas before putting them in place.

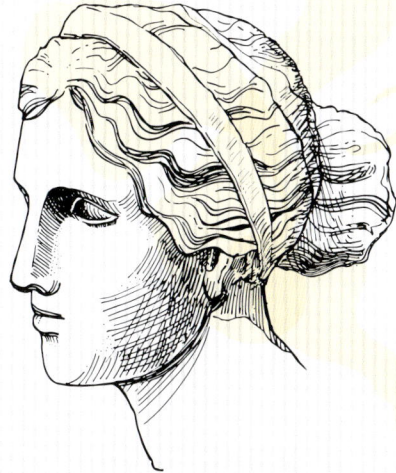

STEAM STAR: PHILIPPE STARCK
(1949–)

French designer Philippe Starck has worked in a wide range of design fields, including furniture, product and interior design. He has designed the interiors of world-renowned hotels, exclusive restaurants and even luxury yachts. However, Starck does not just design for the rich and famous. He has created ranges of stylish low-cost furniture and developed affordable wooden eco-houses that consume just one third of the energy of a traditional house.

Stylist

Do you love flicking through glossy magazines or browsing them online? The food, clothes and other products in the photos have all been made to look their very best by a stylist. As a stylist, it is your job to choose the items to be featured, selecting objects that show off the latest trends. You'll be out on photo shoots for much of the day, coordinating with the photographer to create images for the magazine.

CLOTHES STYLIST

Do you have a passion for clothes? Fashion stylists coordinate outfits from a selection of clothing and accessories. They may dress mannequins for shop displays or coordinate photo shoots for fashion magazines. A fashion stylist can also help individual customers to select the clothes that suit their body shape. Celebrity stylists choose the outfits for famous actors to wear to film premieres or TV appearances.

STEAM STAR: CHERYL KONTEH

British stylist Cheryl Konteh started her career at a national newspaper magazine, but soon moved on to more glamorous work. She discovered that she had a flair for fashion and now she travels the world styling the looks of famous actors. Today, Konteh dresses some of the biggest names in Hollywood, including Idris Elba, Kate Winslet and Brad Pitt. The next time you watch the Oscars on TV, you will see a host of stars who have been dressed by Cheryl Konteh.

..... Film star Kate Winslet wears an outfit styled by Konteh.

STYLING FOOD

Food stylists create appealing displays of food for magazines and cookbooks that make you want to lick the page! As a food stylist, you need to love to cook – everything from pizza to patisserie. As well as following the recipes perfectly, you need to arrange all the ingredients on the plate to make them look their best. Food stylists have a few sneaky tricks up their sleeve, such as using sprays and glazes to make the food look vibrant and appetising.

Fashion designer

Do you go into clothes shops to check out the fabrics and construction of eye-catching designs? You could turn your obsession into a career in fashion design. With an eye for colour and shape, you will also need hands-on practical skills, such as pattern-cutting and sewing, to turn sketches on a page into the finished garment. One day, people on the high street could be trying on your designs.

HAUTE COUTURE

Haute couture (which is French for 'high fashion') is the cutting edge of the fashion industry. Top designers make haute couture clothes for a very exclusive clients, designing individual items to fit the client's body perfectly. Every piece is made by hand, using only the finest materials. Fashion houses present haute couture collections at fashion shows. The clothes are often daring and unusual and create trends that are later followed by high street clothing companies.

OZWALD BOATENG
(1967–)

British fashion designer Ozwald Boateng is famed for making sharp, stylish suits for men. Working from his London base, Boateng and a team of skilled tailors create made-to-measure suits cut from scratch. Boateng has broken many boundaries in the fashion industry, bringing haute couture glamour into traditional menswear. In 1994, he made history as the first men's tailor to present a catwalk show at Paris Fashion Week.

HIGH STREET DESIGN

Teams of fashion designers develop ready-to-wear clothing ranges for high street and online shops. Often inspired by haute couture designs, the teams take the design process from the initial ideas right through to mass production. They need to keep a close eye on the latest trends and they also need to work to very tight deadlines – every new season demands a fresh new range of clothes.

Photographer

Are you always taking photographs with your phone? Do you have a great eye for the right shot? There are lots of ways you can turn a passion for photography into a career. You could work in fashion, sports, wildlife or portrait photography, or photojournalism. Photographers normally specialise in one or two fields of photography and become experts at capturing the best images.

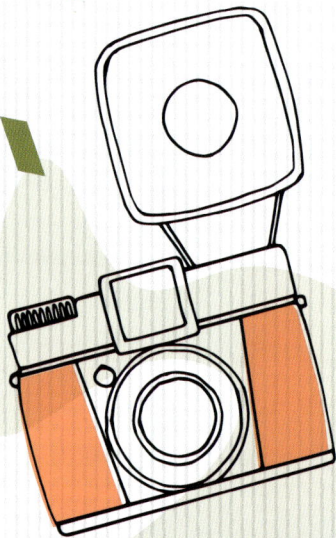

ON THE STREET

Urban photographers specialise in taking images of life in towns and cities. They may record gritty scenes of urban decay or poverty as part of a project, or take images of everyday events, but from different and interesting angles. Whatever they do choose to show, they need to be highly skilled photographers and ready at a moment's notice, as the perfect picture can appear (and disappear!) in a heartbeat.

WILDLIFE PHOTOGRAPHY

Wildlife photographers take photos of creatures in their natural habitats. They are intrepid explorers and often undertake arduous journeys to dangerous places. Photographers use all kinds of technology to capture the secret lives of animals, including hidden cameras that are triggered when an animal walks by. You'll need patience for this job. Wildlife photographers may wait for weeks or even months to capture a single image, such as the moment a bear emerges from her den with her cubs.

Photographing a hummingbird in flight takes skill and patience.

STEAM STAR: DOROTHEA LANGE
(1895–1965)

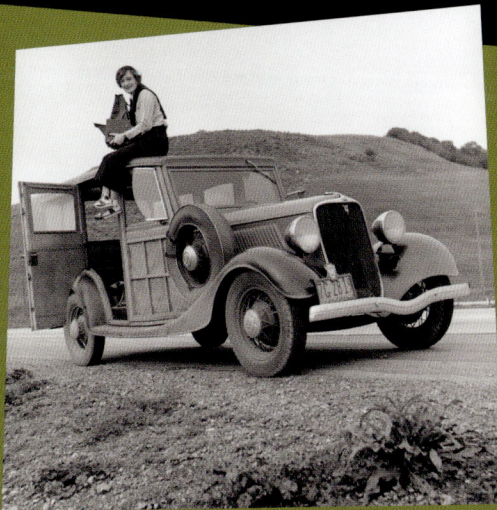

Photojournalists tell stories with pictures. American photographer Dorothea Lange documented the struggles of the poor and disadvantaged in the US. She photographed migrant workers during the Great Depression of the 1930s. Later she made a record of the lives of Japanese-American families who were held in prison in the US during the Second World War (1939–1945). Lange's photographs have since become some of the most recognisable images of that era.

Dorothea Lange on location in 1936

Behind the scenes:
Fashion shoot

A fashion shoot involves a team of creative people. In addition to the photographer and the models, a stylist (see pages 16–17) looks after the clothes and makes sure they are being worn properly, while hairdressers and make-up artists are on hand throughout the day to ensure the models look their best. A fashion shoot can happen anywhere! It might take place in a studio or on location in streets, parks or historic buildings.

IN THE STUDIO

The photographer can control every aspect of the shoot when it is in a studio. Models stand in front of powerful lights that have filters to change the mood, while special effects, such as dry ice, can be introduced to the shoot to create different atmospheres. The photographer will take shots from all kinds of angles as the model adopts a variety of poses.

A model and a photographer at a fashion shoot in a studio setting

ON LOCATION

On location, the photographer has to rely on natural light and has much less control of the environment. This leaves lots of room for the unexpected to happen. Some of the best shots can be the result of a total accident, such as a gust of wind blowing the model's hair out at a dramatic angle.

Location shoots can involve the photographer working on their own or as part of a bigger team of stylists and assistants.

AFTER THE SHOOT

While the models and stylists have finished their work at the end of the shoot, the photographer still has plenty more to do. Together with a production director, they select the best images from hundreds or even thousands of different shots. They then work on the images they have selected on a computer, using a photo editing program. The colour balance and contrast of the images are adjusted, while small imperfections in the clothing or background can be smoothed over.

A photographer digitally edits a photograph.

Landscape architect

Do you love helping out in the garden, digging the soil and planting seeds? Landscape architects design green spaces for plants and wildlife that make towns and cities better places in which to live. Working on public parks, housing developments or wildlife conservation areas, you'll be protecting the environment and improving people's lives.

IMPROVING CITIES

New developments in urban areas need to be eco-friendly. This means that they must have clean air and keep energy use to a minimum. Landscape architects work with town planners to create housing estates that provide every resident with access to green spaces. These include places for the community to come together and recycle their waste, such as city farms that turn food leftovers into compost for crops.

Modern cities combine built-up areas with open spaces.

ANDRÉ LE NÔTRE
(1613–1700)

French landscape architect André Le Nôtre was the head gardener for King Louis XIV (1638–1715). His best-known creation is the garden at the Palace of Versailles, just outside Paris. Covering 8 square km of land, it is a stunning example of a French formal garden, featuring sharp geometric shapes and precisely trimmed hedges. Today, Le Nôtre's garden is one of the most popular tourist destinations in France, attracting more than 6 million visitors every year.

▲ ... A portrait of famed landscape architect, André Le Nôtre

SHOW GARDENS

Each year, some of the best landscape architects in the world are invited to create a show garden for the Chelsea Flower Show in London, UK. The gardens might include fountains, wooden structures or sculptures. One year, an entrant even built a working water wheel! Central to every garden is the stunning selection of plants and flowers. The show gardens are judged by a panel of experts and one garden is declared 'Best in Show'.

A plant wall ....▲ at the Chelsea Flower Show in London, UK

Jewellery designer

Do you love making accessories? Jewellery designers come up with new designs and many make their own pieces in a workshop. You'll need lots of practical skills to work with precious stones and metals and you'll need an eye for detail. To be a great jewellery designer, you need to be a perfectionist!

CREATING THE DESIGN

Designers often come up with their initial designs in a sketchbook, but the best way to sell your ideas is to show them in 3D. When making jewellery for mass production, designers create images of the designs on a computer, using software that can rotate the design to any angle. Some designers create one-off pieces or collections that they sell themselves. Displaying your work in public is a great way to promote yourself – a successful show can lead to lots of new commissions.

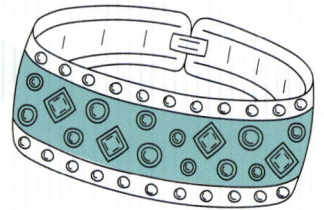

MAKING THE PIECE

Creating a fine piece of jewellery, such as a diamond ring, takes a lot of work. The first stage is called mounting. This involves shaping a precious metal, such as gold or silver, to create the ring, adding the section that secures the stone and any decorative patterns. Next, the diamond needs to be set in place. This involves very intricate work, such as removing tiny slithers of metal. Finally, the whole piece is polished to make it look its best and any letters or inscriptions on the inside of the ring are engraved by hand.

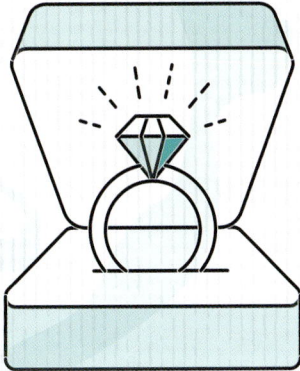

STEAM STAR: KIM POOR
(1952–)

Brazilian artist Kim Poor creates a wide range of artistic work, including paintings, sculptures and jewellery. Much of her work is inspired by the people and animals of the Amazon Rainforest. Poor makes individually sculpted rings, necklaces and brooches. Each piece features an intricate design, often incorporating mythological creatures, such as a winged angel. The design is created by hand using a technique called chasing.

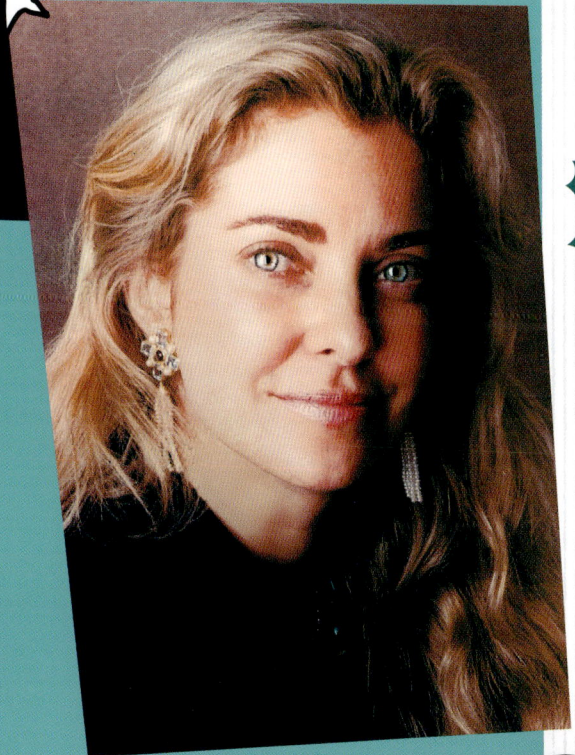

Product designer

If you look around a room, most of the things you see, from your chair to the light you are reading with, had to be designed. Product designers combine design skills with technical knowledge to create products that look good and perform their function superbly. These might be furniture, new ranges of cutlery or specialist medical or electronics equipment.

FURNITURE DESIGNER

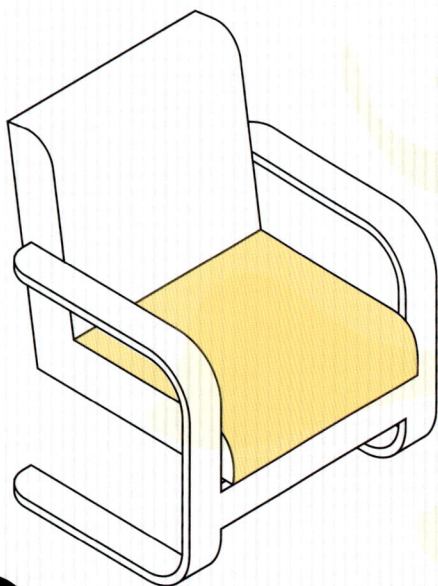

Furniture designers create new designs for mass-produced items, furniture made in small quantities or one-off pieces. Designers take their ideas from an initial sketch to make test models before their designs go into production. As well as design skills, you'll need lots of technical know-how about how furniture is made and the qualities of different materials. Many furniture designers start their careers as apprentices, learning the craft of furniture-making before they turn their hand to design.

ERWAN (1976–) AND RONAN (1971–) BOUROULLEC

French brothers Erwan (left) and Ronan Bouroullec (right) have won multiple awards for their elegant modern furniture. They often incorporate surprising shapes into their designs, which include wavy-edged interlocking ceramic vases and a table with a bowl moulded into it. By doing this, the Bouroullecs hope to encourage their customers to think creatively, finding new uses for their furniture that the designers hadn't thought of. In addition to furniture, the brothers are also noted for their minimalist lighting designs.

INDUSTRIAL DESIGNER

Industrial designers work on products that are mass-produced in factories. In addition to designing the item, an industrial designer must come up with a production process that is cost-effective. One of today's biggest challenges involves creating green production processes that reduce waste and energy use and employ more sustainable materials. In this way, industrial design provides a link between science and creativity.

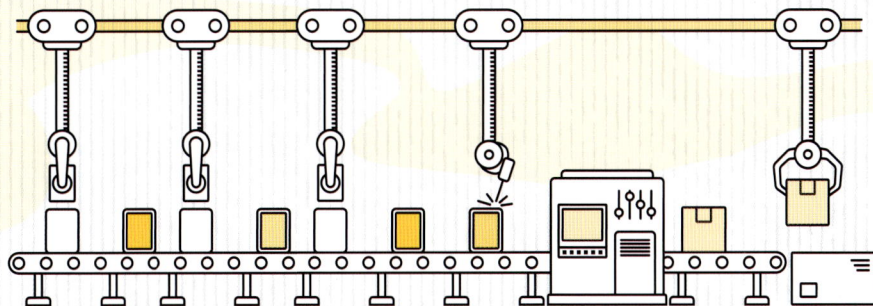

Behind the scenes:
Herman Miller

US manufacturer Herman Miller makes furniture for offices and the home. The company is known for its innovative, stylish ranges that have changed the way people work by rearranging office spaces. Herman Miller's factory has manufactured the designs of many famous furniture designers.

DESIGN CLASSIC

Herman Miller's best-selling piece of furniture is an office chair called the Aeron Chair, which was first made in 1992. The fully adjustable revolving chair is made from recycled materials and can be recycled itself when it reaches the end of its life. The company makes more than 1 million Aeron Chairs each year in its factory, which can put together a whole chair in just 21 seconds!

The Aeron Chair ....

TESTED TO DESTRUCTION

In a special testing laboratory, Herman Miller put their furniture through a rigorous set of tests to ensure it is worthy of the company's 12-year guarantee. An office chair might receive up to 1 million different movements to test the weight it can support and to make sure the materials it is made from are up to standard.

Herman Miller's testing facility

ART AND SCIENCE

It takes the design team at Herman Miller up to three years to develop a new piece of furniture. The designs need to look good, feel good and be easy to manufacture. The designers take advice from a range of experts, including doctors and psychologists, to create furniture that keeps people happy and healthy, whether they are at work or at home.

Herman Miller designers study models of future chair designs

Graphic designer

Do you make collages or collect your favourite images in a scrapbook? Graphic designers put their eye for a great image to use in a range of illustrated works, including books, magazines, posters, websites, film posters and album covers. They combine images with words to create fantastic, eye-catching, informative designs.

WORDS AND IMAGES

For magazines, newspapers and other publications, graphic designers work with both images and words. They select the fonts, colours and size of the typeface, and place text on or around the images. You'll often need to get creative to make new images such as infographics – fun ways of visually displaying information in the form of graphs and diagrams. Many designers work for several different publications, so you will work in many different styles.

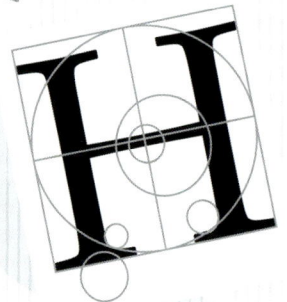

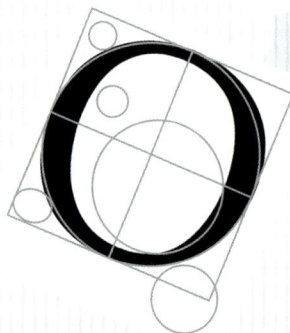

CAROLYN DAVIDSON
(1941–)

American graphic designer Carolyn Davidson designed the Nike Swoosh, one of the most famous logos in the world. In 1971, Davidson was a student at Portland State University, Oregon, when she was asked to design the logo by Nike founder Phil Knight. She was paid a fee of just US$35 for the job. Later, after Nike had become a successful worldwide company, Knight gave Davidson shares in the company in recognition of the importance of her logo design.

◄ ·············· **Serena Williams wearing Nike clothing**

POSTER DESIGN

As you walk down a high street, you're surrounded by images. These could be huge billboards advertising new goods, such as smartphones, or posters for the latest films or music concerts. These posters were put together by graphic designers. Designing film posters is considered a form of art and the best posters may still be on show decades after they were made. That's a great way to make your name as a graphic designer!

Illustrator

Do you find yourself doodling sketches whenever you have a spare minute? You could turn those doodles into a career as an illustrator. Working by hand or digitally, illustrators put their drawing skills to use producing original artwork for books, magazines, websites, posters or greeting cards. You'll need to be flexible in your style and able to work to a client's brief.

TECHNICAL ILLUSTRATOR

Technical illustrators produce highly detailed images to show how things work. These might be cross-sections of body parts for medical journals or step-by-step diagrams for instruction manuals. Technical illustrators work to a very precise brief to make accurate images that are easy to understand. You'll often need detailed knowledge of the subject area and many technical illustrators specialise in one subject, such as medicine, botany or engineering.

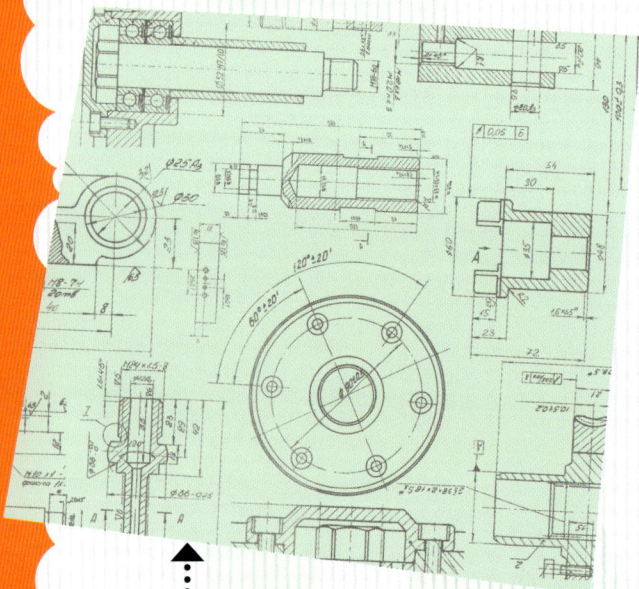

A technical drawing of a mechanical device

ILLUSTRATED FICTION

Freed from the constraints of technical illustration, an artist's imagination can run wild when they are illustrating fiction. Storybooks for young children are usually illustrated, with just a few words on each page to help tell the story. Graphic novels are books written in comic-strip style, with dialogue appearing in speech bubbles. Graphic novels may be written for children or adults.

STEAM STAR: AXEL SCHEFFLER (1957–)

German illustrator Axel Scheffler works with authors to make illustrated fiction for children. He has collaborated with British author Julia Donaldson on a number of books, including *The Gruffalo*, an international best-seller about a cunning mouse who fools a giant creature called a gruffalo on a walk in the woods.

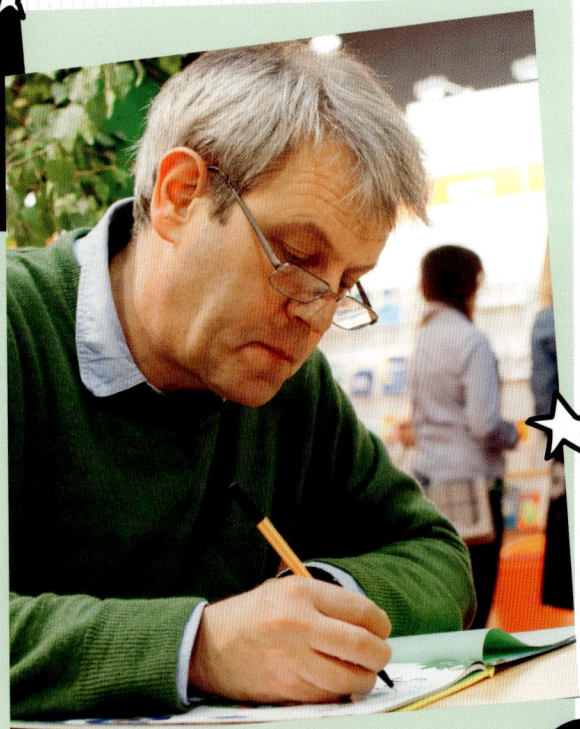

Art director

Are there magazines you pick up simply because you love their style? Art directors create the visual style for magazines, books or advertising campaigns. Working with writers, graphic designers, stylists and photographers, the art director is in charge of signing off the final designs before they go to print.

MODERN MEDIA

Today's media are normally produced for a range of platforms. A magazine doesn't just appear in print. Art directors must make sure their designs look just as good on a tablet or a smartphone as they do on a printed page. They also need to engage with social media, maintaining a lively online presence to make sure their magazine is seen by as many people as possible.

ADVERTISING

In advertising, the art director works closely with copywriters to come up with striking and memorable images and catchphrases for a wide range of media. An advertising campaign might include posters, TV adverts and web pages. The art director creates a memorable look to go across the whole campaign. They need a wide range of skills, as they may be laying out a poster design one day and directing a photo shoot the next.

STEAM STAR: NEVILLE BRODY (1957–)

British graphic designer Neville Brody made his name as art director for the music and style magazine *The Face*. He created visually striking layouts in which the photos took centre stage. Brody's work helped to change the way magazines are laid out, making them much more image-conscious. Today, he runs an international design company, developing fresh new looks for a variety of companies, newspapers and magazines.

Behind the scenes:
Designing a brand

A company's brand is its recognisable public image. Companies spend a lot of money developing and protecting their brand. They employ advertising agencies to come up with new ideas for promoting the brand. Once they have created a recognisable logo, the companies seek to give the logo positive exposure. They often do this by sponsoring sports, theatre or other cultural events.

Advertising in New York's Times Square means millions will see your brand every day.

CREATING A BRAND

Developing a trusted brand is crucial for a company's success, creating confidence in their products. Brand designers work on all aspects of a company's public face, from the look and message of advertising campaigns to the sponsorship of public events. An overall brand manager coordinates each aspect of the brand, making sure every detail is correct – right down to using exactly the right font in the adverts.

CLEVER BRANDING

Advertising professionals speak of Volkswagen's 1960 advertising campaign in the US as one of the best ever. Most Americans at the time liked big, powerful cars, but Volkswagen were selling the compact Beetle. They made a virtue of its size in adverts that made the car appear tiny, alongside the slogan 'Think small'. Within a few years, the Beetle, or Bug as it was called in the US, had become the most popular imported car in the country. Small cars were hip!

Volkswagen Beetle . . . . .

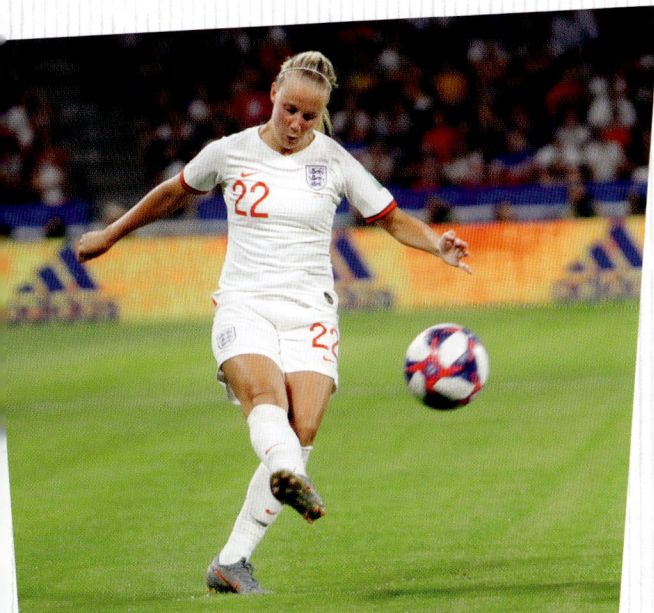

MERCHANDISING

Companies often promote their brands by creating a range of merchandise that carries their company logo. This might include anything from hats and T-shirts to notebooks or USB drives. Companies often pay large sums of money to place their merchandise at big public events, such as a football World Cup. But it needs to be good quality stuff, otherwise customers will associate the brand with something that doesn't work!

Advertising hoardings . . . . . .
surround pitches at
major sporting events.

Fine artist

Do you love painting pictures and showing them off to your friends and family? Fine artists create original works of art, such as paintings and sculptures, which can be sold to private collectors or displayed in art galleries. You'll need to be really determined to make it as a fine artist as it can be hard to make a living. Many fine artists teach or work in galleries to support their fine art careers.

PUBLIC ART

Sculptors are often commissioned to create a work to be displayed in a particular public place, such as a square or a park. These could be sculptures of a famous person or to commemorate famous events. Sometimes the sculptures are just intended to provide some fun or amazement. In 2007, Georgian artist Tamara Kvesitadze created a moving sculpture of a man and woman. The slices of each figure pass through each other, with the figures emerging intact again on the other side.

.....The moving *Man and Woman* statue in Batumi, Georgia

SHOWING YOUR WORK

Once you have made a collection of works, it is time to put on a show. Fine artists display their latest collections in galleries, either in solo shows or with a group of artists. Many artists get great satisfaction from showing their work and selling their pieces. A lucky few will be featured in the media or have their work bought by a famous museum. If they become well known, they will sell more of their work and command much higher prices.

STEAM STAR: GONÇALO MABUNDA
(1975–)

Mozambican artist and peace activist Gonçalo Mabunda creates sculptures out of guns, rockets and bombs that were used during Mozambique's 16-year civil war. Mabunda's art has been displayed at museums around the world. He works in partnership with the organisation African Artists for Development, which encourages artists to get involved in community projects.

Mabunda's sculpture ....
A Throne for Two Kings

Behind the scenes: Restoring *The Night Watch*

Conservation departments in art galleries conserve and restore works of art. In a special project at the Rijksmuseum in Amsterdam, The Netherlands, a painting called *The Night Watch* is being restored by a team of experts in full view of the public. The team includes scientists, art historians and specialist restorers. You can tune in and watch their progress live on the Internet. The restoration is expected to take several years to complete.

THE PAINTING

The Night Watch is the Rijksmuseum's most prized possession. Painted in 1642 by Rembrandt van Rijn (1606–1669), it is a huge canvas – more than 4 metres wide and 3 metres high – depicting a group of city militiamen walking through a crowd. *The Night Watch* is famed for its use of light and shadow, contrasting brightly lit figures with a menacingly dark background, a technique called tenebrism. The restoration is being carried out because parts of the painting's background have faded.

The Night Watch by Rembrandt ....

X-RAY SCAN

Working inside a protective glass case, the experts will first scan the whole painting millimetre by millimetre using a special machine called an X-ray fluorescence scanner. The machine uses high-energy X-rays to identify the chemical elements in the paint, such as iron, potassium or cobalt. In total, 56 different scans will be carried out to fully analyse every layer of paint.

Conservation artists may have to remove old, damaged paint before replacing it.

MATCHING THE COLOURS

Once the scanning and analysis are complete, the restorers will know exactly how Rembrandt made each of his colours. They plan to recreate Rembrandt's paints in order to carry out the restoration using authentic methods. For instance, they know that, for his blue paint, Rembrandt used cobalt, which he ground from smalt – a kind of glass.

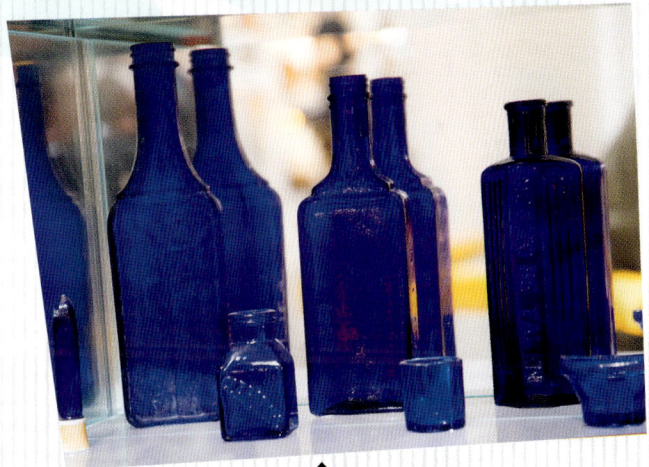

Smalt was used to make bottles and glasses and could be ground up to make cobalt pigment.

Art therapist

Does creating art make you feel good? Art therapists tap into the healing power of art to help people to feel better about themselves. They work with children or adults, using art to help them express their emotions and explore their innermost fears. Art therapists may be artists who have trained in psychology, or nurses or teachers who have trained in art.

HEATH SERVICES

The term 'art therapy' was coined by British artist Adrian Hill in 1942, who discovered the benefits of making art for patients who were recovering from tuberculosis. At first, art therapists like Hill were self-taught, but today art therapists study the subject at university, learning psychotherapy techniques. Health services around the world employ art therapists to help patients with a wide range of difficulties, including mentally ill people, people with learning disabilities and people with chronic illnesses.

OUTSIDER ART

While art therapy is focussed on helping people to feel better, it can also produce some amazing works of art. The term 'outsider art' refers to art made by people with no artistic training. Many outsider artists first start making art in art therapy classes. Autistic British artist Stephen Wiltshire started drawing before he had learned to talk, and his first ever word was 'paper'. Today, he has his own gallery, displaying his incredibly detailed drawings. He is able to draw an entire cityscape from memory after a single helicopter ride over the area.

British artist ....
Stephen Wiltshire

STEAM STAR: EDWARD ADAMSON
(1911–1996)

Edward Adamson was the first artist to be employed by the UK's National Health Service, working with patients in Netherne psychiatric hospital from the 1940s to the 1990s. Adamson helped the patients to express themselves in art works that were later exhibited to the public in group shows. In 1984, he wrote an influential book about his work called *Art as Healing*. His pioneering work helped to win funding for many other art therapy projects.

Glossary

animation
The joining together of a series of pictures to create the effect of a moving image

app
Short for 'application', a computer program that does a particular job (such as making digital art)

apprentice
A person who works for a skilled tradesperson, often for low wages, in order to learn the trade

autism
A condition that causes difficulties in learning how to communicate with others and behave in social situations

botany
The study of plants

catwalk
A narrow stage at a fashion show, down which models walk. The catwalk allows everybody in the audience to get a close look at the clothes.

ceramics
Pots or other items shaped from soft clay that has been baked in a kiln to make it hard

chasing
The creation of a pattern in a sheet of metal by hammering from the reverse side to create a raised design. It is also called repoussage.

chronic illness
A long-term health condition that may not have a cure. Patients with chronic illnesses may become depressed about their condition and can be helped with art therapy.

cobalt
A metallic chemical element that is used to make blue pigments

collage
A piece of art created by pasting different objects next to one another on a flat surface, such as a piece of paper or wood

colour theory
The science behind the way we see colours. Colour theory explains how to combine colours to create different effects.

commission
An order from a client to do a particular job

conservation area
An area of special interest that is protected. It may be countryside with unique wildlife or an urban zone with historic buildings.

copywriter
The person who writes the text to go alongside images in advertising or other publicity material

curator
The person in charge of a particular collection in a museum or a gallery

ergonomics
The study of how people work and how to design a work environment

formal garden
A garden in which the plants have all been specially chosen and are trimmed to create geometric shapes

geometric shapes
Shapes, such as circles, squares and hexagons that are created according to mathematical rules

glaze
A treatment applied to items of food, ceramics and other materials to make their surfaces smooth and shiny

Great Depression
A period during the 1930s during which many parts of the world experienced economic hardship, with high unemployment and widespread hunger

infographic
A visual way of showing information that makes it easy to understand

logo
A symbol or design that instantly identifies a company or organisation

merchandise
Goods that have been made to be bought and sold

minimalist
A style in art, design or music that has deliberately been kept simple

photojournalist
A photographer who tells news stories by taking a series of photos

pigment
A substance with a particular colour. Pigments are often made in powder form.

precious metal
A metal that is only found on Earth in small quantities and that is highly valued for its chemical properties

prosthetic
An artificial body part, such as an arm or a foot

psychiatric hospital
A hospital that cares for patients suffering from mental illness

psychology
The scientific study of the human mind and the ways in which humans behave in different situations

psychotherapy
Also called 'talking therapy', treatment of mental illnesses using psychological methods rather than medical means, such as drugs

recycling
Turning waste materials into useful new things

restoration
Returning an old object, such as an artwork, to its original condition

sculpture
A three-dimensional work of art

set
A specially created scene that has been designed for a film or a play

sustainability
A way of creating human development that meets our needs for today without destroying resources that we will need in the future

tailor
A person who designs and makes clothing for men, such as suits

tenebrism
A technique in painting in which areas of shadow are contrasted with brightly coloured areas to create dramatic effects

tuberculosis
An infectious disease – usually of the lungs – that is caused by bacteria

X-rays
A form of high-energy radiation that can be used to look inside bodies or underneath layers of paint in an artwork

Index

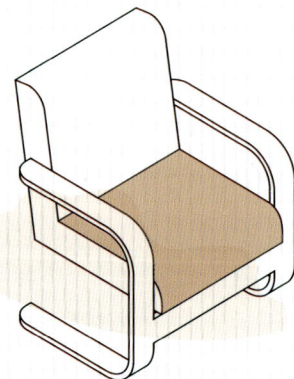

KV-578-668

This revision and classroom companion is matched to the new **OCR GCSE Chemistry Specification (J634)**, from the Twenty First Century Science Suite.*

As a revision guide, this book focuses on the skills and material on which you will be examined. It does not cover the practical data analysis and case study (Unit 4) or the practical investigation (Unit 5), which will be internally assessed by your science teacher and count(s) for 33.3% of your total mark.

All seven modules from the specification are covered in this guide. You will need to study, and sit exams for, **all** of these modules.

An overview of the exams for OCR GCSE Chemistry A is provided below, with details of where the relevant material can be found in this guide.

The Ideas in Context exam paper will focus on the ideas covered in all of the modules you have studied. It will test your knowledge of the content and your ability to apply that knowledge, for example, to evaluate information about a current social–science issue effectively. This paper is looked at in more detail on pages 82–88 of this revision guide.

The **contents list and page headers** in this revision guide clearly identify the separate modules, to help you to revise for the different exam papers.

This guide can be used to revise for both the Foundation and Higher Tier exam papers.

HT Content that will only be tested on the Higher Tier papers appears in a coloured box, and can easily be identified by the Higher Tier symbol **HT**.

- You will find a **glossary** at the end of the book providing clear definitions of essential words and phrases. There is also a copy of the Periodic Table at the back of this book for reference.

- Don't just read the information in this guide – **learn actively**! Jot down anything you think will help you to remember, no matter how trivial it may seem, and constantly test yourself without looking at the text.

Good luck in your exams!

*All material correct at time of going to print.

Title	What is Being Assessed?	How it is Assessed	Weighting	Total Mark	Page No.
Unit 1	C1, C2, C3	40 minutes written paper	16.7%	42	4–28
Unit 2	C4, C5, C6	40 minutes written paper	16.7%	42	29–60
Unit 3	C7 and Ideas in Context	60 minutes written paper	33.3%	55	61–88
Unit 4 **OR**	Practical Data Analysis and Case Study	Assessed internally	33.3%	40	——
Unit 5	Practical Investigation	Assessed internally	33.3%	40	——

Unit 1

Unit 2

Unit 3

Contents

Contents

Air Quality

Air pollutants can affect the environment and our health. However, there are options available for improving air quality in the future. This module looks at…

- the chemicals that make up air and the ones that are pollutants
- data about air pollution
- the chemical reactions that produce air pollutants
- what happens to pollutants in the atmosphere
- the steps that can be taken to improve air quality.

Pollutants in the Air

Pollutants are chemicals that can harm the environment and our health. They enter the atmosphere as a result of human activity, e.g. burning **fossil fuels**.

Pollutants that harm the environment can also harm humans indirectly. For example, acid rain makes the water in rivers and lakes too acidic for plants and animals to survive. This has a direct impact on our food chain and natural resources like trees.

Common pollutants and the problems they cause are listed in the table below.

Chemicals in the Air

The Earth is surrounded by a thin layer of gases called the **atmosphere**. It contains about 78% **nitrogen**, 21% **oxygen**, 1% **argon** and **other noble gases**. There are also small amounts of **water vapour**, **carbon dioxide**, and **other gases**. The amount of water vapour and polluting gases varies.

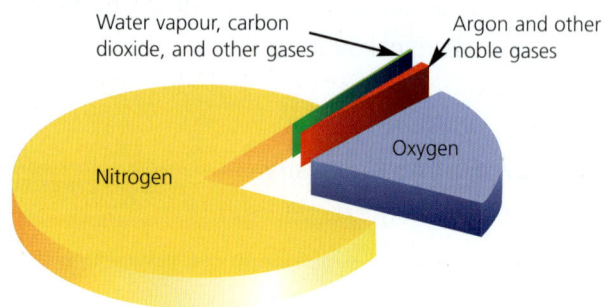

Water vapour, carbon dioxide, and other gases

Argon and other noble gases

Oxygen

Nitrogen

Measuring Pollutants

By measuring the **concentrations** of pollutants in the air it is possible to assess air quality. The units of measurement used are **ppb** (**parts per billion**) or **ppm** (**parts per million**). For example, a sulfur dioxide concentration of 16ppb means that in every one billion (1 000 000 000) **molecules** of air, 16 will be sulfur dioxide molecules.

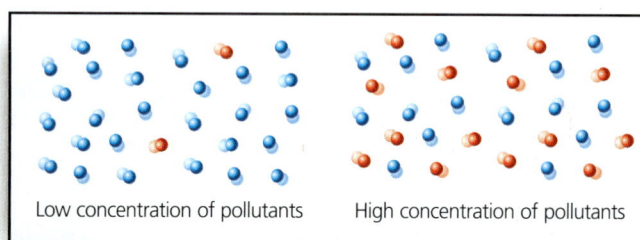

Low concentration of pollutants   High concentration of pollutants

Pollutant	Harmful to...	Why?
Carbon dioxide	Environment	Traps heat in the Earth's atmosphere (a greenhouse gas).
Nitrogen oxides	Environment Humans	Causes acid rain. Causes breathing problems and can make asthma worse.
Sulfur dioxide	Environment	Causes acid rain.
Particulates (small particles of solids, e.g. carbon)	Environment Humans	Makes buildings dirty. Can make asthma and other lung infections worse if inhaled.
Carbon monoxide	Humans	Displaces oxygen in the blood which can result in death.

Data about Pollution

Data is very important to scientists because it can be used to test a theory or explanation.

Example: One theory states that carbon monoxide (CO) is an example of a pollutant caused by human activity.

If this is true, carbon monoxide concentrations are likely to be higher in densely populated areas, e.g. cities.

The data below was collected on the same day using a carbon monoxide meter:

Location	Time	Carbon Monoxide Concentration (ppm)
City centre	9.00am	5.2
	10.00am	4.9
	11.00am	5.0
	12.00pm	2.6
	1.00pm	4.8
Country park	9.00am	0.2
	10.00am	0.1
	11.00am	0.1
	12.00pm	0.0
	1.00pm	0.1

Measurements like this can vary because...
- **variables** (factors that change), like volume of traffic and weather, affect concentrations
- all measuring **equipment** has a limited degree of accuracy
- the user's **skill** will affect the accuracy of the measurement.

Because the measurements vary, it is not possible to give a **true value** for the concentration of carbon monoxide in the air. However, the true value is likely to lie somewhere within the **range** of the collected data, i.e. between 4.8 and 5.2 in the city centre and between 0 and 0.2 in the country park.

The measurement of 2.6ppm has been excluded from the data range for the city centre, because it is an **outlier**. Outliers are measurements that stand out as being very different from the rest of the data.

They fall well outside the range of the other measurements and normally indicate some sort of error. You must be able to say why 2.6ppm is an outlier, e.g. the operator may have misread the scale. It is unlikely that the volume of traffic would have decreased at midday. In fact, you might expect it to increase as people leave their workplaces for lunch.

It is important that measurements are repeated. If you look at one measurement on its own, you cannot tell if it is reliable. However, if you look at lots of repeated measurements, any errors should stand out.

By calculating the **mean** (finding the average) of a set of repeated measurements, you can overcome small variations and get a **best estimate** of the true value.

$$\text{Mean} = \frac{\text{Sum of all values}}{\text{Number of values}}$$ Do not use outliers in mean calculations!

$$\text{City} = \frac{5.2 + 4.9 + 5.0 + 4.8}{4} = \textbf{5.0ppm}$$

$$\text{Country} = \frac{0.2 + 0.1 + 0.1 + 0.0 + 0.1}{5} = \textbf{0.1ppm}$$

The mean carbon monoxide concentration in the city centre is significantly higher than the mean carbon monoxide concentration in the country park. So, this data supports the theory that carbon monoxide is a pollutant caused by human activity.

In fact, about half of all carbon monoxide emissions in the UK are produced by road transport, with the rest coming from homes and other industries.

HT There is a **real difference** between the mean CO concentrations in the city centre and the park, because the difference between the mean values is a lot bigger than the range of each set of data. If the difference between the mean values had been smaller than the range there would have been no real difference. The result would have been insignificant and the data would not support the theory.

Air Quality

Chemicals

Elements are the 'building blocks' of *all* materials. There are over 100 elements and each one is made up of very tiny particles called **atoms**. All the atoms of a particular element are the **same** and are unique to that element.

Each element is represented by a different **chemical symbol**, e.g. C for carbon, O for oxygen and Fe for iron.

Atoms can join together to form bigger building blocks called **molecules**.

Compounds are formed when the atoms of **two or more different elements** are **chemically combined** to form molecules. The properties of a compound are very different to the properties of the individual elements it is made from.

Chemical symbols and numbers are used to write **formulae**. Formulae show…
- the different elements that make up a compound
- the number of atoms of each different element in one molecule.

Example

A water molecule, H_2O:

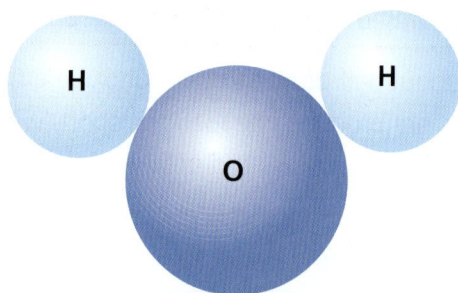

H_2O

Each molecule has…   two hydrogen atoms   one oxygen atom

Chemical Change

During a **chemical reaction** new substances are formed from old ones. This is because the atoms in the reactants (starting substances) are rearranged in some way:
- joined atoms may be separated
- separate atoms may be joined
- joined atoms may be separated and then joined again in different ways.

These chemical changes are **not** easily reversible.

You can show what happens during a chemical reaction by using a word equation. The **reactants** are on one side of the equation and the **products** (newly formed chemicals) are on the other.

Reactants   ⟶   Products

Combustion

Combustion is a chemical reaction which occurs when fuels burn, releasing energy as heat. For combustion to take place, **oxygen** must be present.

Coal is a fossil fuel that consists mainly of carbon. The following equation shows what happens when coal is burned:

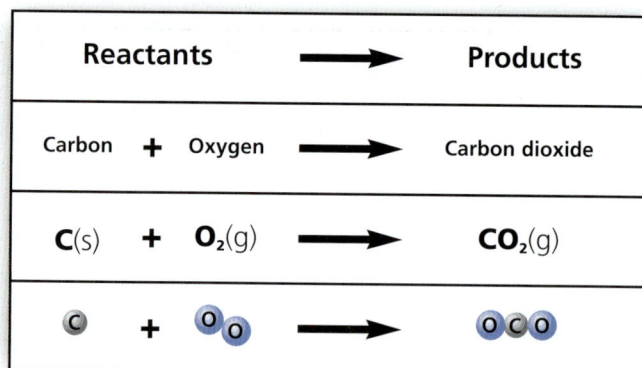

Reactants	⟶	Products
Carbon **+** Oxygen	⟶	Carbon dioxide
C(s) **+** O_2(g)	⟶	CO_2(g)
	⟶	

This equation tells us that one atom of carbon (solid) and one molecule of oxygen (gas) produces one molecule of carbon dioxide (gas).

No atoms are lost or produced during a chemical reaction. So, there will **always** be the same number of atoms on each side of the equation.

Burning Fossil Fuels

Many of the pollutants in the atmosphere are produced through the combustion of fossil fuels, e.g. in power stations, cars, aeroplanes etc.

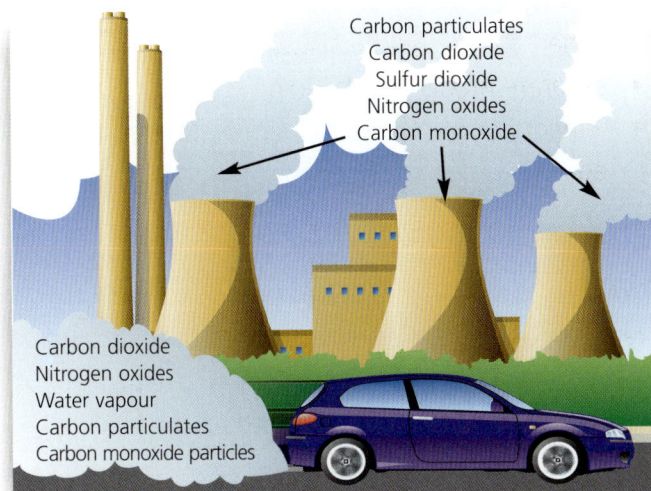

Carbon particulates
Carbon dioxide
Sulfur dioxide
Nitrogen oxides
Carbon monoxide

Carbon dioxide
Nitrogen oxides
Water vapour
Carbon particulates
Carbon monoxide particles

Complete Combustion

Fossil fuels such as petrol, diesel fuel, natural gas and fuel oil consist mainly of compounds called **hydrocarbons**. A hydrocarbon contains *only* **hydrogen** atoms and **carbon** atoms. So, when it is burned in air, **carbon dioxide** and **water** (hydrogen oxide) are produced (**complete combustion**). Remember, carbon dioxide is a pollutant!

Methane	+	Oxygen		Carbon dioxide	+	Water
CH_4(g)	+	$2O_2$(g)		CO_2(g)	+	$2H_2O$(l)

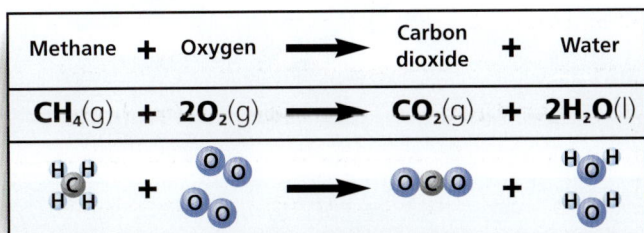

Incomplete Combustion

If a fuel is burned and there is not enough oxygen in the air, **carbon particulates (C)** or **carbon monoxide (CO)** may be produced. This is called **incomplete combustion**.

Methane	+	Oxygen		Carbon	+	Water
CH_4(g)	+	O_2(g)		C(s)	+	$2H_2O$(l)

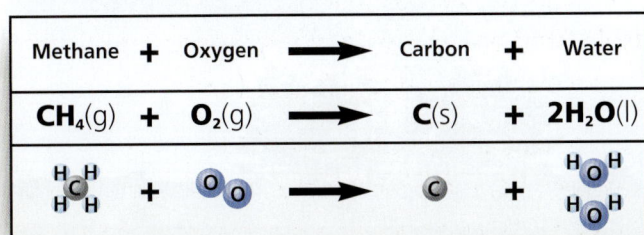

Methane	+	Oxygen		Carbon monoxide	+	Water
$2CH_4$(g)	+	$3O_2$(g)		$2CO$(g)	+	$4H_2O$(l)

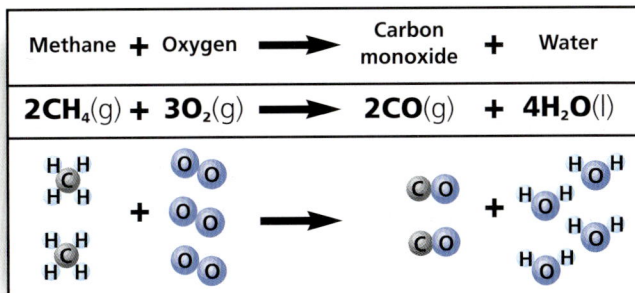

Incomplete combustion occurs in car engines, so exhaust emissions contain carbon particulates and carbon monoxide as well as carbon dioxide.

Many samples of coal contain sulfur, so sulfur dioxide is released into the atmosphere when they are burned.

Sulfur	+	Oxygen		Sulfur dioxide
S(g)	+	O_2(g)		SO_2(g)

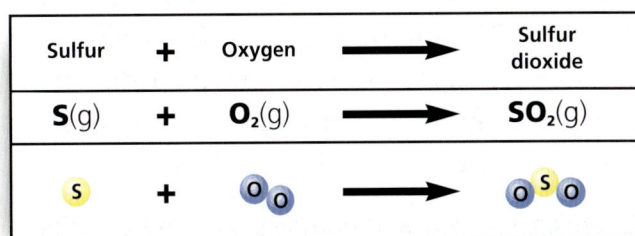

During the combustion of fuels, high temperatures (e.g. in a car engine or power station) can cause **nitrogen** in the atmosphere to react with **oxygen** and produce **nitrogen monoxide**.

Nitrogen	+	Oxygen		Nitrogen monoxide
N_2(g)	+	O_2(g)		$2NO$(g)

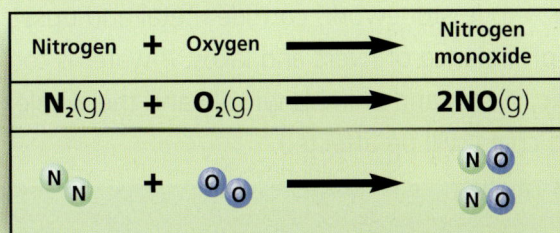

Nitrogen monoxide is then **oxidised** to produce **nitrogen dioxide**.

Nitrogen monoxide	+ Oxygen	Nitrogen dioxide
$2NO$(g)	+ O_2(g)	$2NO_2$(g)

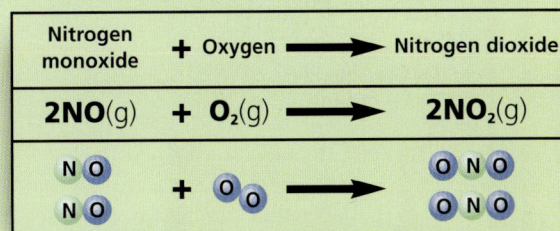

When NO and NO_2 occur together they are called **NOx**.

Air Quality

What Happens to Pollutants?

Once pollutants have been released into the atmosphere they cannot just disappear, they have to go somewhere. This is when they can start causing **problems** for the environment.

Carbon particulates are deposited on surfaces such as stone buildings, making them dirty. The appearance of many beautiful, old buildings has been changed due to this.

Some **carbon dioxide** is removed by natural processes; it is needed by plants for **photosynthesis** and some also **dissolves** in rain water and sea water, where it reacts with other chemicals in the water.

However, because we are producing too much carbon dioxide not all of it is used up naturally. The rest remains in the atmosphere, so each year the concentration of CO_2 in the atmosphere increases.

Because carbon dioxide is a **greenhouse gas** (it traps heat in the atmosphere) the rise in concentration is contributing to **global warming**, which is leading to **climate change**.

Sulfur dioxide and **nitrogen dioxide** dissolve in water to produce **acid rain**. Acid rain can damage trees, erode stonework, corrode metal and upset the pH balance of rivers and lakes. If water is too acidic, plants and animals will die and the whole food chain will be affected.

Carbon particulates are deposited

CO_2

Photosynthesis

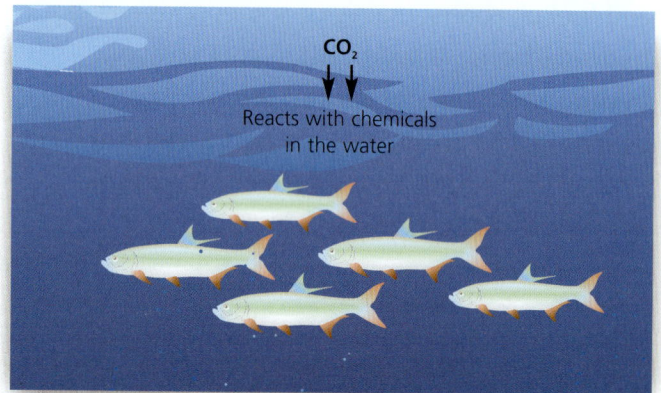

CO_2

Reacts with chemicals in the water

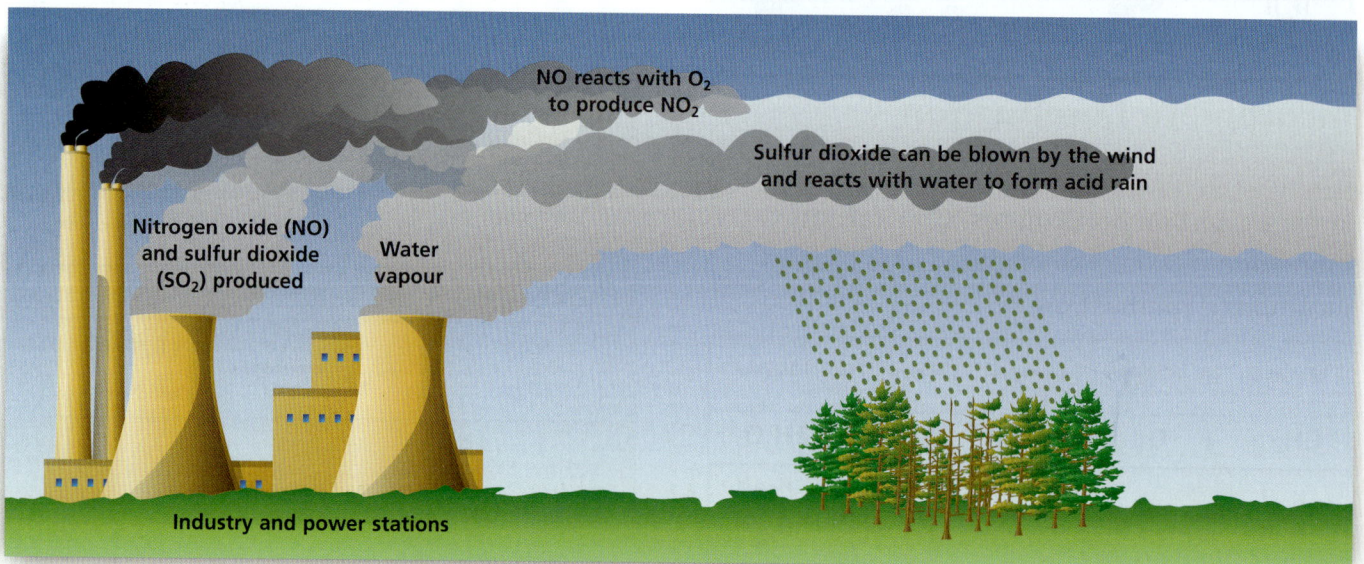

NO reacts with O_2 to produce NO_2

Sulfur dioxide can be blown by the wind and reacts with water to form acid rain

Nitrogen oxide (NO) and sulfur dioxide (SO_2) produced

Water vapour

Industry and power stations

Identifying Health Hazards

Because humans need to breathe in air to get oxygen, it is reasonable to assume that air quality will have some effect on the body.

To find out exactly how air quality affects us, scientists look for **correlations** (patterns) that might link a **factor** (e.g. a pollutant in the air) to an **outcome** (e.g. a respiratory complaint like asthma).

Example
We now know that **pollen** in the air causes **hay fever** in people who have a pollen **allergy**.

However, to reach this conclusion, scientists had to look at thousands of medical records. The data showed that most cases of hay fever occurred in the summer months when pollen counts were high.

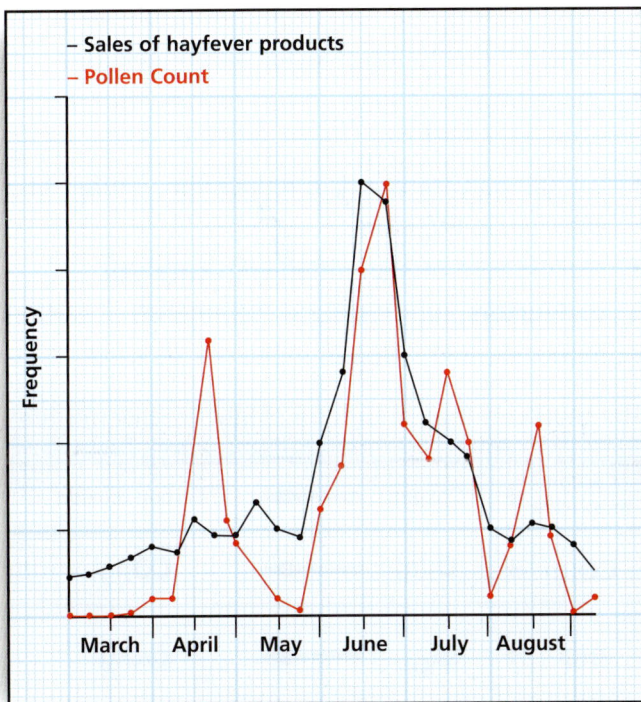

This correlation suggested that pollen **might** cause hay fever. However, it did not provide conclusive evidence because there were lots of other variables that could have influenced the outcome, e.g. temperature, humidity, other pollutants.

Further investigations, in the form of **skin tests**, were carried out to find out how pollen can affect health.

Pollen was collected in spore traps. The pollen was then stuck to the skin of volunteers using plasters.

In some volunteers the skin became red and inflamed indicating an **allergic reaction**. The results showed that people with a pollen allergy also suffered from hay fever. Those who did not have a pollen allergy did not get hay fever. This provided much stronger evidence of a link between pollen and hay fever.

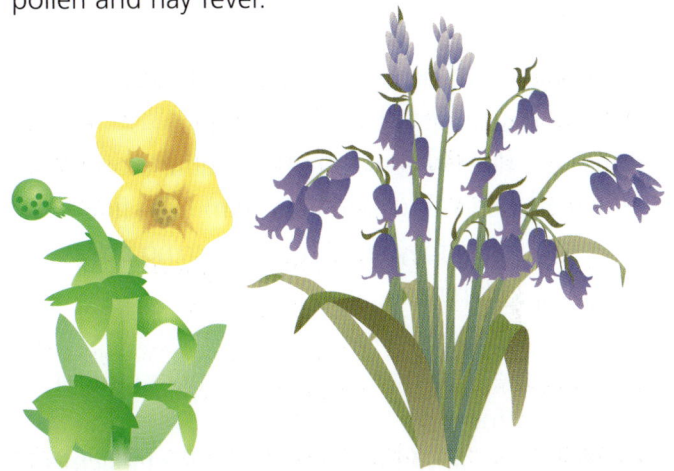

When these findings were released, other scientists studied the data and repeated the skin test experiments. The fact that the tests always produced the same results proved that they were reliable.

Another condition that is linked to air quality is asthma. However, this example is more complicated. Studies of asthma have shown that when the concentration of NO_2 (nitrogen dioxide) increases in the air, more asthma attacks are triggered.

However, people still have asthma attacks when the levels of NO_2 are very low. This suggests that although NO_2 can increase the chance of an asthma attack occurring, it is not the primary **cause**.

There are many factors that can trigger an asthma attack. To fully understand what factors **cause** asthma and what factors may **aggravate** the condition, scientists need to study a large sample of people.

Air Quality

Improving Air Quality

Air pollution is everywhere. It affects everyone, so we all have a responsibility to reduce it.

Motor vehicles and power stations that burn fossil fuels are two major sources of atmospheric pollution, so we need to look at how emissions from these sources can be reduced.

Emissions from power stations can be reduced by…

- using less electricity so fewer fossil fuels need to be burned
- using a filter system to remove sulfur dioxide and particulates (carbon and ash) from flue gases before they leave a coal-burning power station's chimney
- removing toxic chemicals before they are burned, e.g. removing the sulfur from natural gas and fuel oil
- using alternative renewable sources of electricity, e.g. solar energy, wind energy and hydroelectric energy, to replace fossil fuels.

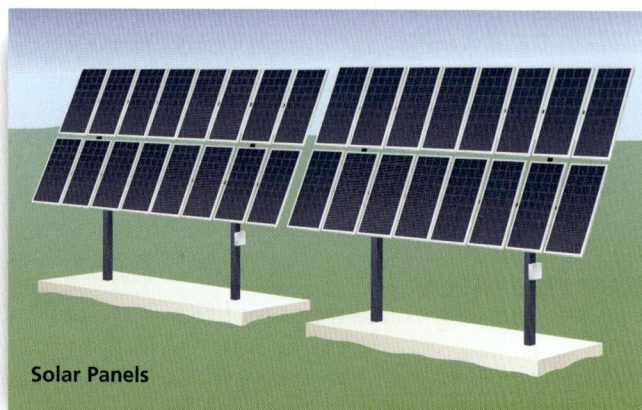
Solar Panels

Wind Turbines

Emissions from motor vehicles can be reduced by…

- buying a car with a modern engine that is more efficient and burns less fuel
- buying a hybrid car, which uses electric power in the city centre and can then switch to running on petrol for longer journeys
- using a low sulfur fuel (readily available) to reduce the amount of sulfur dioxide released
- converting the engine to run on biodiesel, a renewable fuel
- using public transport to reduce the number of vehicles on the road
- making sure cars are fitted with **catalytic converters**, which reduce the amount of carbon monoxide and nitrogen monoxide emitted.

The reactions that occur in a catalytic converter are:

Carbon monoxide	+	Oxygen		Carbon dioxide
$CO(g)$	+	$O_2(g)$		$CO_2(g)$
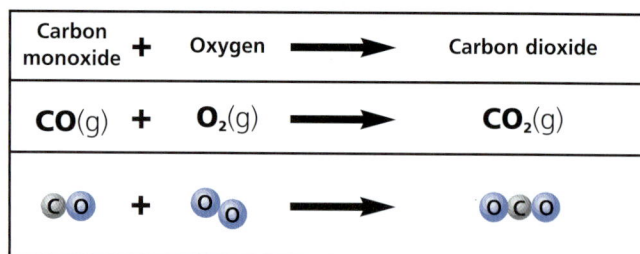				

Nitrogen monoxide	+	Carbon monoxide		Nitrogen	+	Carbon dioxide
$2NO(g)$	+	$2CO(g)$		$N_2(g)$	+	$2CO_2(g)$
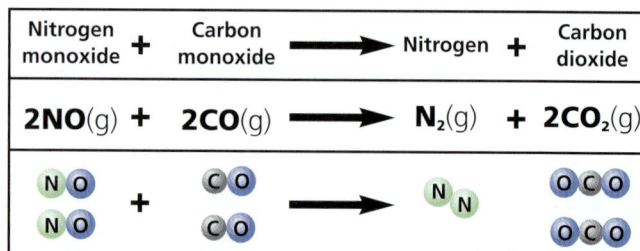						

The only way of reducing carbon dioxide emissions is to burn fewer fossil fuels.

Air Quality

Global Choices

In 1997 there was an international meeting about climate change in **Kyoto**, Japan. People from many nations agreed to reduce CO_2 emissions, and targets were set for individual countries. The governments of the countries are required to take appropriate measures to meet the targets.

National Choices

Here are just some of the rules and regulations that have been put in place by different countries to help meet their targets:

- setting legal limits for vehicle exhaust emissions, which are enforced by statutory MOT tests
- making catalytic converters compulsory on new vehicles
- using subsidies (grants) or reduced taxes to encourage power companies to use 'cleaner' fuels
- introducing a car tax system that encourages drivers to buy smaller cars with smaller engines
- encouraging investment in non-polluting renewable energy such as wind and solar energy.

These laws and regulations impact on many areas of science and industry. For example, when new cars are developed the technology used must meet all the legal requirements.

Some governments are concerned that steps taken to reduce carbon dioxide emissions will result in a decline in manufacturing and production, employment and the national economy.

Local Choices

Many local authorities are trying to encourage us to make environmentally friendly choices by providing…

- door step collections of paper, bottles, metals and plastics for recycling
- regular bus or train services
- electric trams (in some cities)
- congestion charges
- 'park and ride' schemes
- cycle paths and cycle parks.

Personal Choices

It is clear that the **choices** we make as **individuals** affect the amount of pollution in the air.

Using less energy in the home reduces the demand for energy from power stations, e.g. turning televisions off and not leaving them on standby.

Making sure your car is energy efficient and has a catalytic converter or choosing an alternative mode of transport, e.g. bicycle, cuts down on vehicle emissions.

Recycling materials like paper, bottles, metals and plastics helps to conserve natural resources, but also saves energy, e.g. it takes about 95% less energy to recycle an aluminium can than to make a new one.

There are other benefits to the 'green' options too. For example, walking and cycling instead of travelling by car help to keep us fit!

Air Quality – Summary

Science Explanations

Chemicals

- All materials are made from about 100 different chemicals called elements.
- Each element is represented by a different chemical symbol, e.g. Fe, H or Pb.
- An element is made up of very tiny particles called atoms.
- The atoms in each element are the same and are unique to that element.
- Atoms of different elements join together to make compounds.
- There are many different compounds because the atoms can join together in different ways.
- The properties of a compound are very different from the properties of the elements they are made from.
- In many compounds, different atoms of elements join together to form molecules.
- The composition of molecules can be shown using formulae, e.g. H_2O.

Chemical Change

- Chemical reactions produce new chemicals.
- In a chemical reaction, the atoms in the reactants are rearranged in some way.
  - Atoms that were joined together at the start may have separated.
  - Atoms that were separate at the start may have joined together.
  - Atoms that were joined at the start may have separated and then joined together in different ways.
- No atoms are destroyed or created in a chemical reaction.
- When hydrocarbon fuels burn, carbon and hydrogen atoms from the fuel combine with oxygen in the air to produce carbon dioxide and water.
- When fuels contain sulfur, they produce sulfur dioxide when burned.

Ideas about Science

Data and its Limitations

- Data is used to test scientific theories and explanations.
- Measurements do not always provide a true value.
- Repeated measurements of the same quantity often vary due to the skill of the scientist, the limitations of the equipment and external variables, e.g. fluctuations in air pollutants due to weather changes and emission levels.
- A best estimate of the true value can be found by calculating the mean of repeated measurements.
- If a measurement lies well outside the expected range of the true value it is probably incorrect and may be discarded.

Correlation and Cause

- A correlation (matching pattern) between a factor and an outcome suggests that one may cause or influence the other.
- Correlations have to be investigated further to eliminate any other factors that might influence the results.

> **HT** • A correlation between a factor and an outcome does not always mean that one causes the other.

The Scientific Community

- Scientists should be able to repeat experiments conducted by other scientists and get the same results.

> **HT** • If an experiment cannot be repeated, scientists may question its validity.

Science and Technology

- In many areas of scientific work, official regulations and laws control how science is used, e.g. legal limits on emissions restrict developments in car design and industry.

Module C2

We use materials for a variety of different functions everyday. Materials are often selected for a job because of the properties that they possess. This module looks at...

- the properties and structure of materials
- how polymers are created
- how the properties of materials can be altered
- the life cycle of a product
- how waste materials are disposed of.

Natural and Synthetic Materials

The materials that we use are chemicals, or mixtures of chemicals. Some materials can be made or obtained from living things, e.g. cotton (plant), paper (wood), silk (a silk worm) or wool (sheep). Synthetic materials, produced by chemical synthesis, can be made as alternatives to these.

Crude Oil

When extracted, crude oil is a thick, black, sticky liquid. It contains mainly **hydrocarbons**, which are chain molecules containing only hydrogen and carbon atoms.

Different hydrocarbons have different boiling points, because their molecular chains are different lengths. This means that hydrocarbons can be separated by fractional distillation into different parts, or **fractions** (groups of hydrocarbons of similar lengths).

The petrochemical industry refines naturally-occurring crude oil to produce fuels, lubricants and raw materials for chemical synthesis. Only a small proportion of crude oil is used in chemical synthesis.

Properties of Materials

Different solid materials have different properties; they have different melting points and densities, and they can be strong or weak, rigid (stiff) or flexible, hard or soft.

The properties of a particular material mean that it will be better suited to some uses than others.

Examples

Unvulcanised Rubbers

Properties:	Uses:
• Low tensile strength • Soft • Flexible / elastic	• Erasers • Rubber bands

Vulcanised Rubbers

Properties:	Uses:
• High tensile strength • Hard • Flexible / elastic	• Car tyres • Conveyor belts • Shock absorbers

Plastic – Polythene

Properties:	Uses:
• Light • Flexible • Easily moulded	• Plastic bags • Moulded containers

Plastic – Polystyrene

Properties:	Uses:
• Light • Hard • When foamed provides exceptional insulation properties • Water resistant	• Meat trays • Egg cartons • Coffee cups • Protecting appliances and electronics

Synthetic Fibres – Nylon

Properties:	Uses
• Lightweight • Tough • Waterproof • Blocks UV light	• Clothing • Climbing ropes

Synthetic Fibres – Polyester

Properties:	Uses:
• Lightweight • Waterproof • Tough	• Clothing • Bottles

Material Choices

Properties of Materials (cont.)

The properties of the materials used will affect the durability and effectiveness of the end product, so manufacturers always test and assess them carefully beforehand.

Example

A supermarket needs to produce carrier bags. They can use either polythene or biodegradable plastic.

One factor which will determine their choice of material is strength, so they carry out the following investigation: a 2cm x 20cm strip of each type of plastic is placed in a clamp. (Each strip used must be exactly the same size to ensure a fair test). Weights are then gradually attached to the bottom of each strip to find the total weight it can support before breaking. The experiment is repeated a number of times to ensure the results are reliable.

Measurement	Maximum Weight (g)	
	Polythene	Biodegradable Plastic
1	2545g	1980g
2	2550g	1975g
3	2540g	1980g
4	5250g	1985g
5	2550g	1990g

When analysing data like this, look to see if any values stand out as being unusual, i.e. they look like **outliers** (see p.5). In the data collected for polythene the fourth measurement is an outlier. This is likely to have been caused by human error, e.g. the investigator writing the measurement down incorrectly, so it can be discounted.

The range (or span) of each set of data is from the lowest value to the highest value. The **true value** of the measured quantity is likely to lie within this range. Calculating the mean of a set of data helps to overcome any small variations and obtain a best estimate for the true value of the measured quantity (see p.5).

$$\text{Mean Weight Polythene} = \frac{10185}{4}$$
$$= \mathbf{2546g}$$
$$\text{Mean Weight Biodegradable Plastic} = \frac{9910}{5}$$
$$= \mathbf{1982g}$$

This data shows that polythene can hold more weight than the biodegradable plastic before breaking. In terms of strength, this makes it the most suitable material from which to make carrier bags. However, there are lots of other considerations the supermarket must take into account before making its final decision.

Polymerisation

Polymerisation is an important chemical process in which small hydrocarbon molecules, called **monomers**, are joined together to make very long molecules called **polymers**.

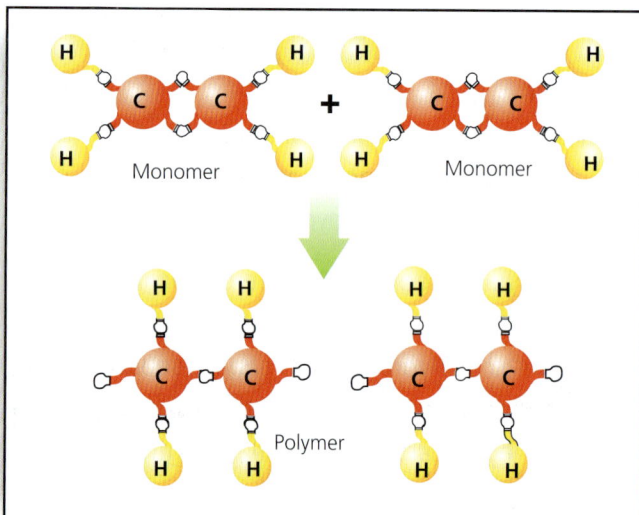

Monomer + Monomer

Polymer

In this example the resulting long-chain molecule polymer is polyethene, often called polythene.

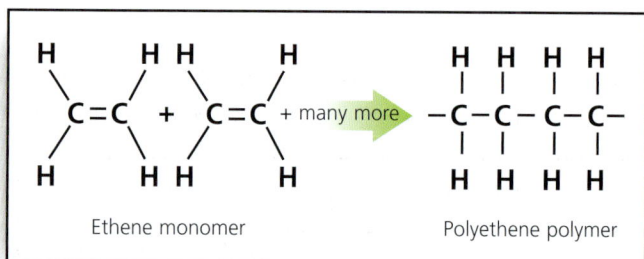

Ethene monomer   Polyethene polymer

Remember that during a chemical reaction the number of atoms of each element in the products must be the same as in the reactants. Count the atoms!

Using Polymerisation

Polymerisation can be used to create a wide range of different materials which have different properties and therefore can be used for different purposes.

Many traditional (natural) materials have been replaced by polymers because of their superior properties.

Use	Traditional Material	Monomer	Polymer	Reason
Carrier bags	Paper	Ethene	Polyethene	Stronger; waterproof
Window frames	Wood	Chloroethene	Polychloroethene	Unreactive; does not rot

Molecular Structure of Materials

The properties of solid materials depend on how the particles they are made from are arranged and held together.

Natural rubber is very flexible. It consists of a tangled mass of long-chain molecules. Although the atoms in each molecule are held together by strong covalent bonds, there are very weak forces between the molecules so they can easily slide over one another allowing the material to stretch. Rubber has a low melting point as little energy is needed to separate the molecules.

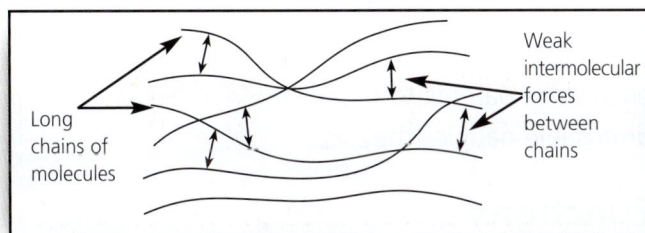

Materials with strong forces between the molecules (covalent bonds or cross-linking bridges) have high melting points as lots of energy is needed to separate them. As the molecules cannot slide over one another, they are rigid and cannot be stretched.

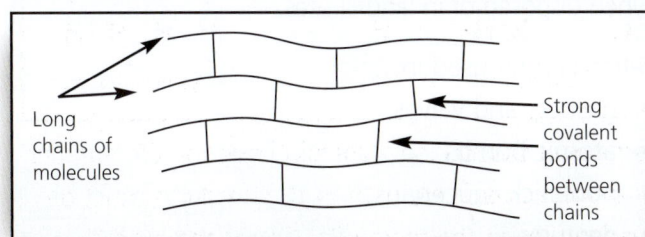

Modifications in Polymers

Modifications can produce changes to the properties of polymers. These modifications can include...

- **increasing the chain length** – longer molecules are stronger than shorter ones
- **crosslinking** – crosslinks are formed by atoms bonding between the polymer molecules, so they are no longer able to move. This makes a harder material. An example of this is **vulcanisation**, when sulfur atoms form crosslinks between rubber molecules. Vulcanised rubber is used to make car tyres and conveyor belts
- **plasticizers** – adding plasticizers makes a polymer softer and more flexible. A plasticizer is a small molecule which sits between the molecules and forces the chains further apart. The forces between the chains are, therefore, weaker and so the molecules can move more easily. Plasticized PVC is used to make children's toys, and un-plasticized PVC (uPVC) is used to make window frames.

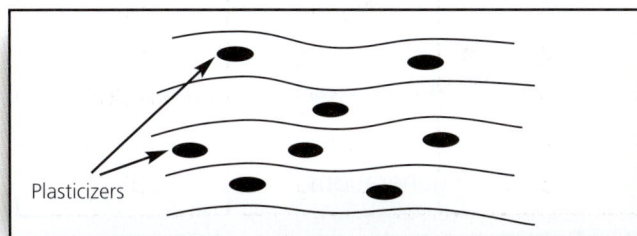

A polymer can also be modified by packing the molecules more closely together to form a **crystalline polymer**. The intermolecular forces are slightly stronger so the polymer is stronger, more dense and has a slightly higher melting point.

Material Choices

Life Cycle of a Product

Before a new product is produced, the manufacturing company must carry out a Life Cycle Assessment (LCA). The life cycle of a product, often known as Cradle to Grave, has three phases – **Manufacture, Use,** and **Disposal**. The LCA involves examining each of these three phases in detail, including the impact on the environment.

Each part of the life cycle of a product is carefully considered and assessed on the amount of energy and materials that will be used and how materials will be obtained and disposed of.

> **HT** The outcome of the LCA is dependent on several factors, including the use of the end product.

LCAs were introduced in the 1960s to encourage companies to reduce waste and be aware of environmental impact. New laws were put in place to protect the environment, cash incentives were offered to encourage recycling, and in 1996 a tax was introduced to discourage the use of landfill sites.

The purpose of an LCA is to ensure the most **sustainable** method is used, which means meeting the needs of today's society whilst allowing for the needs of future generations.

The diagram below shows what is being assessed in each stage of an LCA.

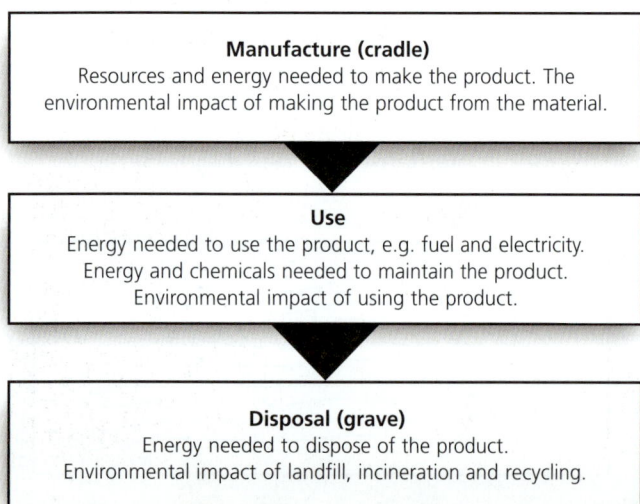

Manufacture (cradle)
Resources and energy needed to make the product. The environmental impact of making the product from the material.

Use
Energy needed to use the product, e.g. fuel and electricity. Energy and chemicals needed to maintain the product. Environmental impact of using the product.

Disposal (grave)
Energy needed to dispose of the product. Environmental impact of landfill, incineration and recycling.

Materials

Different materials can often be used to perform the same job. For example, disposable nappies are made from cellulose fibres, a super-absorbent polymer and fluff pulp whilst re-usable nappies are made from cloth. Disposable nappies may be more convenient but in a life cycle assessment which one is better for the environment?

The results of one study are shown below.

Impact per baby, per year	Re-usable nappies	Disposable nappies
Energy needed to produce product	2532MJ	8900MJ
Waste water	12.4m^3	28m^3
Raw materials used	29kg	569kg
Domestic solid waste produced	4kg	361kg

The evidence here shows that using re-usable nappies uses less energy, water and natural resources, whilst also producing less waste. This would suggest that people should be encouraged to use re-usable nappies.

Since 2003 it has been Government policy to encourage parents to reduce the number of disposable nappies they use.

Functions

The same material can be used to perform different jobs, for example, Teflon® (polytetrafluoroethene) was accidentally discovered in 1938 by Roy Plunkett. It is **chemically inert** and temperature resistant and there is also little impact of environmental damage when disposed of in landfill sites.

Teflon can be used in…

* gaskets and valves
* atomic bombs
* non-stick saucepans
* dentures.

Waste Management

To manage the waste that arises from our use of products we need to assess the environmental impact of each method of disposal, as well as the overall cost and loss of raw materials. There are three main methods for disposing of waste products and materials:

1 Use of Landfill Sites

Many materials such as plastics are non-biodegradable. Microorganisms have no effect on them so they will not decompose or rot away. The use of landfill sites for these non-biodegradable products can result in the waste of valuable resources, because nothing is being re-used or returned to the environment.

Some materials that do slowly degrade produce landfill gas (methane). Methane can be used to generate electricity, but if too much gas builds up underground it can cause an explosion.

If landfill sites are properly lined, they cause no harm to the environment and eventually the land can be reclaimed, e.g. for parks. However, in the past toxic waste has escaped when the site has been poorly engineered. Landfill is also taxed.

2 Incineration

Incineration, or burning materials, produces air pollution. The production of carbon dioxide contributes to the Greenhouse Effect, which results in global warming.

Some plastics produce toxic fumes when they are burned, e.g. the burning of poly(chloroethene), PVC, produces hydrogen chloride gas. Incineration again wastes valuable resources.

Newly built incinerators burn waste material at high temperatures to avoid the production of many harmful gases. The heat released from an incinerator could be used to produce steam to drive an electricity generator; this can save on the burning of fossil fuels to produce electricity. Apart from any gases, the only other waste product produced will be the ash.

3 Recycling

Recycling a product means that no new material needs to be made. This conserves our raw materials, money and energy. People should be encouraged to re-use products such as polyethene carrier bags and glass bottles.

However, it is very expensive to recycle some materials, e.g. plastics need to be sorted into their different types before they can be recycled. This is often done by hand and is very time consuming. Every time polyethene is recycled its long molecules tend to get torn, so it becomes weaker, and the quality of the product is reduced.

Material Choices

Example LCA: A Polypropylene Food Box

Stage of Life Cycle	Assessment questions – Energy requirements	Assessment questions – What is the environmental impact of each stage?
Manufacture	How much energy would be needed… • to drill the oil? • to distil the oil? • for polymerisation? • to mould the box? • to transport the materials between stages?	• How much oil will need to be taken from natural reserves? • What is the risk of oil spillage during transportation? • What method of transportation is required and how does it affect the environment? • What pollutants are produced during manufacture and transportation?
Use	How much energy would be required… • to fill the boxes with food? • to store the boxes, e.g. in a fridge or freezer? • to transport the boxes between the factory, shop and consumer's home?	• How will the product be transported between the factory, shop and consumer's home and how does this affect the environment? • What pollutants are produced during filling and transportation?
Disposal	How much energy would be used or recovered if the box was… • reused? • recycled? • incinerated? • thrown away?	• Would incineration produce pollutants / toxic gases? • How much energy could be reclaimed through incineration? • How much energy is needed to recycle the boxes and what is the cost? • What is the value of materials and energy wasted if the box is thrown away? • How much landfill would it generate?

Although the government regulates industrial processes (e.g. there is a limit on emissions of pollutants) the manufacturers still have choices to make.

They must evaluate the answers to all of these questions and compare LCAs for producing the same product but using different materials. In some cases the most environmentally friendly materials and methods may be too expensive so a different method will be used.

The examples above are all questions that can be answered using scientific models and investigations. However, there are some answers that cannot be found in this way. For example, the manufacturer needs to decide whether the amount of energy and resources used, and the impact on the environment, is justified to produce a convenience product.

Material Choices – Summary

Science Explanations

Materials and Properties

- All materials that we use are chemicals or mixtures of chemicals.
- Natural materials are found in the world around us, in non-living things such as the Earth's crust or living things such as plants and animals.
- Synthetic materials are alternatives to natural materials.
- A material may be chosen for its particular properties such as melting point; strength (tension and compression); stiffness; hardness; density.
- The properties of solid materials depend on how the molecules are arranged.
- Materials which have strong forces between the molecules require more energy to separate them and they therefore have high melting points.
- The properties of a material can be modified to increase its usefulness, e.g. making it stronger or more flexible.
- Modifications can include increasing chain length; cross-linking; the use of plasticizers.

> **HT** • Increased **crystallinity** can be used to modify a polymer.

- Crude oil consists mainly of hydrocarbons.
- A hydrocarbon is a chain molecule containing only hydrogen and carbon atoms.
- In hydrocarbons the length of the chain determines the boiling points.
- Small molecules that can be joined together are called monomers.
- Monomers can be joined together to form long-chains of molecules called polymers. This process is called polymerisation.

Life Cycle

- The life cycle of a product has three phrases – manufacture, use and disposal.
- Different materials can be used for the same job.
- The same material can be used for different jobs.

- There is an environmental impact associated with all the methods of disposing of waste – landfill sites, incineration and recycling.

Ideas about Science

Data and its Limitations

- Data is used to gain a better understanding of the properties of materials.
- Measurements do not provide a true value.
- Repeated measurements of the same quantity often vary due to the skill of the scientist, the limitations of the equipment, and external variables, e.g. different batches of a polymer made at different times.
- A best estimate of the true value can be found by calculating the mean of repeated measurements.
- If a measurement lies well outside the expected range of a true value it is probably incorrect and may be discarded.

Correlation and Cause

- It is important to control all the factors that are likely to affect the outcome, i.e. to carry out a fair test. This allows reliable and meaningful measurements to be taken.

Science and Technology

- When a new product is developed, by Law, a Life Cycle Assessment must be carried out.
- The environmental impact of a product, from manufacture to disposal, needs to be assessed.
- The beneficial effects of the product need to be weighed against economic and environmental costs.
- Sustainable ways of manufacturing products are encouraged to conserve our natural resources for future generations.

Food Matters

Different farming methods and the chemicals and additives that are added to our food can affect our health. This module looks at...

- issues facing farmers in the production of large amounts of good quality food
- chemicals found in foods: both natural chemicals and additives
- the role of the Food Standards Agency
- what happens to our food when we eat it
- health risks associated with eating.

The Nitrogen Cycle

Nitrogen is a vital element in all living things. It is used in the production of amino acids and proteins, which are needed for plants and animals to grow. Fertile soil containing a range of nutrients is needed for crops to grow. There is a continual cycle of elements through consumption of living organisms and decay. This is clearly seen in the nitrogen cycle, which shows how nitrogen and its compounds are recycled in nature.

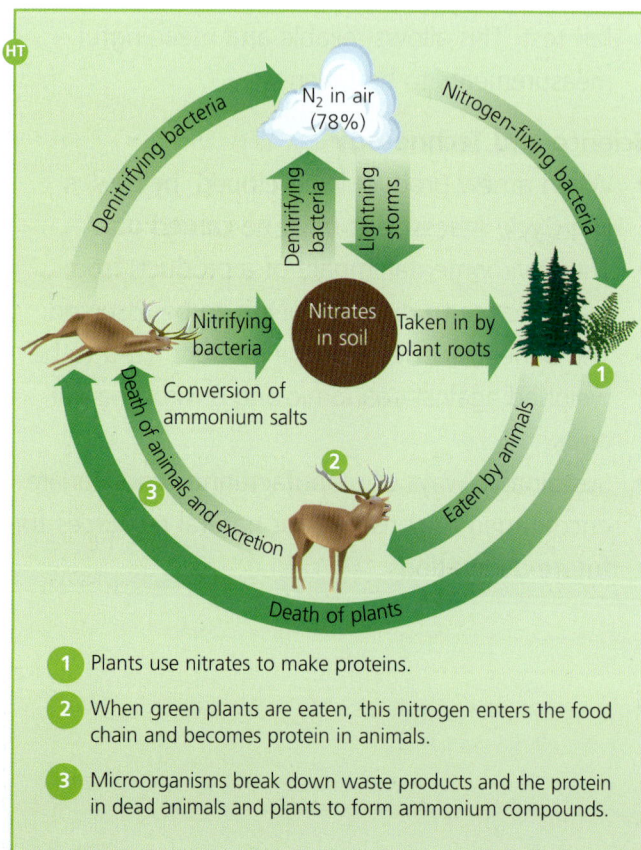

HT

N_2 in air (78%)

Denitrifying bacteria

Nitrogen-fixing bacteria

Denitrifying bacteria

Lightning storms

Nitrifying bacteria

Nitrates in soil

Taken in by plant roots

Conversion of ammonium salts

Death of animals and excretion

Eaten by animals

Death of plants

1 Plants use nitrates to make proteins.

2 When green plants are eaten, this nitrogen enters the food chain and becomes protein in animals.

3 Microorganisms break down waste products and the protein in dead animals and plants to form ammonium compounds.

Intensive and Organic Farming

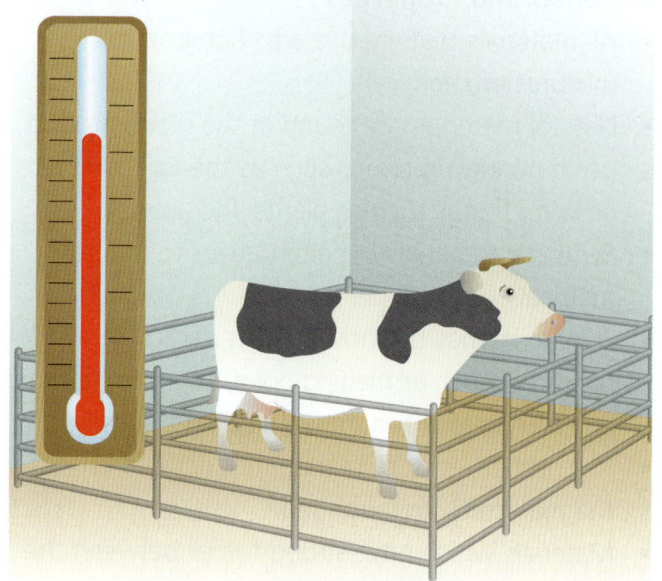

Farmers are increasingly faced with the challenge of producing greater quantities of food at lower costs. To help achieve this, farmers can use **intensive farming** practices which include the use of fertilisers, pesticides and herbicides. They can also keep animals in carefully controlled environments where their temperature and movement are limited. However, some people find this morally unacceptable as the animals have a poor quality of life.

Organic farming uses more natural methods which have little environmental impact. However, the costs are higher as more farm workers need to be employed.

Farms must pass the UK National, and International Standards if they want to be recognised as organic farms; the Soil Association is one of the agencies that monitors the standards of these farms.

Farming Issues

There are several issues facing farming today which intensive farms and organic farms try to solve in different ways. These can affect the environment, and benefit groups of people, in different ways.

Maintaining Fertile Soil

The land becomes less fertile when crops are harvested because plants remove nutrients such as nitrogen from the soil and they are not returned through the natural process of decay. Intensive farmers use manufactured fertilisers to replace the lost nitrogen compounds and other nutrients. Organic farmers use manure from animals to add nutrients to the soil. They also rotate their crops, e.g. grass / clover → wheat → root crops (beet) → grass / clover.

HT Harvested crops also remove **potassium** and **phosphorus** from the soil.

Crop Yields

Pests (such as insects) may carry disease and can damage crops. This means that fewer crops are produced or there is a lower yield. Intensive farms use **pesticides** (chemicals that kill the pests) while organic farmers use **biological control** (introduction of a predator). Intensive farms generally produce high yields at low cost, which benefits consumers. Organic farms are more labour intensive and produce lower yields at higher costs.

The Environment (Intensive)

Intensive farms are often small, leaving more room for woodland. However, hedgerows are often removed to create larger fields, to maximise the amount of crops planted per area of land. The farmers' use of fertilisers can lead to **eutrophication** and pesticides can harm other organisms that are not pests. Pesticides can accumulate in the food chain passing the toxins to animals further up the chain. Over 50% of the energy used in intensive farming is used to make fertilisers. Most of this energy comes from burning fossil fuels (see p.7).

The Environment (Organic)

Organic farms have smaller fields with less destruction of hedgerows. Food chains are not affected. They do not use pesticides and fertilisers so there is less eutrophication, and there is more local employment. This is more **sustainable development**.

HT There is a difference between what can be done and what should be done, and different social and economic circumstances also need to be considered.

Chemicals in Living Things

Many chemicals in living organisms are natural polymers, (see p.14), e.g. carbohydrates and proteins. Cellulose, starch and sugars are carbohydrates which contain the elements carbon, hydrogen and oxygen, e.g. glucose $C_6H_{12}O_6$.

Glucose molecules join together in a long chain to form starch.

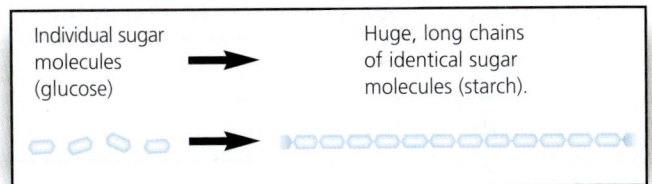

| Individual sugar molecules (glucose) | → | Huge, long chains of identical sugar molecules (starch). |

Cellulose is formed when the glucose molecules form long chains which are cross-linked.

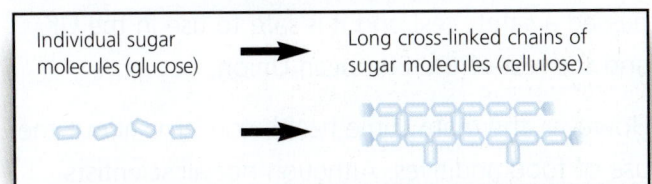

| Individual sugar molecules (glucose) | → | Long cross-linked chains of sugar molecules (cellulose). |

Proteins are polymers made from long chains of amino acids. They contain the elements carbon, hydrogen, oxygen, nitrogen and sometimes other elements such as sulfur.

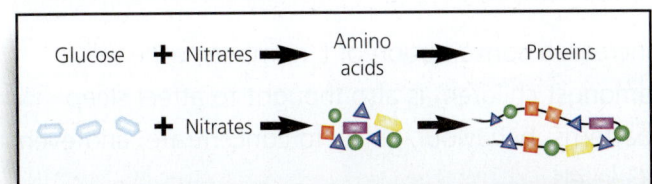

| Glucose | + Nitrates | → | Amino acids | → | Proteins |

Food Matters

Chemicals in Food

Chemicals, or additives, are added to food for a number of reasons (see table below):

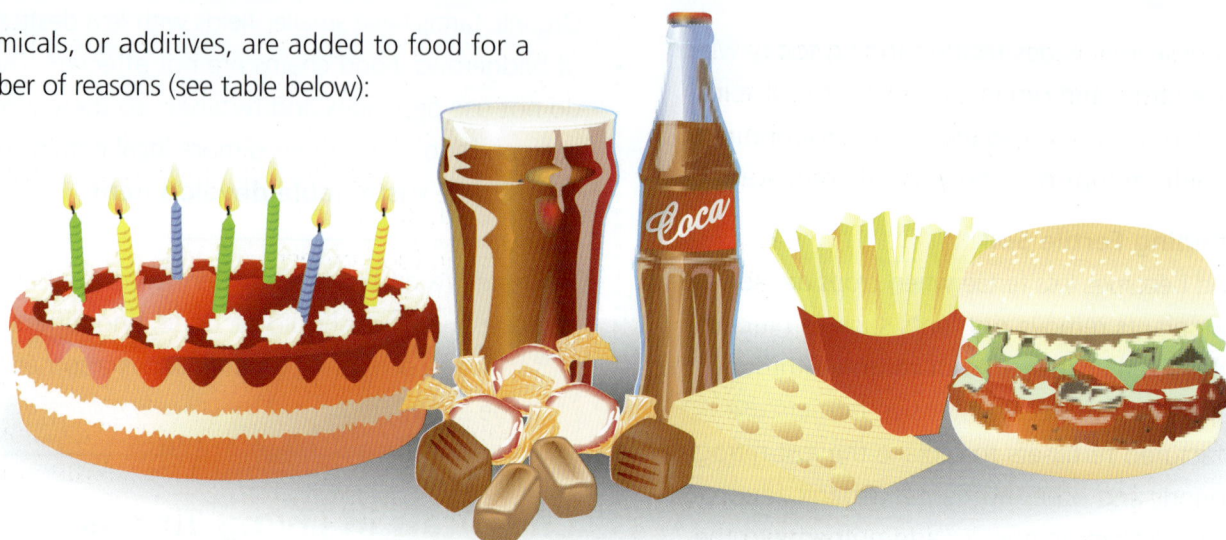

Additive	Reason
Colouring	Replaces colour lost during processing or storage. Colourful food looks more attractive.
Flavouring	Gives a particular taste or flavour. Replaces flavours lost during processing.
Emulsifier	Used to mix together ingredients that would normally separate, e.g. oil and water.
Stabiliser	Helps to stop ingredients from separating again.
Preservative	Stops mould or bacteria growing in food, so foods are kept safe and fresher for longer.
Sweetener	Used to reduce the amount of sugar added to processed foods and drinks.
Antioxidant	Added to foods containing fats or oils to stop them from reacting with oxygen in the air.

Health Concerns

If an additive has an **E number**, this means it has passed a safety test and it is safe to use in the UK and the rest of the European Union.

However, there are some health concerns about the use of food additives. Although not all scientists agree, some think, for example, that the flavouring monosodium glutamate (E621), can have harmful effects, and that sodium benzoate (E211) and carmoisine (E122) can be linked to hyperactivity and skin problems.

Increased consumption of E numbers, especially amongst children, is also thought to affect sleep patterns, behaviour, ability to concentrate, and even IQ levels.

Sweeties

INGREDIENTS:
Sugar, Milk, Cocoa Butter, Modified starch, Colours (E104 Quinoline Yellow, E110 Sunset Yellow FCF, E120 Carminic acid, E122 Carmoisine, E124 Cochineal Red A, E133 Brilliant Blue FCF, E171 Titanium dioxide), Glazing agents (E901 Beeswax, E903 Carnauba wax), Flavouring.

The Food We Eat

Many plants are eaten for food. Some can be eaten raw, e.g. fruit and vegetables, but there are some plants which contain natural chemicals which may be toxic, and cause harm if they are not cooked properly.

Some of these chemicals may also give rise to problems for some people. Examples are listed in the table below:

Plant	Natural Chemical	Effect
Cassava (a woody shrub)	Poisonous compounds release cyanide	Cyanide poisoning if eaten raw. Heating removes the toxin.
Wheat	Gluten	Damages the small intestine in people who suffer from intolerance (known as coeliac disease).
Peanuts	Proteins in the nuts	Allergic reaction from fresh, cooked and roasted peanuts as the proteins are not destroyed by cooking.

There are many opportunities for harmful chemicals to get into our food, and it is impossible for any food to be completely safe:

- Contamination during storage – moulds growing on cereals, dried fruit and nuts can produce a carcinogen called aflatoxin.
- The use of pesticides and herbicides by farmers can mean that chemicals sprayed onto crops may remain in the products we eat.
- Food processing and cooking may produce harmful chemicals.
- Poor storage of cooked food may result in contamination by bacteria, which can lead to **food poisoning**.

Organic farming and the way in which food is stored and processed can reduce the risks of harmful chemicals getting into the food.

There are also a number of steps that people can take to reduce their exposure to harmful chemicals. These include…

- keeping a hygienic kitchen and quickly disposing of waste food
- cooking food properly
- not re-freezing previously frozen meats
- regularly cleaning out the fridge to avoid keeping cooked foods too long
- reading food labels – particularly important for people who suffer from coeliac disease or have known allergies.

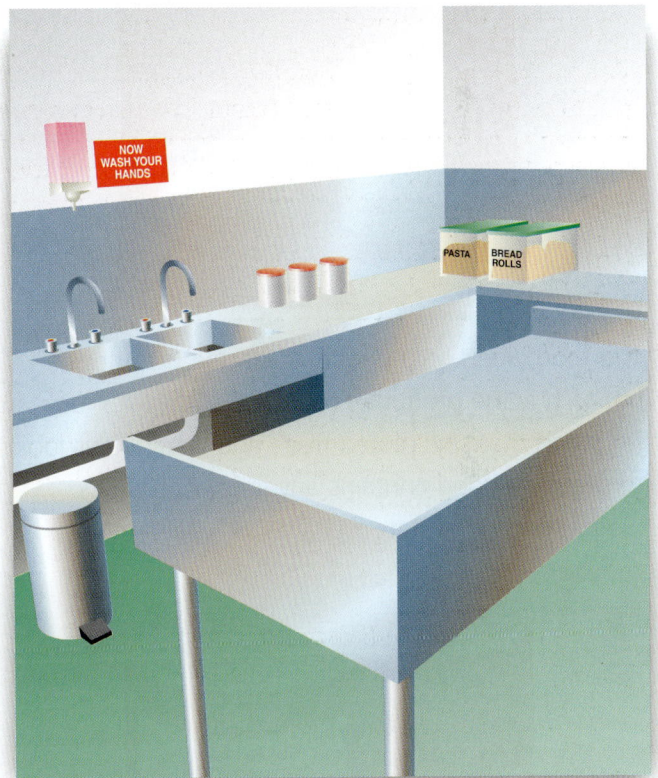

The **risk** from different chemicals in our food can vary from person to person. For example, most of the time eating out is a low-risk activity because there are laws about food hygiene, and kitchens must meet Health and Safety standards. However, it is not always possible to know all the ingredients that have gone into preparing food. Therefore, if you are allergic to a common ingredient in food such as wheat, eggs, nuts, etc. eating out may be a higher risk for you than for other people.

Food Matters

Food Standards Agency

The Food Standards Agency (FSA) is an independent food safety watchdog set up by an Act of Parliament in 2000.

The FSA helps to make sure that our food is safe, healthy and fairly marketed. It also makes sure that food producers are acting within the law. The FSA promotes healthy eating and aims to minimise illnesses such as food poisoning. It makes sure that food labels are clear and that they say exactly what is in the food.

The food labels help people to decide whether or not to buy the product. For example, coeliacs look for labels that say 'gluten free'; and vegetarians look to see if the food contains any animal products. (Some foods also state 'suitable for vegetarians'.)

The FSA wants to give the public the most up-to-date information about food safety. In order to do this the agency employs scientists to carry out research into food issues such as **genetically modified** (GM) foods.

Sometimes the research findings are controversial and the results are uncertain. Scientists may even disagree about what the results actually mean. Further problems may be encountered from manufacturers who may not want to accept the research findings, as it may not be in their economic interest.

If there is any doubt about food safety then one of the scientific advisory committees is asked to carry out a risk assessment. They must decide...

- if the food contains any chemicals that could cause harm
- how harmful the chemicals are
- how much of the food must be eaten before it is likely to harm people
- if any groups of people are particularly vulnerable, e.g. the elderly, children, or those suffering from a previous illnesses.

HT The outcome of a risk assessment is often based on experience gained from people or animals eating the food.

Sometimes the scientific evidence is uncertain and the risk is unknown, in which case the **precautionary principle** is applied. Both experts and the public are consulted before the regulators make a decision about food safety.

They have to weigh up the costs and benefits of any decision, as the priority is to protect public safety and not just let the new foods be mass produced and put on the market.

For example, many people ask the question, 'Are GM foods safe to eat?'

For many GM foods, scientists simply do not know enough about the science of altering genes, which may lead to health problems in the future. There is also not much data yet on the potential risks to humans, and this is why the precautionary principle is sometimes applied.

Digestion

When we eat food, it gets digested.

Physical digestion includes chewing and squeezing food in the stomach. This breaks the food into smaller pieces so that it can pass more easily through the gut, and increases the surface area of the food to help enzymes work more quickly.

Chemical digestion uses enzymes to break down the large insoluble molecules into smaller soluble molecules.

The smaller molecules can diffuse through the walls of the small intestines into the blood, where they are transported to different parts of the body.

Enzymes in the saliva and stomach break down starch into glucose.

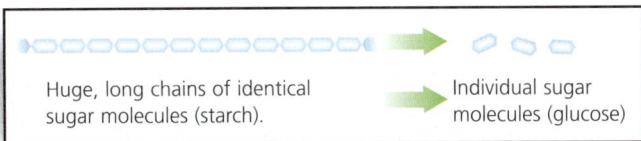

Huge, long chains of identical sugar molecules (starch).

Individual sugar molecules (glucose)

Enzymes in the small intestine break down proteins into amino acids.

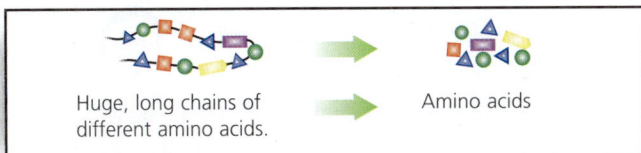

Huge, long chains of different amino acids.

Amino acids

The glucose is used in respiration to release energy and the amino acids are used to build new cells and repair damaged ones.

Amino acids are taken from the bloodstream by cells as they grow. The amino acids build up in the cells until proteins are made. Many parts of the body, including muscle, tendons, skin, hair, and haemoglobin in the blood, consist mainly of proteins.

In a healthy person the excess amino acids are transported to the liver where they are broken down to form urea. Urea is transported in the blood to the kidneys where it is filtered out before being excreted in urine. If the liver did not function correctly, harmful chemicals could be formed during the breakdown of the amino acids.

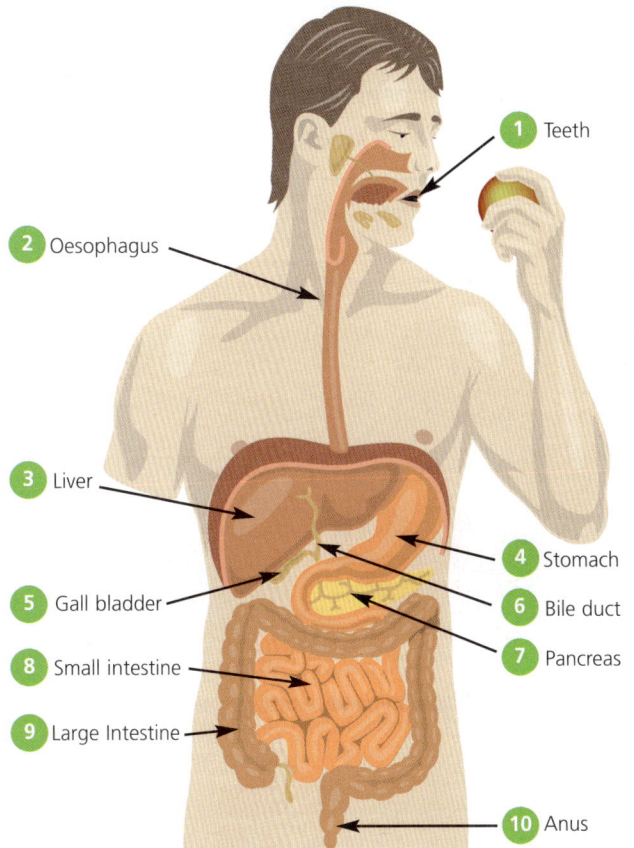

1 Teeth
2 Oesophagus
3 Liver
4 Stomach
5 Gall bladder
6 Bile duct
7 Pancreas
8 Small intestine
9 Large Intestine
10 Anus

1 **Teeth** – used for grinding up food.

2 **Oesophagus** – carries food from the mouth to the stomach.

3 **Liver** – produces bile which helps digest fat.

4 **Stomach** – stores food. It produces an enzyme to help digest food. Hydrochloric acid is released by cells in the wall of the stomach. It kills bacteria and provides the best conditions for the enzyme to work.

5 **Gall bladder** – stores bile, before releasing it into the small intestine.

6 **Bile duct** – takes bile from the gall bladder to the small intestine.

7 **Pancreas** – produces enzymes which are released into the small intestine to help digest food.

8 **Small intestine** – produces more enzymes which complete the chemical digestion of food. The small, soluble molecules produced by digestion are absorbed by the small intestine.

9 **Large intestine** – excess water from the contents of the intestines is reabsorbed into the blood here. Faeces are stored before passing out of the body.

10 **Anus** – faeces leave the body here.

Food Matters

Importance of a Healthy Diet

In order to remain healthy it is important to eat a balanced diet. This includes…

Carbohydrates – bread, pasta, potatoes

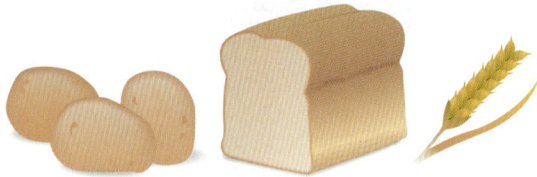

Proteins – eggs, meat, fish

Vitamins and minerals – fruit, vegetables, milk

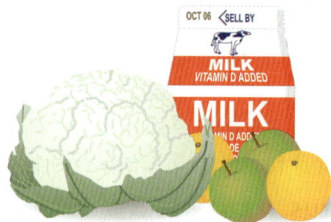

Fats – milk, butter, cheese

Water

Roughage (cellulose) – green vegetables, fibre, etc.

Eating the wrong foods can lead to many different types of diseases.

For example, in the UK, **obesity** (being very overweight) is now a major problem, even amongst children. The main cause is eating too much, especially fatty, sugary foods, and not exercising enough.

Even though the link between heart disease and obesity is well known, many people still choose to over-eat and do not exercise. There are a number of reasons for this; people often think that it will not happen to them and that the short-term benefits outweigh the risks:

- Foods that contain a lot of fat, salt and sugar such as crisps, soft drinks and sweets taste good.
- Fruit and vegetables can be expensive to buy.
- Exercising is hard work and people cannot be bothered.
- Processed microwave meals are quick and easy.
- Making meals from fresh ingredients takes time.

HT Obese people are endangering their health and increasing their chances of developing heart disease, cancer and diabetes.

If you eat a lot of the wrong type of foods, you may be putting yourself at risk of becoming obese. Questions you might ask yourself include…

- how healthy is my lifestyle?
- is there a family history of cancer, heart disease or diabetes, etc?
- am I in a high risk age group?

If you are at high risk and choose not to change your lifestyle, then you may later pay the consequences of poor health.

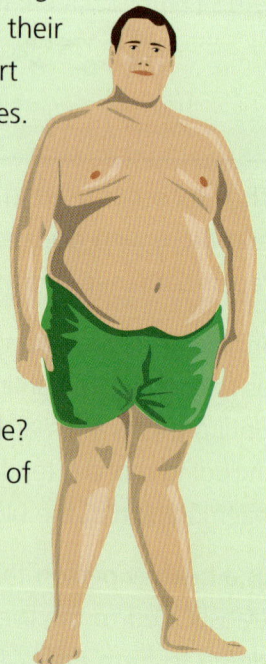

Diabetes

Diabetes is a disease that is caused by the pancreas not producing and releasing enough **insulin**, which allows the blood sugar level to fluctuate. This can lead to a person's blood sugar level rising fatally high, resulting in a coma, and even death.

Many processed foods contain high levels of sugar, which is quickly absorbed into the bloodstream, causing a rapid rise in the blood sugar level.

Even though there is some evidence to suggest that there is a link between diabetes and poor diet, many people still eat too much processed food.

There are two types of diabetes:

- **Type 1 diabetes** is where the pancreas stops producing insulin altogether as the special cells in the pancreas are destroyed. This is more likely to start in young people and the blood sugar level can be controlled by injecting insulin.
- **Type 2 diabetes** is where the pancreas does not make enough insulin or the cells do not respond. This can often be treated by diet and exercise although medicine and insulin injections are usually also needed.

The latter type of diabetes is late-onset diabetes and is more likely to start in older people. However, it is now also being seen in younger people. This is because there are more young people who are obese; this group of people has a higher **risk factor** than those who are the correct weight and have regular exercise. Other risk factors include genetics and age, for example, some ethnic minority groups develop type 2 diabetes at a younger age.

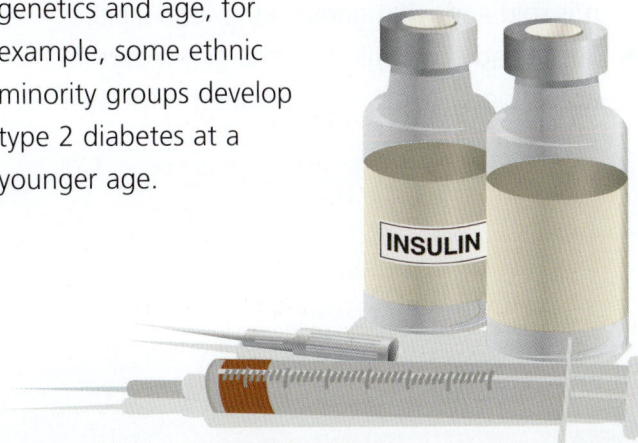

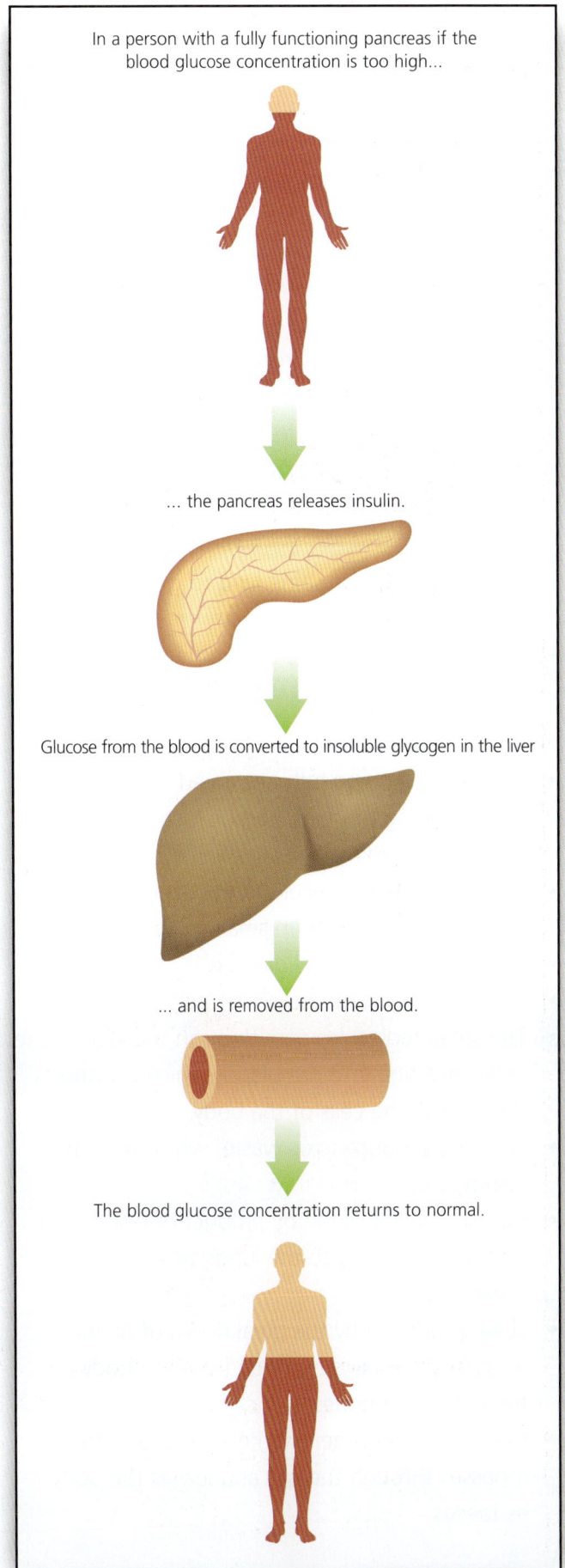

INSULIN

In a person with a fully functioning pancreas if the blood glucose concentration is too high...

... the pancreas releases insulin.

Glucose from the blood is converted to insoluble glycogen in the liver

... and is removed from the blood.

The blood glucose concentration returns to normal.

Food Matters – Summary

Science Explanations

Chemical Cycles

- Decomposers (microorganisms) break down the dead bodies of plants and animals. They play a very important role in the recycling of materials.
- Protein molecules are important in all living cells. They contain nitrogen atoms.

> **HT**
> - Compounds containing nitrogen are continually recycled. This process is known as the nitrogen cycle.
> - Potassium and phosphorus are important in living cells. They are also continually recycled.

- Farmers re-use the same land to grow plants and rear animals for food.
- The removal of nitrogen from the soil by farming makes it less fertile.

Maintenance of Life

- Animals, including humans, need a balanced diet including proteins, carbohydrates, fats, minerals, vitamins, and water.
- Large insoluble molecules are broken down in the gut by enzymes to form small soluble molecules.
- Starch is digested into glucose.
- Protein is digested into amino acids.
- The small molecules pass through the wall of the small intestine into the blood, which transports them to all the cells of the body.
- The cells produce toxic waste, which must be disposed of.
- Carbon dioxide is the by-product of respiration and is transported to the lungs where it is exhaled.
- Urea, produced by the breakdown of amino acids in the liver, is excreted from the body by the kidneys in urine.
- Undigested food never enters the bloodstream; it passes through the gut and leaves the body as faeces.

Ideas about Science

Risk

- Everything we do carries a risk of accident or harm; nothing is risk free.
- New technologies based on science often introduce new risks.
- Risk can often be assessed over a period of time.

> **HT**
> - To make a decision about a risk, we need to take account of the chance of it happening and the consequences if it did.

- People are willing to accept risk if they enjoy, or benefit from, the associated activity.
- People are more willing to accept risk associated with the things they choose to do rather than the things they must do.

> **HT**
> - The precautionary principle tells us to avoid doing an activity if we are unsure about the associated risks.

Science and Technology

- The benefits of science-based technology need to be weighed against the costs.
- Scientists may identify unintended impacts of human activity on the environment. Sustainable development is concerned with using natural resources to reduce the impact.
- Scientific research is subject to official regulations and laws. There are laws about how farmers produce food, how the food is processed, how it is sold and what goes on the food label.
- Social and economic contexts play a part in accepting or rejecting applications in science.

Chemical Patterns

Module C4

Theories of atomic structure can be used to explain the properties and behaviour of elements. This module looks at...

* the pattern of properties in elements
* the Periodic Table
* alkali metals and halogens
* ionic bonding.

The Periodic Table

Elements are the 'building blocks' of all materials.

The atoms of each of the 100 or so elements have a different proton number. The elements are arranged in order of ascending **atomic** (or **proton**) **number**, which gives repeating patterns in the properties of elements.

Groups

A **vertical column** of elements is called a **group**. For example, lithium (Li), sodium (Na) and potassium (K) are all elements found in Group 1.

Elements in the same group have the same number of electrons in their outermost shell (see p.30) (except helium). This number also coincides with the group number, e.g. Group 1 elements have 1 electron in their outer shell, and Group 7 elements have 7 electrons in their outer shell. Elements in the same group have similar properties.

Periods

A **horizontal row** of elements is called a **period**. For example, lithium (Li), carbon (C) and neon (Ne) are all elements in the same period.

The period to which an element belongs corresponds to the number of shells of electrons it has, e.g. sodium (Na), aluminium (Al) and chlorine (Cl) all have three shells of electrons, and so they are found in the third period.

The Periodic Table can be used as a reference table to obtain important information about the elements. For example:

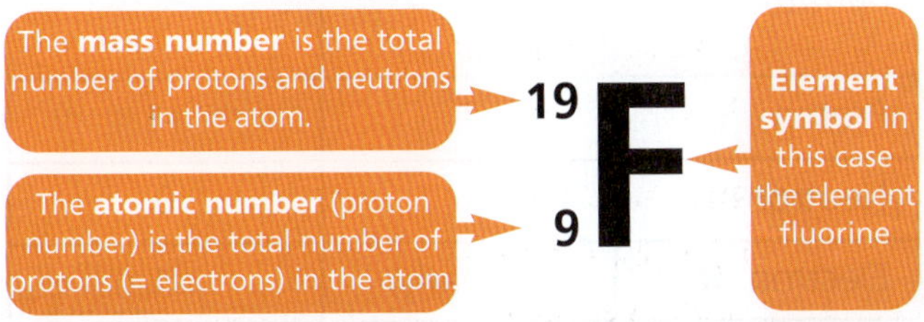

The **mass number** is the total number of protons and neutrons in the atom. → 19 F — Element symbol in this case the element fluorine

The **atomic number** (proton number) is the total number of protons (= electrons) in the atom. → 9

You can also tell if elements are metals or non-metals by looking at their position in the table.

You will be given a copy of the Periodic Table in the exam.

The Periodic Table

Key

Relative atomic mass → 1 / Symbol → H / Name → hydrogen / Atomic (proton) number → 1

non-metals

metals

1	2												3	4	5	6	7	8 or 0
																		4 He helium 2
7 Li lithium 3	9 Be beryllium 4												11 B boron 5	12 C carbon 6	14 N nitrogen 7	16 O oxygen 8	19 F fluorine 9	20 Ne neon 10
23 Na sodium 11	24 Mg magnesium 12												27 Al aluminium 13	28 Si silicon 14	31 P phosphorus 15	32 S sulfur 16	35.5 Cl chlorine 17	40 Ar argon 18
39 K potassium 19	40 Ca calcium 20	45 Sc scandium 21	48 Ti titanium 22	51 V vanadium 23	52 Cr chromium 24	55 Mn manganese 25	56 Fe iron 26	59 Co cobalt 27	59 Ni nickel 28	63.5 Cu copper 29	65 Zn zinc 30		70 Ga gallium 31	73 Ge germanium 32	75 As arsenic 33	79 Se selenium 34	80 Br bromine 35	84 Kr krypton 36
85 Rb rubidium 37	88 Sr strontium 38	89 Y yttrium 39	91 Zr zirconium 40	93 Nb niobium 41	96 Mo molybdenum 42	98 Tc technetium 43	101 Ru ruthenium 44	103 Rh rhodium 45	106 Pd palladium 46	108 Ag silver 47	112 Cd cadmium 48		115 In indium 49	119 Sn tin 50	122 Sb antimony 51	128 Te tellurium 52	127 I iodine 53	131 Xe xenon 54
133 Cs caesium 55	137 Ba barium 56	139 La* lanthanum 57	178 Hf hafnium 72	181 Ta tantalum 73	184 W tungsten 74	186 Re rhenium 75	190 Os osmium 76	192 Ir iridium 77	195 Pt platinum 78	197 Au gold 79	201 Hg mercury 80		204 Tl thallium 81	207 Pb lead 82	209 Bi bismuth 83	210 Po polonium 84	210 At astatine 85	222 Rn radon 86
223 Fr francium 87	226 Ra radium 88	227 Ac* actinium 89	261 Rf rutherfordium 104	262 Db dubnium 105	265 Sg seaborgium 106	264 Bh bohrium 107	277 Hs hassium 108	268 Mt meitnerium 109	271 Ds darmstadtium 110	272 Rg roentgenium 111								

Chemical Patterns

Atoms

All substances are made up of **atoms** (very small particles). Each atom has a small central nucleus, made up of **protons** and **neutrons** (with the exception of hydrogen), which is surrounded by **electrons** arranged in **shells** (or **energy levels**).

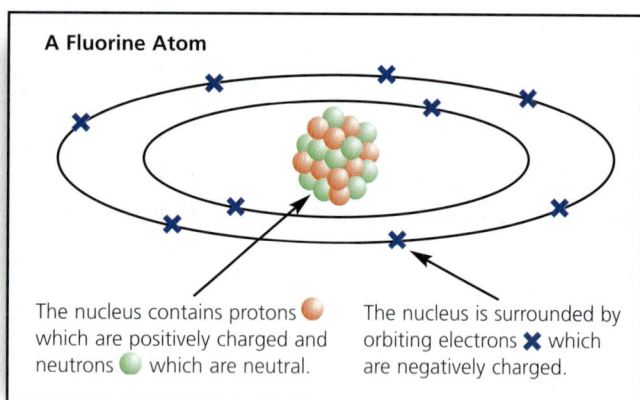

A Fluorine Atom

The nucleus contains protons which are positively charged and neutrons which are neutral.

The nucleus is surrounded by orbiting electrons ✖ which are negatively charged.

Atomic Particle	Relative Mass	Relative Charge
Proton	1	+1
Neutron	1	0
Electron ✖	0 (nearly)	-1

- An atom has the same number of protons as electrons, so the atom as a whole is neutral (i.e. it has no electrical charge).
- A proton has the same mass as a neutron.
- The mass of an electron is negligible, i.e. nearly nothing, when compared to a proton or neutron.
- A substance which contains only one sort of atom is called an element.
- All atoms of the same element have the same number of protons.
- Atoms of different elements have different numbers of protons.
- The elements are arranged in the Periodic Table in order of increasing atomic (proton) number.

Spectroscopy

When some elements are heated they emit distinctive coloured flames. Lithium, sodium, and potassium compounds can be recognised by the distinctive colours they produce in a flame test.

A piece of nichrome (a nickel-chromium alloy) wire is dipped in the compound and then put into a Bunsen flame to produce the following distinctive colours:

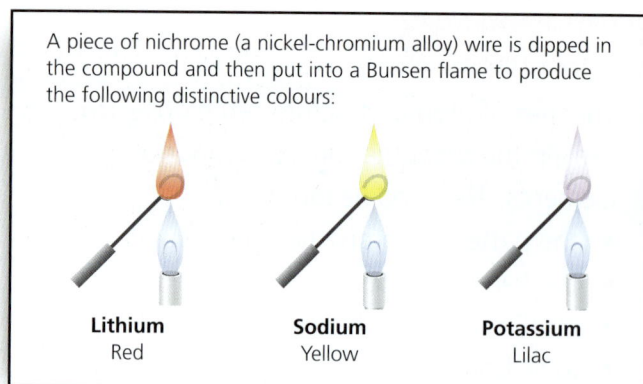

Lithium Red   **Sodium** Yellow   **Potassium** Lilac

The light emitted from the flame of an element produces a characteristic line spectrum. Each line in the spectrum represents an energy change as excited electrons fall from high energy levels to lower energy levels. The study of spectra has helped chemists to discover new elements.

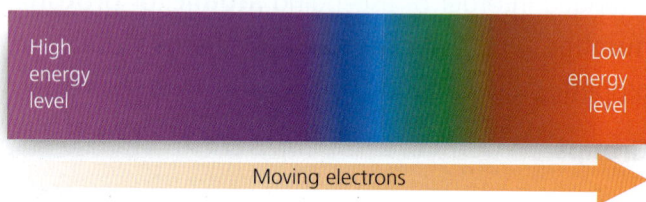

High energy level   Low energy level

Moving electrons

Electron Configuration

Electron configuration tells us how the electrons are arranged around the nucleus of an atom in shells (energy levels).

- The electrons in an atom occupy the lowest available shells (i.e. shells closest to the nucleus).
- The first level (or shell) can only contain a maximum of 2 electrons.
- The shells after this can hold a maximum of 8 electrons.
- The electron configuration is written as a series of numbers, e.g. oxygen is 2.6; aluminium is 2.8.3; and potassium is 2.8.8.1.

There is a connection between the number of outer electrons and the position of an element in a group. You can also deduce the period to which an element belongs from its electron configuration, e.g. oxygen is 2.6, which means it is found in the second period, potassium is 2.8.8.1, which means it is found in the fourth period, and so on (i.e. the number of energy levels occupied by electrons equals the number of the period).

Chemical Patterns

Electron Configuration of the First 20 Elements

GROUP 8

Helium, He
Atomic No. = 2
No. of electrons = 2

2

Neon, Ne
Atomic No. = 10
No. of electrons = 10

2.8

Argon, Ar
Atomic No. = 18
No. of electrons = 18

2.8.8

GROUP 7

Fluorine, F
Atomic No. = 9
No. of electrons = 9

2.7

Chlorine, Cl
Atomic No. = 17
No. of electrons = 17

2.8.7

GROUP 6

Oxygen, O
Atomic No. = 8
No. of electrons = 8

2.6

Sulfur, S
Atomic No. = 16
No. of electrons = 16

2.8.6

GROUP 5

Nitrogen, N
Atomic No. = 7
No. of electrons = 7

2.5

Phosphorus, P
Atomic No. = 15
No. of electrons = 15

2.8.5

GROUP 4

Carbon, C
Atomic No. = 6
No. of electrons = 6

2.4

Silicon, Si
Atomic No. = 14
No. of electrons = 14

2.8.4

GROUP 3

Boron, B
Atomic No = 5
No. of electrons = 5

2.3

Aluminium, Al
Atomic No. = 13
No. of electrons = 13

2.8.3

Electron configuration of oxygen
is 2.6 because there are...
- 2 electrons in this shell
- 6 electrons in this shell.

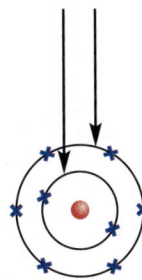

Hydrogen, H
Atomic No = 1
No. of electrons = 1

1

GROUP 1

Lithium, Li
Atomic No. = 3
No. of electrons = 3

2.1

Sodium, Na
Atomic No. = 11
No. of electrons = 11

2.8.1

Potassium, K
Atomic No. = 19
No. of electrons = 19

2.8.8.1

GROUP 2

Beryllium, Be
Atomic No. = 4
No. of electrons = 4

2.2

Magnesium, Mg
Atomic No. = 12
No. of electrons = 12

2.8.2

Calcium, Ca
Atomic No. = 20
No. of electrons = 20

2.8.8.2

Chemical Patterns

Balanced Equations

The total mass of the products of a chemical reaction is always equal to the total mass of the reactants.

This is because the products of a chemical reaction are made up from the atoms of the reactants – no atoms are lost or made. So, chemical symbol equations must always be balanced: there must be the same number of atoms of each element on the reactant side of the equation as there is on the product side (see Example 1).

Writing Balanced Equations

Follow these steps to write a balanced equation (see Example 2):

1. Write a word equation for the chemical reaction.
2. Substitute in formulae for the elements or compounds involved.
3. Balance the equation by adding numbers in front of the reactants and/or products.
4. Write a balanced symbol equation.

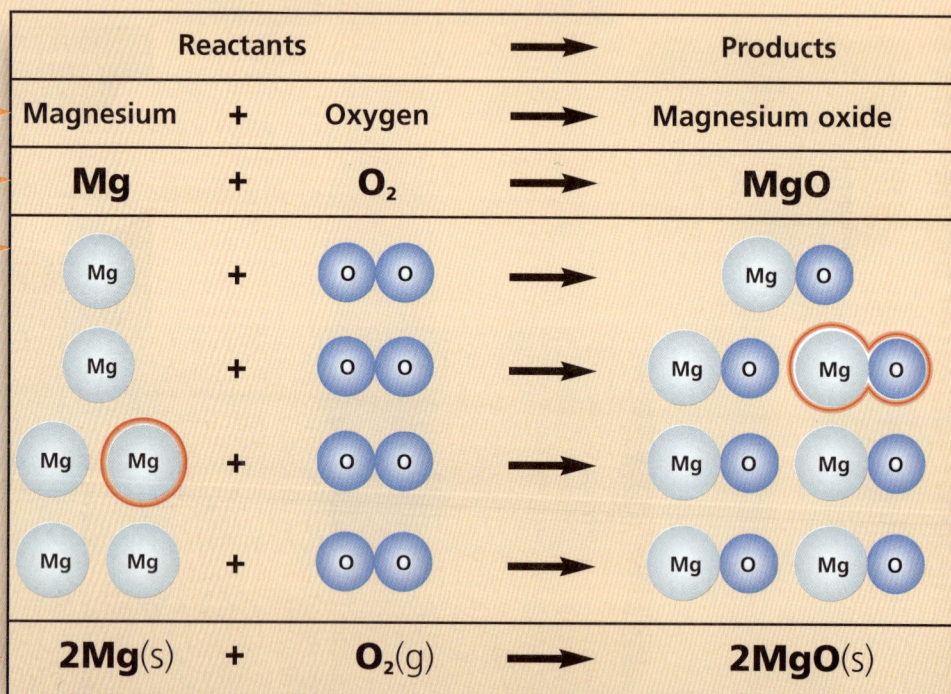

Example 1

	Reactants				Products	

Word equation...

| Sodium | + | Water | $\longrightarrow$ | Sodium hydroxide | + | Hydrogen |

Symbol equation...

| $2Na(s)$ | + | $2H_2O(l)$ | $\longrightarrow$ | $2NaOH(aq)$ | + | $H_2(g)$ |

This means that...

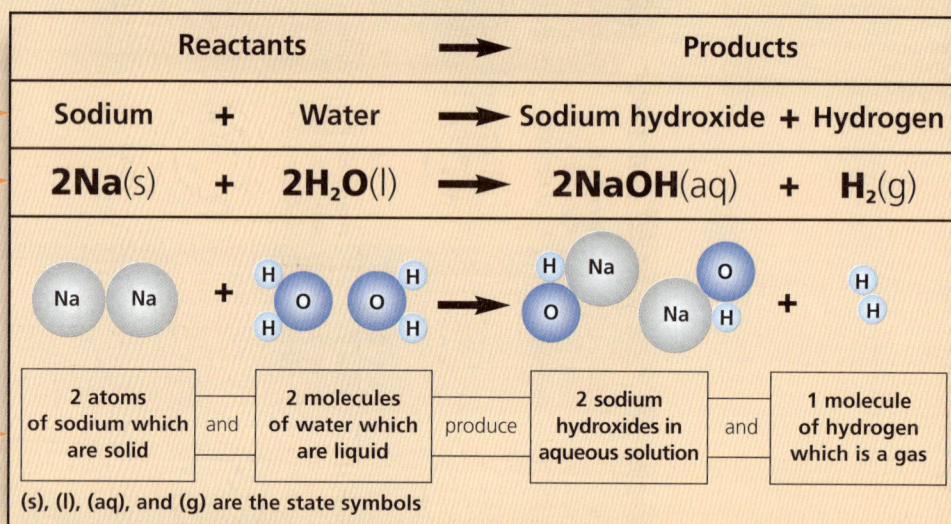

| 2 atoms of sodium which are solid | and | 2 molecules of water which are liquid | produce | 2 sodium hydroxides in aqueous solution | and | 1 molecule of hydrogen which is a gas |

(s), (l), (aq), and (g) are the state symbols

Example 2

	Reactants			Products

1 Write a word equation

| Magnesium | + | Oxygen | $\longrightarrow$ | Magnesium oxide |

2 Substitute in formulae

| Mg | + | O_2 | $\longrightarrow$ | MgO |

3 Balance the equation

- There are 2 **O**s on the reactant side, but only 1 **O** on the product side. We need to add another **MgO** to the product side to balance the **O**s.
- We now need to add another **Mg** on the reactant side to balance the **Mg**s.
- There are 2 Mg atoms and 2 O atoms on each side – **it is balanced**.

4 Write a balanced symbol equation

| $2Mg(s)$ | + | $O_2(g)$ | $\longrightarrow$ | $2MgO(s)$ |

Chemical Patterns

Hazard Symbols

Hazardous materials will have one of the following hazard symbols on their packaging.

Toxic
These substances can kill when swallowed, breathed in or absorbed through the skin.

Oxidising
These substances provide oxygen, which allows other substances to burn more fiercely.

Harmful
These substances are similar to toxic substances but they are less dangerous.

Highly Flammable
These substances will catch fire easily. They pose a serious fire risk.

Corrosive
These substances attack living tissue, including eyes and skin, and can damage materials.

Irritant
These substances are not corrosive but they can cause blistering of the skin.

Environmental Hazard
These substances may present a danger to the environment.

Safety Precautions

Some common safety precautions are…

- wearing gloves and eye protection, and washing hands after handling chemicals
- using safety screens
- using small amounts and low concentrations of the chemicals
- working in a fume cupboard or ventilating the room
- not eating or drinking when working with chemicals
- not working near naked flames.

Group 1 – The Alkali Metals

There are six metals in Group 1. As we go down the group, the alkali metals become more reactive.

Alkali metals have low melting points. The melting and boiling points decrease as we go down the group.

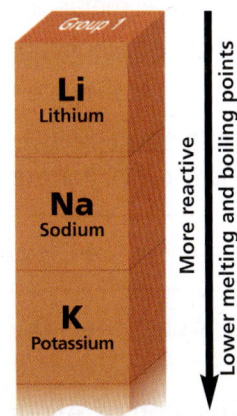

Physical Properties of the Alkali Metals

Element	Melting Point (°C)	Boiling Point (°C)	Density (g/cm³)
Lithium, Li	180	1340	0.53
Sodium, Na	98	883	0.97
Potassium, K	64	760	0.86
Rubidium, Rb	39	688	1.53
Caesium, Cs	29	671	1.90

Alkali Metal Compounds

When alkali metals react they form compounds that are similar. The reactivity of the reaction increases as we go down the group. The table below shows the compounds formed when alkali metals react with water, oxygen and chlorine.

Element	+ Water	+ Oxygen	+ Chlorine
Lithium, Li	LiOH	Li_2O	LiCl
Sodium, Na	NaOH	Na_2O	NaCl
Potassium, K	KOH	K_2O	KCl

Reaction of Alkali Metals with Chlorine

Chlorine reacts vigorously with alkali metals to form colourless crystalline salts called metal chlorides, for example:

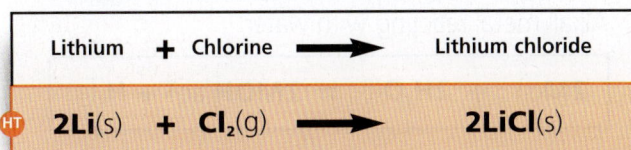

Lithium + Chlorine ⟶ Lithium chloride

HT $2Li(s) + Cl_2(g) \longrightarrow 2LiCl(s)$

Chemical Patterns

Reaction of Alkali Metals with Oxygen

The alkali metals are stored under oil because they react very vigorously with oxygen and water. When freshly cut they are shiny. However, they quickly tarnish in moist air, go dull and become covered in a layer of metal oxide. For example:

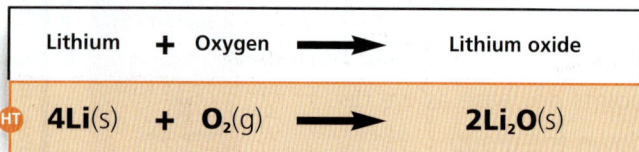

Lithium	+	Oxygen	$\longrightarrow$	Lithium oxide

HT $4Li(s) + O_2(g) \longrightarrow 2Li_2O(s)$

Reaction of Alkali Metals with Water

Lithium, sodium and potassium float on top of cold water (due to their low density). They melt because the heat from the reaction is great enough to turn them into liquids. Lithium reacts gently, sodium more aggressively and potassium so aggressively it melts and catches fire.

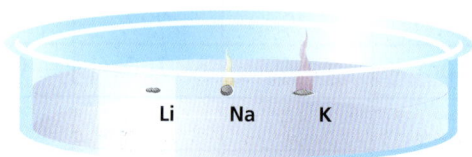

Li   Na   K

When alkali metals react with water, a metal hydroxide and hydrogen gas are formed. The metal hydroxide dissolves in water to form an alkaline solution, for example:

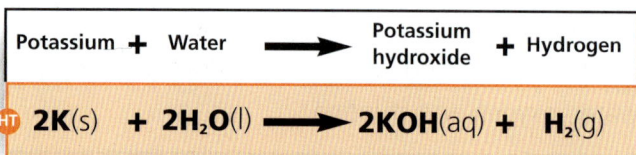

Potassium	+	Water	$\longrightarrow$	Potassium hydroxide	+	Hydrogen

HT $2K(s) + 2H_2O(l) \longrightarrow 2KOH(aq) + H_2(g)$

Since all the reactions of alkali metals are similar, a general equation or formula is sometimes used. In each case M refers to the alkali metal.

HT Alkali metal reacting with chlorine:

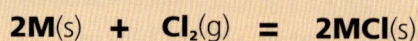

$$2M(s) + Cl_2(g) = 2MCl(s)$$

Alkali metal reacting with oxygen:

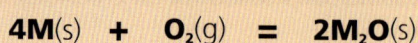

$$4M(s) + O_2(g) = 2M_2O(s)$$

Alkali metal reacting with water:

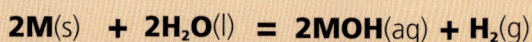

$$2M(s) + 2H_2O(l) = 2MOH(aq) + H_2(g)$$

Follow these steps to check the pH level of the solution formed when an alkali metal is added to water.

1. Put some universal indicator into a beaker containing water (H_2O). Universal indicator should be green to show neutral pH (pH 7).

2. Put a small piece of potassium into the beaker. It will react with the water and give off hydrogen gas (H_2).

3. When it has finished reacting, the beaker will contain potassium hydroxide solution, i.e. KOH(aq). The solution will now be purple, which indicates it is alkaline.

The hydrogen gas ignites and burns with the heat from the reaction

Potassium

The alkali metals carry the following hazard symbols:

Chemical	Hazard Symbol
Lithium	🔥 ⚗
Lithium chloride	✖
Sodium	🔥 ⚗
Sodium hydroxide	⚗
Potassium	🔥 ⚗

When working with Group 1 metals, the following precautions should be taken:

- use small amounts of very dilute concentrations
- wear safety glasses and use safety screens
- watch teacher demonstrations carefully
- avoid working near naked flames.

Chemical Patterns

Group 7 – The Halogens

There are five non-metals in this group.

At room temperature and room pressure, chlorine is a green gas, bromine is an orange liquid and iodine is a dark purple solid.

Chlorine is used to sterilise water and to make pesticides and plastics.

Iodine is used as an antiseptic to sterilise wounds.

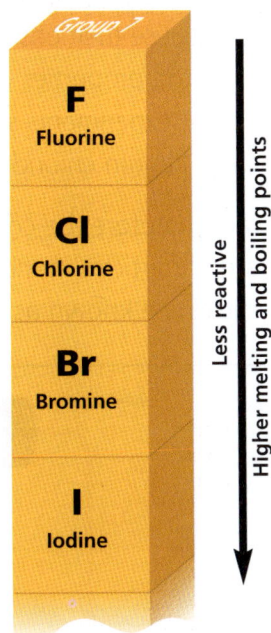

All halogens consist of **diatomic molecules** (i.e. they only exist in pairs of atoms), e.g. Cl_2, Br_2, I_2, and they can be used to bleach dyes and kill bacteria in water.

Physical Properties of the Halogens

The physical properties of the halogens alter as we go down the group. The table below shows their melting points, boiling points and densities:

Element	Melting Point (°C)	Boiling Point (°C)	Density (g/cm³)
Fluorine, F	-220	-188	0.0016
Chlorine, Cl	-101	-34	0.003
Bromine, Br	-7	59	3.12
Iodine, I	114	184	4.95
Astatine, At	302 (estimated)	337 (estimated)	not known

- The melting points and boiling points of the halogens increase as we go down the group. Astatine is estimated to have the highest melting point and boiling point.
- The densities increase as we go down the group. (However, due to the unstable nature of astatine, its density is not known.)

The halogens carry the following hazard symbols:

Element	Hazard Symbol		
Fluorine, F			
Chlorine, Cl			
Bromine, Br			

When working with halogens, the following precautions should be taken:

- wear safety glasses
- work in a fume cupboard
- make sure the room is well ventilated
- use small amounts of very dilute concentrations
- avoid working near naked flames
- watch teacher demonstrations carefully.

Displacement Reactions of Halogens

A more reactive halogen will displace a less reactive halogen from an aqueous solution of its salt. Therefore, chlorine will displace both bromine and iodine, while bromine will displace iodine.

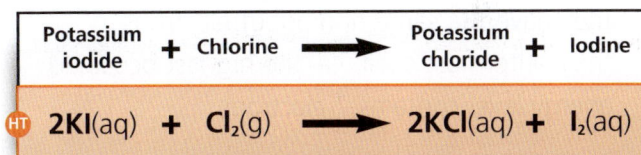

Potassium iodide + Chlorine ⟶ Potassium chloride + Iodine

$$2KI(aq) + Cl_2(g) \longrightarrow 2KCl(aq) + I_2(aq)$$

Halogen Compounds

When halogens react they form compounds that are similar. The reactivity decreases as we go down the group. The table below shows the compounds that are formed when halogens react with Group 1 metals and metal hydroxides.

	Chlorine	Bromine	Iodine
Lithium	LiCl	LiBr	LiI
Sodium	NaCl	NaBr	NaI
Potassium	KCl	KBr	KI
Metal hydroxide	MCl MClO	MBr MBrO	MI MIO

Chemical Patterns

Trends in Group 1

Alkali metals have similar properties because they have the same number of electrons in their outermost shell, i.e. the highest occupied energy level contains 1 electron.

The alkali metals become more reactive as we go down the group because the outermost electron shell gets further away from the influence of the nucleus and so an electron is more easily lost.

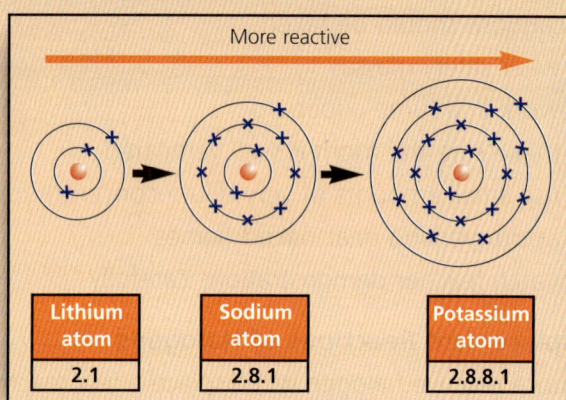

Lithium atom	Sodium atom	Potassium atom
2.1	2.8.1	2.8.8.1

Trends in Group 7

The halogens have similar properties, because they have the same number of electrons in their outermost shell, i.e. the highest occupied energy level contains 7 electrons.

The halogens become less reactive as we go down the group, because the outermost electron shell gets further away from the influence of the nucleus and so an electron is less easily gained.

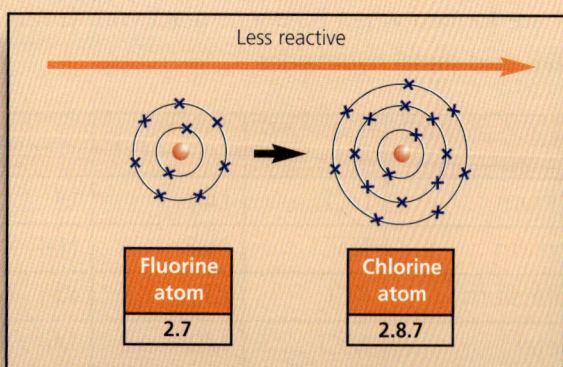

Fluorine atom	Chlorine atom
2.7	2.8.7

The Properties of Compounds

Chemists use their observations to develop theories to explain the properties of different compounds. For example, experiments show that molten compounds, such as lithium chloride, conduct electricity.

It can, therefore, be concluded that there must be charged particles in molten compounds. These particles are known as **ions**.

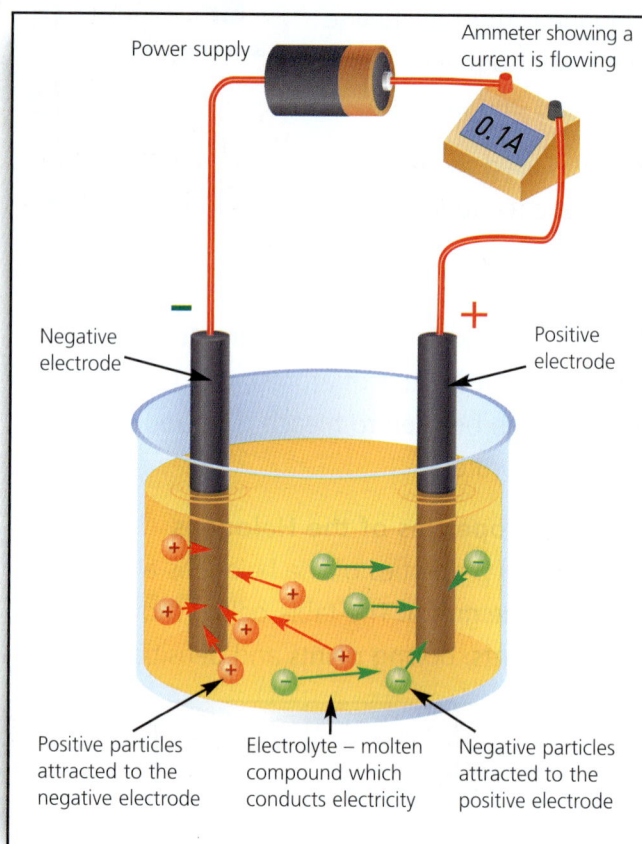

Ions

If an atom loses or gains one or more electrons it will carry an overall charge because the proton and electron numbers are no longer equal. When this happens, the atom becomes an ion.

If the ion has been formed by an atom losing electron(s), it will have an overall positive (+) charge because it now has more protons that electrons. It is called a **cation,** e.g. Na^+. If the ion has been formed by an atom gaining an electron(s), it will have an overall negative (–) charge because it now has more electrons than protons. It is called an **anion** e.g. Cl^-.

The Ionic Bond

An ionic bond occurs between a metal and a non-metal and involves the transfer of electrons from one atom to another to form electrically charged ions.

Each electrically charged ion has a complete outermost energy level or shell, i.e. the first shell has 2 electrons and each outer shell has 8 electrons. Compounds of Group 1 metals and Group 7 elements are **ionic compounds**.

Example 1

Sodium and chlorine bond ionically to form sodium chloride, NaCl. The sodium (Na) atom has 1 electron in its outer shell which is transferred to the chlorine (Cl) atom so they both have 8 electrons in their outer shell. The atoms become ions, Na^+ and Cl^-, and the compound formed is sodium chloride, NaCl.

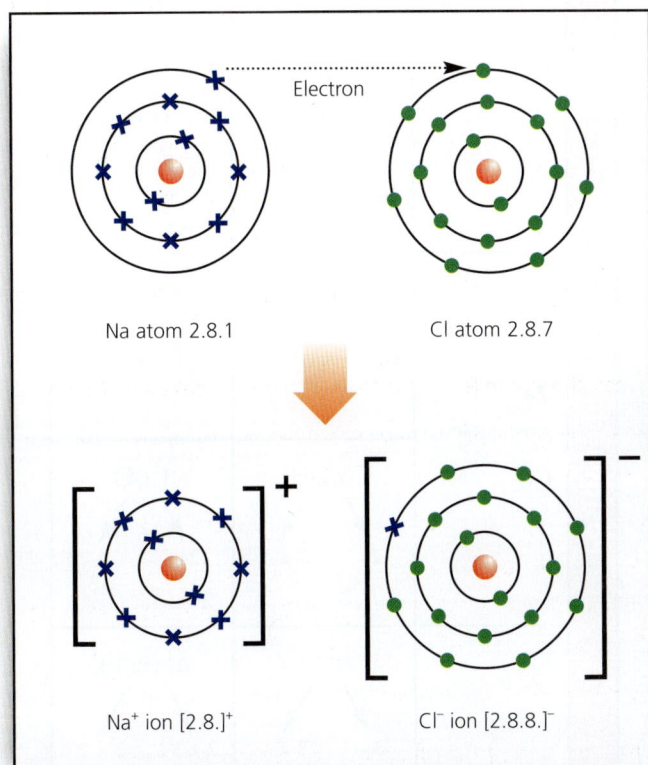

Na atom 2.8.1   Cl atom 2.8.7

Na^+ ion $[2.8.]^+$ Cl^- ion $[2.8.8.]^-$

The positive ion and the negative ion are then electrostatically attracted to each other to form a giant crystal lattice.

Sodium Chloride

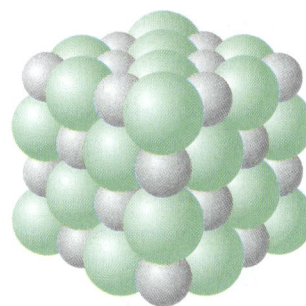

○ Na^+ ion, i.e. a sodium atom that has lost 1 electron

● Cl^- ion, i.e. a chlorine atom that has gained 1 electron

Sodium chloride has a high melting point and dissolves in water. It conducts electricity when it is in solution or is molten, but not when it is a solid.

Example 2

Sodium and oxygen bond ionically to form sodium oxide, Na_2O. Each sodium (Na) atom has 1 electron in its outer shell. An oxygen (O) atom wants 2 electrons, therefore 2 Na atoms are needed. The atoms become ions (Na^+, Na^+ and O^{2-}) and the compound formed is sodium oxide, Na_2O.

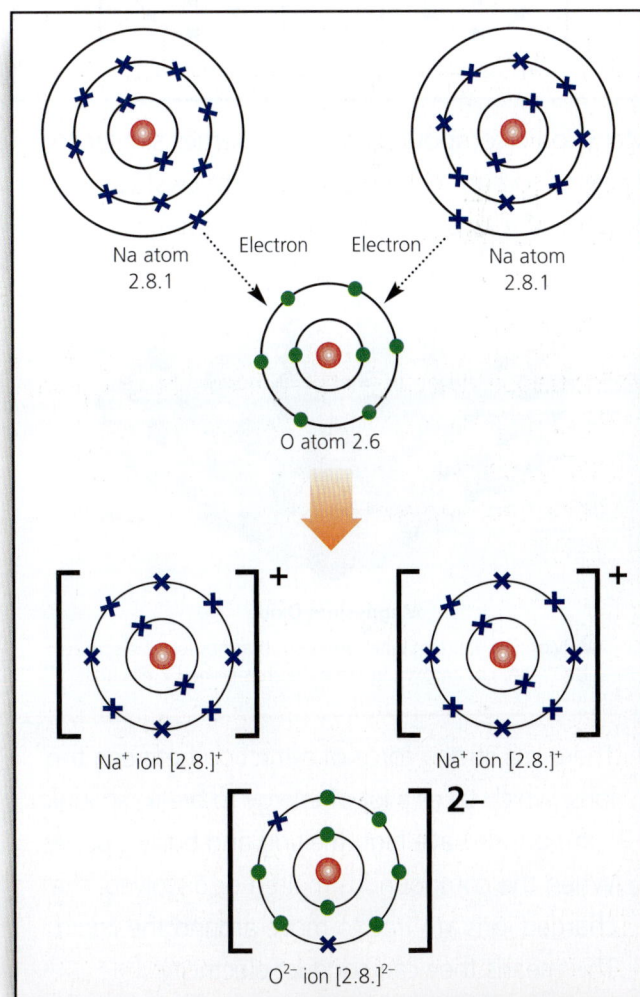

Na atom 2.8.1   Electron   Electron   Na atom 2.8.1

O atom 2.6

Na^+ ion $[2.8.]^+$ Na^+ ion $[2.8.]^+$

O^{2-} ion $[2.8.]^{2-}$

Chemical Patterns

Example 3

Magnesium and oxygen bond ionically to form magnesium oxide, MgO. The magnesium (Mg) atom has 2 electrons in its outer shell. The oxygen atom only has 6 electrons in its outer shell so the 2 electrons from the Mg atom are transferred to the O atom, so they both have 8 electrons in their outer shell. The atoms become ions Mg^{2+} and O^{2-} and the compound formed is magnesium oxide, MgO.

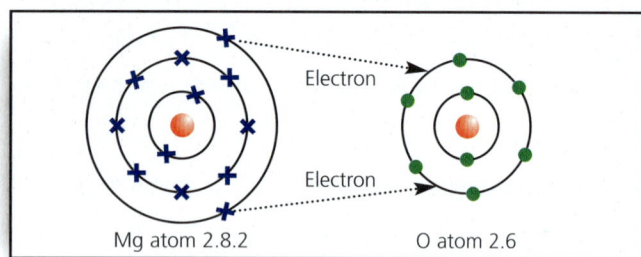

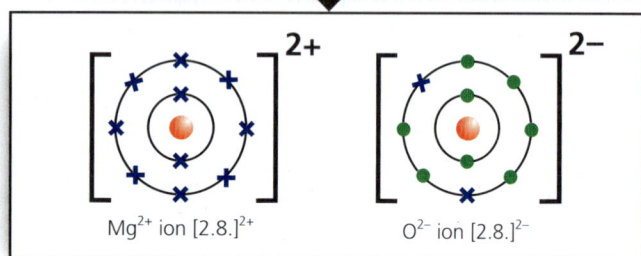

Mg atom 2.8.2   O atom 2.6

Mg^{2+} ion $[2.8.]^{2+}$ O^{2-} ion $[2.8.]^{2-}$

Many ionic compounds have properties similar to those of sodium chloride. They form crystals because the ions are arranged into a regular lattice.

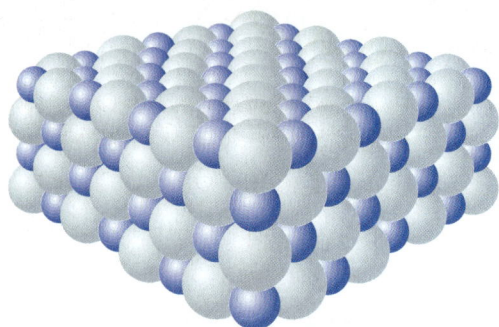

Magnesium Oxide

- Mg^{2+} ion, i.e. a magnesium atom that has lost 2 electrons
- O^{2-} ion, i.e. an oxygen atom that has gained 2 electrons

HT There is a strong force of attraction between the ions, which takes a lot of energy to break, so ionic compounds have high melting and boiling points. When the compound is molten or dissolved, the charged ions are free to move around the liquid. This means they can conduct electricity.

HT ## Deducing the Formula of an Ionic Compound

If you know the charge given on both ions you can work out the formula, or if you know the formula and the charge on one of the ions, you can work out the charge on the other ion.

This is because all ionic compounds are neutral substances where the charge on the positive ion(s) is equal to the charge on the negative ion(s). (See table below.)

		Negative Ions	
		1– e.g. Cl^-, OH^-	2– e.g. SO_4^{2-}, O^{2-}
Positive Ions	**1+** e.g. K^+, Na^+	KCl 1+ 1–	K_2SO_4 2 x 1+ 2– = 2+
		NaOH 1+ 1–	Na_2O 2 x 1+ 2– = 2+
	2+ e.g. Mg^{2+}, Cu^{2+}	$MgCl_2$ 2+ 2 x 1– = 2–	$MgSO_4$ 2+ 2–
		$Cu(OH)_2$ 2+ 2 x 1– = 2–	CuO 2+ 2–
	3+ e.g. Al^{3+}, Fe^{3+}	$AlCl_3$ 3+ 3 x 1– = 3–	$Al_2(SO_4)_3$ 2 x 3+ 3 x 2– = 6+ = 6–
		$Fe(OH)_3$ 3+ 3 x 1– = 3–	Fe_2O_3 2 x 3+ 3 x 2– = 6+ = 6–

Chemicals of the Natural Environment

We can get a better understanding of the impact human activity can have on the natural environment by knowing more about the chemicals that make up our planet. This module looks at…

- the structure of the Earth and the properties of the chemicals found in the atmosphere, hydrosphere, lithosphere and biosphere
- the natural cycle of elements between the spheres
- how to extract useful minerals
- properties of metals.

The Earth's Resources

1 Atmosphere – a layer of gas surrounding the Earth. It is made up of the elements nitrogen (N), oxygen (O), traces of argon (Ar) and some compounds, e.g. carbon dioxide (CO_2) and water vapour (H_2O).

2 Hydrosphere – all the water on the Earth, including oceans, rivers, lakes and underground reserves. The water contains dissolved compounds.

3 Biosphere – all living organisms on the Earth, including plants, animals and microorganisms. They are all made up of compounds containing the elements carbon (C), hydrogen (H), oxygen (O) and nitrogen (N), with small amounts of phosphorus (P) and sulfur (S).

4 Lithosphere – the rigid outer layer of the Earth made up of the crust and the part of the mantle just below it. It is a mixture of minerals, such as silicon dioxide. Abundant elements in the lithosphere include silicon (Si), oxygen (O) and aluminium (Al).

Chemicals of the Natural Environment

Chemical Cycles

In order to sustain life, chemicals constantly move between the different spheres. For example, carbon dioxide in the atmosphere is moved into the biosphere by green plants during photosynthesis. During respiration it is returned to the atmosphere.

Sometimes human activity upsets the balance of natural cycles, e.g. burning fossil fuels puts carbon dioxide into the atmosphere more quickly than it is removed.

N.B. You need to be able to interpret the type of diagram shown below.

The Carbon Cycle

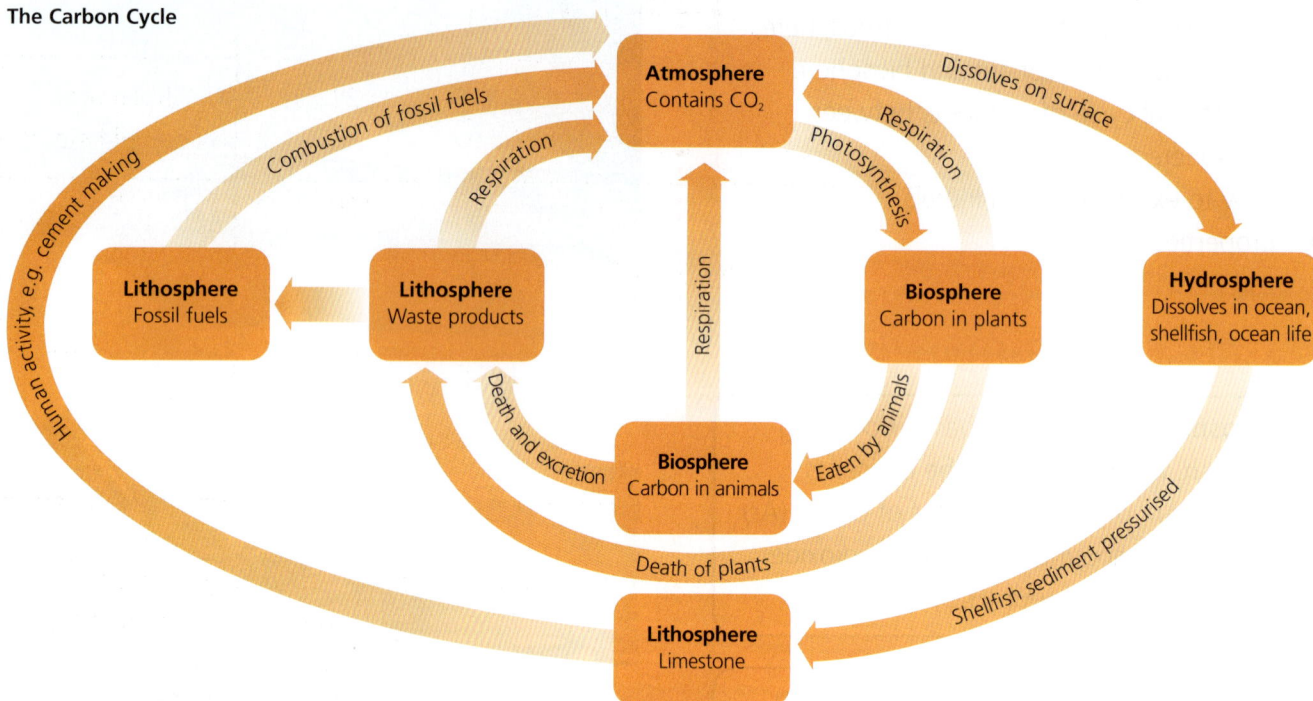

Human activity, e.g. cement making

Combustion of fossil fuels

Respiration

Respiration

Photosynthesis

Respiration

Dissolves on surface

Atmosphere Contains CO_2

Lithosphere Fossil fuels

Lithosphere Waste products

Biosphere Carbon in plants

Hydrosphere Dissolves in ocean, shellfish, ocean life

Death and excretion

Biosphere Carbon in animals

Eaten by animals

Death of plants

Shellfish sediment pressurised

Lithosphere Limestone

The Nitrogen Cycle

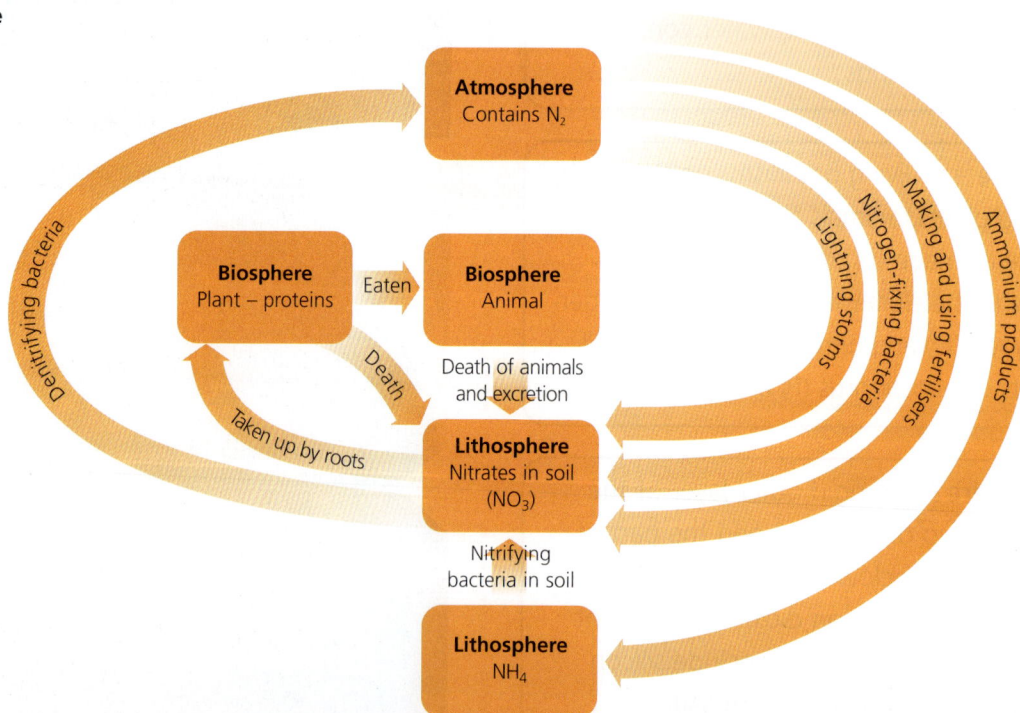

Atmosphere Contains N_2

Denitrifying bacteria

Lightning storms

Nitrogen-fixing bacteria

Making and using fertilisers

Ammonium products

Biosphere Plant – proteins

Eaten

Biosphere Animal

Death

Death of animals and excretion

Taken up by roots

Lithosphere Nitrates in soil (NO_3)

Nitrifying bacteria in soil

Lithosphere NH_4

Chemicals of the Natural Environment

Chemicals of the Atmosphere

Chemical	2-D Molecular Diagram	3-D Molecular Diagram	Boiling Point (°C)	Melting Point (°C)
Oxygen O_2	O=O		−182.9	−218.3
Nitrogen N_2	N≡N		−195.8	−210.1
Carbon dioxide CO_2	O=C=O		−78	Sublimes (no liquid state)
Water vapour H_2O	H–O–H		100	0
Argon Ar	Ar		−185.8	−189.3

The chemicals that make up the atmosphere consist of non-metal elements and molecular compounds made up from non-metal elements.

From the information in the table above we can deduce that the molecules (with the exception of water) that make up the atmosphere are gases at 20°C because they have very low boiling points, i.e. they boil below 20°C. This can be explained by looking at the structure of the molecules.

Gases consist of small molecules with weak forces of attraction between the molecules. Only small amounts of energy are needed to break these forces, which allows the molecules to move freely through the air.

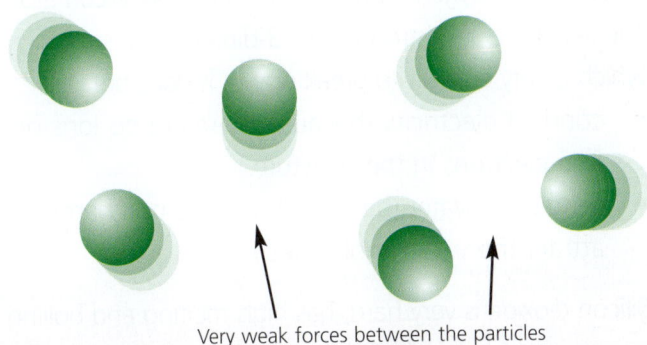

Very weak forces between the particles

HT The atoms within molecules (e.g. hydrogen) are connected by strong covalent bonds that arise because the electrons are shared between the nuclei. This causes a strong, electrostatic attraction between the nuclei and shared electrons.

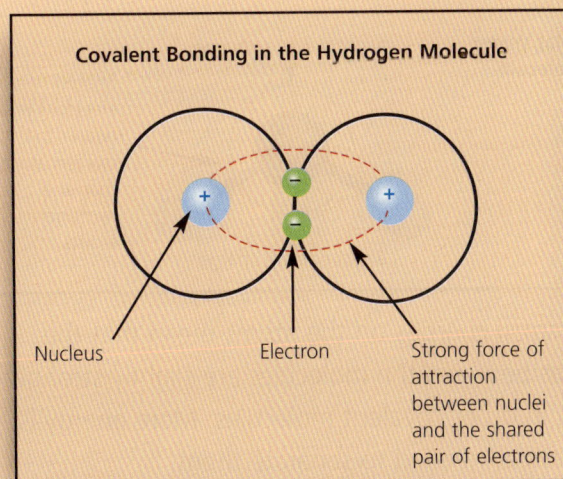

Covalent Bonding in the Hydrogen Molecule

Nucleus   Electron   Strong force of attraction between nuclei and the shared pair of electrons

Unlike ionic compounds, pure molecular compounds do not conduct electricity because their molecules are not charged.

Chemicals of the Natural Environment

Chemicals of the Hydrosphere

Sea water in the hydrosphere is 'salty' because it contains dissolved ionic compounds called **salts**. A litre of sea water contains approximately 40g of salts. These salts include...

- sodium chloride, $NaCl$
- magnesium chloride, $MgCl_2$
- magnesium sulfate, $MgSO_4$
- potassium chloride, KCl
- potassium bromide, KBr.

HT When given a table of charges, you must be able to work out the formulae for the following ionic compounds: sodium chloride, magnesium sulfate, potassium chloride and potassium bromide (see method on p.38).

The Water Molecule

Water has some unexpected properties. For example, the table on p.41 shows that the boiling point of water is 100°C. This is a much higher boiling point than for the other molecules listed. Water is also a good **solvent** for salts. The properties can be explained by its structure.

The water molecule is bent, because the electrons in the covalent bond are nearer to the oxygen atom than the hydrogen atoms. The result is a **polar molecule**.

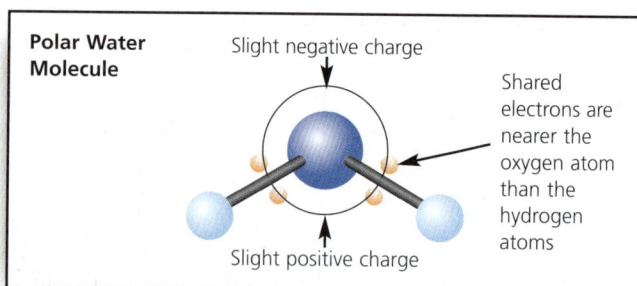

Polar Water Molecule

Slight negative charge

Shared electrons are nearer the oxygen atom than the hydrogen atoms

Slight positive charge

The small charges on the atoms mean that the forces between the molecules are slightly stronger than in other covalent molecules. More energy is, therefore, needed to separate them.

The small charges also help water to **dissolve** ionic compounds as the water molecules attract the charges on the ions. The ions can then move freely through the liquid (see p.37 for ionic bonding).

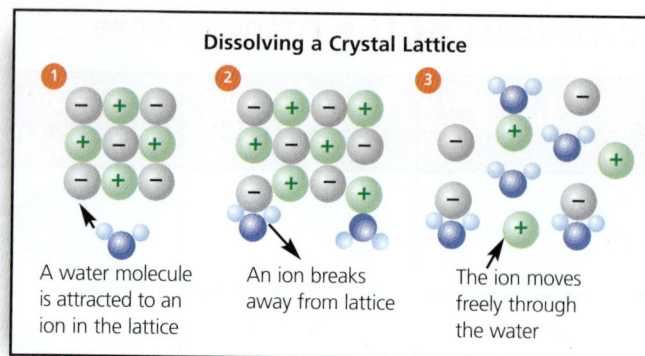

Dissolving a Crystal Lattice

① A water molecule is attracted to an ion in the lattice

② An ion breaks away from lattice

③ The ion moves freely through the water

Chemicals of the Lithosphere

Element	Abundance in Lithosphere (ppm)
Oxygen, O	455 000
Silicon, Si	272 000
Aluminium, Al	83 000
Iron, Fe	62 000
Calcium, Ca	46 600
Magnesium, Mg	27 640
Sodium, Na	22 700
Potassium, K	18 400
Titanium, Ti	6 320
Hydrogen, H	1 520

N.B. You may be asked to interpret data like this in your exam.

The table shows that the three most abundant elements in the Earth's crust are oxygen, silicon and aluminium. Much of silicon and oxygen is present as the compound silicon dioxide (SiO_2). Silicon dioxide exists in different forms, such as **quartz** in granite, and it is the main constituent of sandstone.

Silicon dioxide forms a **giant covalent structure**, where each silicon atom is covalently bonded to four oxygen atoms. Each oxygen atom is bonded to two silicon atoms. The result is a very strong, rigid 3-dimensional structure, which is very difficult to break down. It does not...

- conduct electricity (because there are no ions or free electrons in the structure.)
- dissolve in water (because there are no charges to attract the water molecules.)

Silicon dioxide is very hard, has high melting and boiling points, is an electrical insulator and is insoluble in water.

Chemicals of the Natural Environment

Chemicals of the Lithosphere (cont.)

These properties can be explained by looking at the structure of silicon dioxide.

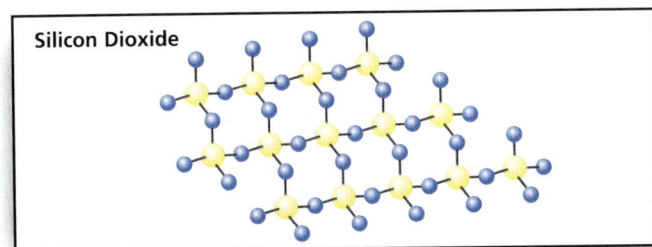

Silicon Dioxide

Amethyst is a form of quartz that is used as a **gemstone**. It is cut, polished and used in jewellery. The violet colour comes from traces of manganese and iron oxides found in the quartz. Some gemstones are very valuable because of their rarity, hardness and shiny appearance.

HT By understanding giant covalent structures, we can explain why we use different materials for certain jobs. The table gives some examples:

Element / Compound	Property	Use	Explanation
Carbon – diamond	Very hard	Drill tips	A lot of energy is needed to break the strong covalent bonds between the atoms.
Silicon dioxide	High melting point (1610°C)	Furnace linings	A lot of energy is needed to break the strong covalent bonds between the atoms.
Silica glass	Does not conduct electricity	Insulator in electrical devices	No free electrons or ions to carry electrical charge.

Chemicals of the Biosphere

Carbohydrates, proteins and DNA are three very important groups of molecules that make up a large part of the biosphere.

Glucose is a carbohydrate because it contains carbon, oxygen and hydrogen (see above opposite).

Glucose, $C_6H_{12}O_6$

- Oxygen
- Carbon
- Hydrogen

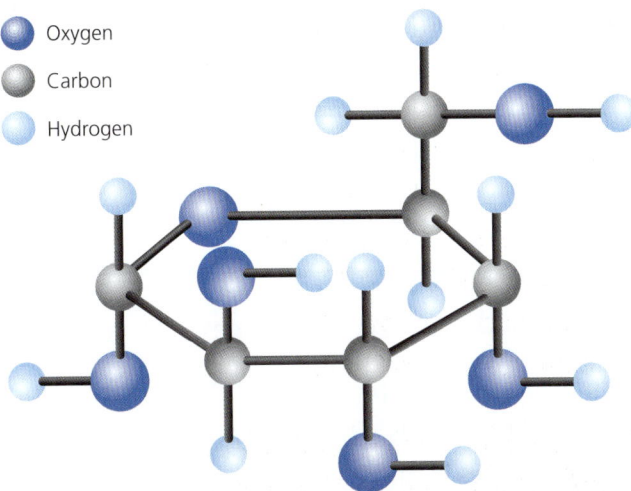

Proteins are polymers made from amino acid monomers joined together. One of the simplest amino acids is glycine.

Glycine, $NH_2CH_2CO_2H$

- Oxygen
- Carbon
- Hydrogen
- Nitrogen

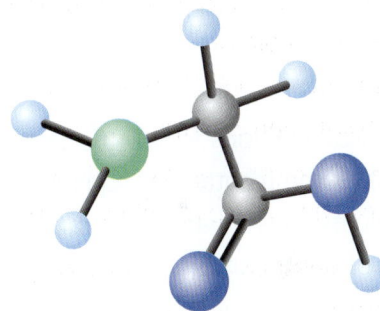

DNA is a large complex molecule.

DNA Molecule

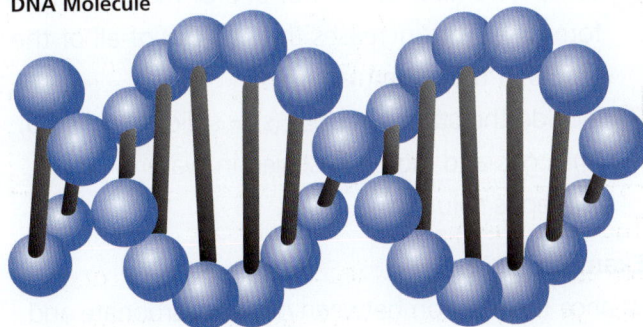

N.B. From a diagram of a molecule, you must be able to identify the elements in the compound and write the formula, as shown in glucose and glycine above.

Chemicals of the Natural Environment

	% Carbon	% Oxygen	% Hydrogen	% Nitrogen	% Phosphorus
Carbohydrate	40.0	53.3	6.7	0	0
Protein 1	32.0	42.7	6.7	18.7	0
Protein 2	40.4	36.0	7.9	15.7	0
Fat	39.0	52.0	8.7	0	0
DNA	41.0	30.7	4.6	29.0	4.2

Chemicals of the Biosphere (cont.)

Carbohydrates, fats, proteins and DNA are made up of different elements. The actual composition of the elements varies as there are many different molecules of carbohydrates, fats, proteins and DNA.

The table above lists the percentage composition of some elements. You must be able to interpret this type of data. For example, the data tells us that Protein 2 contains more carbon than Protein 1; DNA is the only molecule to contain phosphorus, etc.

Balancing Equations

All chemical reactions follow the same simple rule: the mass of the reactants is equal to the mass of the products. This means there must be the same number of atoms on both sides of the equation.

You do not have to do anything if the equation is already balanced. If the equation needs balancing, follow this method:

1. Write a number in front of one or more of the formulae. This increases the number of all of the atoms in that formula.
2. Include the state symbols: (s) = solid, (l) = liquid, (g) = gas and (aq) = dissolved in water (aqueous solution).

Example

Balance the reaction between calcium carbonate and hydrochloric acid.

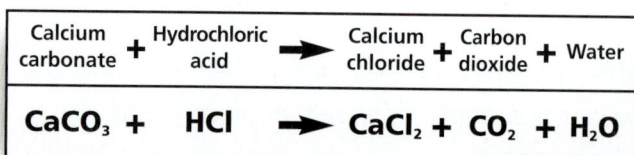

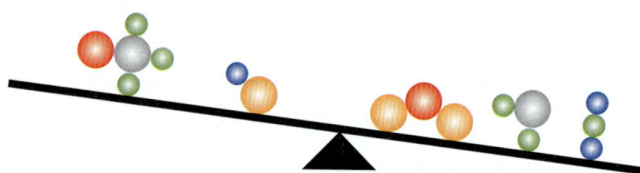

There are more chlorine atoms and hydrogen atoms on the products side than on the reactants side, so balance chlorine by doubling the amount of hydrochloric acid.

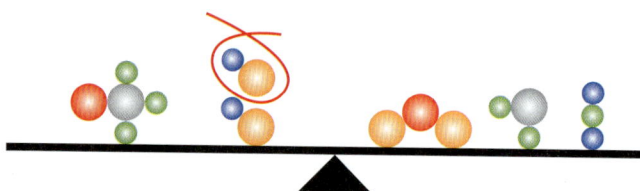

The amount of chlorine and hydrogen on both sides is now equal. This gives you a balanced equation.

$$CaCO_3(s) + 2HCl(aq) \rightarrow CaCl_2(aq) + CO_2(g) + H_2O(l)$$

Relative Atomic Mass

Atoms are too small for their actual atomic mass to be of much use to us. We therefore use the **relative atomic mass, A_r**. This is a number that compares the mass of one atom to the mass of other atoms.

Each element in the Periodic Table has two numbers. The larger of the two (at the top of the symbol) is the mass number, which also doubles up as the relative atomic mass, A_r.

Example

$$^{65}_{30}\text{Zn}$$ Relative atomic mass of zinc is 65.

$$^{16}_{8}\text{O}$$ Relative atomic mass of oxygen is 16.

Chemicals of the Natural Environment

Extracting Useful Materials

The lithosphere contains many naturally occurring elements and compounds called **minerals**. Ores are rocks that contain varying amounts of minerals from which metals can be extracted.

Sometimes very large amounts of ores need to be mined in order to recover a small percentage of valuable minerals, e.g. copper. The method of extraction depends on the metal's position in the reactivity series.

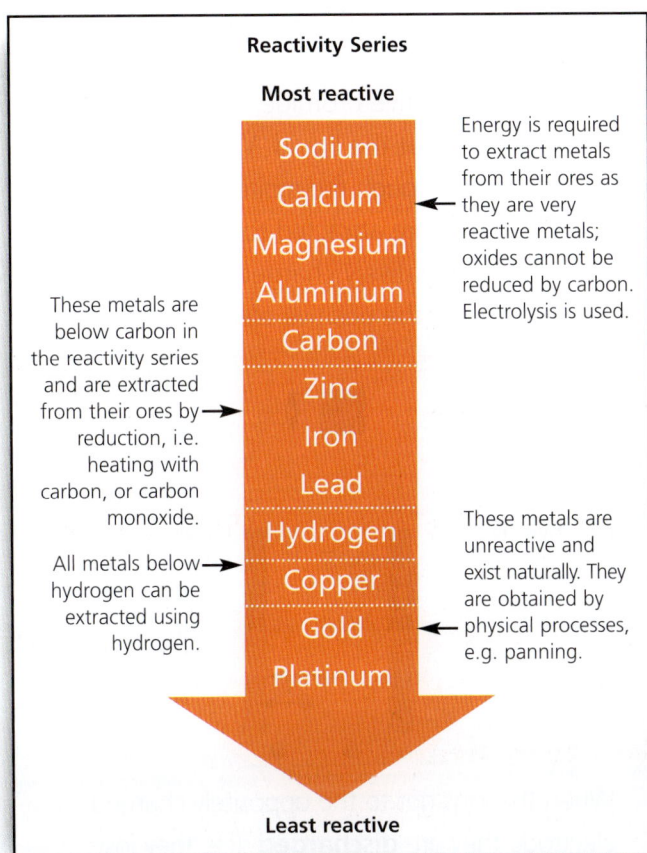

Reactivity Series

Most reactive

Sodium
Calcium
Magnesium
Aluminium
Carbon
Zinc
Iron
Lead
Hydrogen
Copper
Gold
Platinum

Least reactive

Energy is required to extract metals from their ores as they are very reactive metals; oxides cannot be reduced by carbon. Electrolysis is used.

These metals are below carbon in the reactivity series and are extracted from their ores by reduction, i.e. heating with carbon, or carbon monoxide.

All metals below hydrogen can be extracted using hydrogen.

These metals are unreactive and exist naturally. They are obtained by physical processes, e.g. panning.

Example of Extraction by Reduction

Zinc can be extracted from zinc oxide by heating it with carbon. Zinc oxide is reduced because it has lost oxygen. Carbon is oxidised because it has gained oxygen.

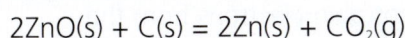

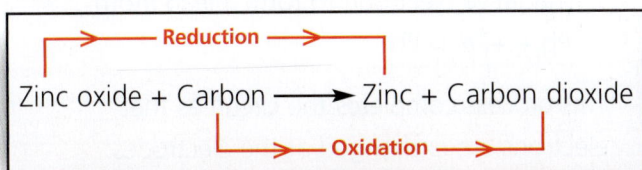

$2ZnO(s) + C(s) = 2Zn(s) + CO_2(g)$

Reduction

Zinc oxide + Carbon ⟶ Zinc + Carbon dioxide

Oxidation

Calculating a Metal's Mass

If you are given its formula, you can calculate the mass of metal that can be extracted from a substance. Follow these steps:

1. Write down the formula.
2. Work out the relative formula mass (see p.54).
3. Work out the percentage mass of metal in the formula.
4. Work out the mass of metal.

Example

Find the mass of Zn that can be extracted from 100g of ZnO.

1. ZnO

2. Relative formula mass $= 65 + 16$
$= 81$

3. Percentage of zinc present

$= \dfrac{A_r \, Zn}{M_r \, ZnO} \times 100$

$= \dfrac{65}{81} \times 100 = 80\%$

4. In 100g of ZnO, there will be $\dfrac{80}{100} \times 100$
$= \textbf{80g of Zn}$

If you were given the equation of a reaction, you could find the ratio of the mass of the reactant to the mass of the product.

$$2ZnO \; + \; C \; \longrightarrow \; 2Zn \; + \; CO_2$$

Relative formula mass:

Work out the M_r of each substance

$(2 \times 81) + 12 = (2 \times 65) + 44$

$162 + 12 = 130 + 44$

$174 = 174$ ✔

Therefore, 162g of ZnO produces 130g of Zn.

So, 1g of ZnO $= \dfrac{130}{162} = 0.8$g of Zn

and 100g of Zn $= 0.8 \times 100 = 80$g of Zn.

Chemicals of the Natural Environment

Metals and the Environment

In order to assess the impact on the environment of extracting and using metals, a life cycle analysis of metal products needs to be carried out. You need to be able to understand and evaluate the sort of data in the table below:

Stage of Life Cycle	Process	Environmental Impact
Manufacture	Mining	• Lots of rock wasted. • Leaves a scar on the landscape. • Air pollution. • Noise pollution.
	Processing	• Pollutants caused by transportation. • Energy usage.
	Extracting the metal	• Electrolysis uses more energy than reduction.
	Manufacturing products	• Energy usage in processing and transportation.
Use	Transport to shops / home	• Pollutants caused by transportation.
	Running product	• Energy usage.
Disposal	Reuse	• No impact.
	Recycle	• Uses a lot less energy than the initial manufacturing.
	Throw away	• Landfill sites remove wildlife habitats and are unsightly.

Extraction by Electrolysis

Electrolysis is the decomposition of an **electrolyte** (solution that conducts electricity) using an electric current. The process is used in industry to extract reactive metals from their ores. Ionic compounds will only conduct electricity when their ions are free to move. This occurs when the compound is either molten or dissolved in solution. During melting of an ionic compound, the electrostatic forces between the charged ions are broken. The crystal lattice is broken down and the ions are free to move.

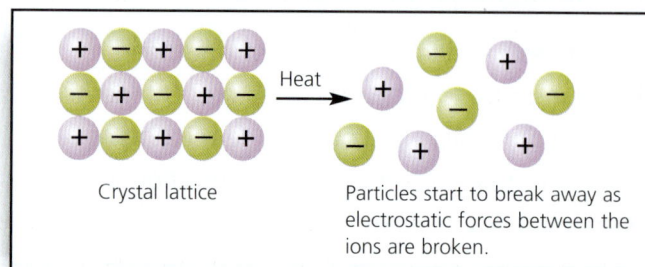

Crystal lattice

Particles start to break away as electrostatic forces between the ions are broken.

Molten lead bromide is a liquid containing positive lead ions and negative bromide ions that are free to move throughout the liquid. When a direct current is passed through the molten salt, the positively charged lead ions are attracted towards the negative electrode. The negatively charged bromide ions are attracted towards the positive electrode.

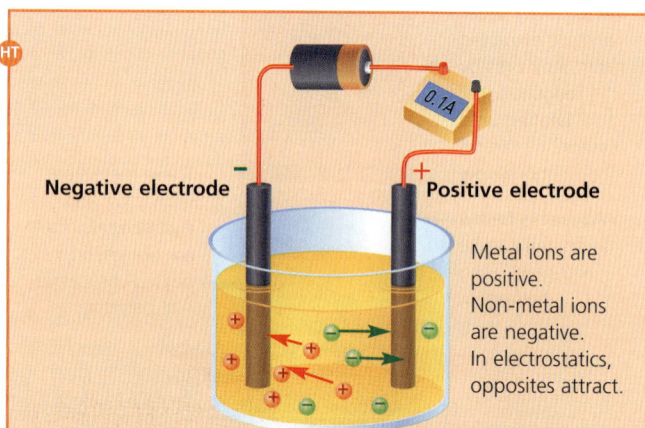

Negative electrode

Positive electrode

Metal ions are positive. Non-metal ions are negative. In electrostatics, opposites attract.

When the ions get to the oppositely charged electrode they are **discharged**, (i.e. they lose their charge).

- The bromide ion loses electrons to the positive electrode to form a bromine atom. The bromine atom then bonds with a second atom to form a bromine molecule.
$2Br^- = Br_2 + 2e^-$
- The lead ions gain electrons from the negative electrode to form a lead atom.
$Pb_2+ +2e^- = Pb$

This process completes the circuit as the electrons are exchanged at the electrodes.

Chemicals of the Natural Environment

Extracting Aluminium by Electrolysis

Aluminium must be obtained from its ore by electrolysis because it is too reactive to be extracted by heating with carbon. (Look at its position in the Reactivity Series, see p.45.)

The steps in the process are as follows:

1. Aluminium ore (bauxite) is purified to leave aluminium oxide.
2. Aluminium oxide is mixed with cryolite (a compound of aluminium) to lower its melting point.
3. The mixture of aluminium oxide and cryolite is melted so that the ions can move.
4. When a current passes through the molten mixture, positively charged aluminium ions move towards the negative electrode (the cathode), and aluminium is formed. Negatively charged oxide ions move towards the positive electrode (the anode), and oxygen is formed.
5. This causes the positive electrodes to burn away quickly. They frequently have to be replaced.

Electrolysis of bauxite to obtain aluminium is quite an expensive process because of the cost of the large amounts of electrical energy needed to carry it out. The equation for this reaction is...

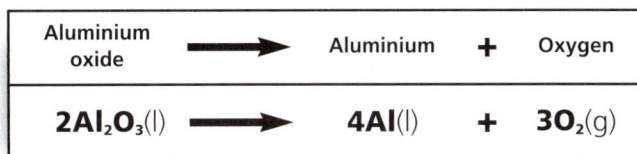

Aluminium oxide	$\longrightarrow$	Aluminium	+	Oxygen
$2Al_2O_3(l)$	$\longrightarrow$	$4Al(l)$	+	$3O_2(g)$

HT The reactions at the electrodes can be written as half equations. This means that we write separate equations for what is happening at each of the electrodes during electrolysis.

At the cathode...

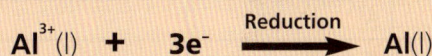

$$Al^{3+}(l) + 3e^- \xrightarrow{\text{Reduction}} Al(l)$$

At the anode...

$$2O^{2-}(l) - 4e^- \xrightarrow{\text{Oxidation}} O_2(g)$$

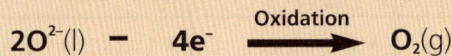

Electrolysis of Bauxite (Aluminium Oxide)

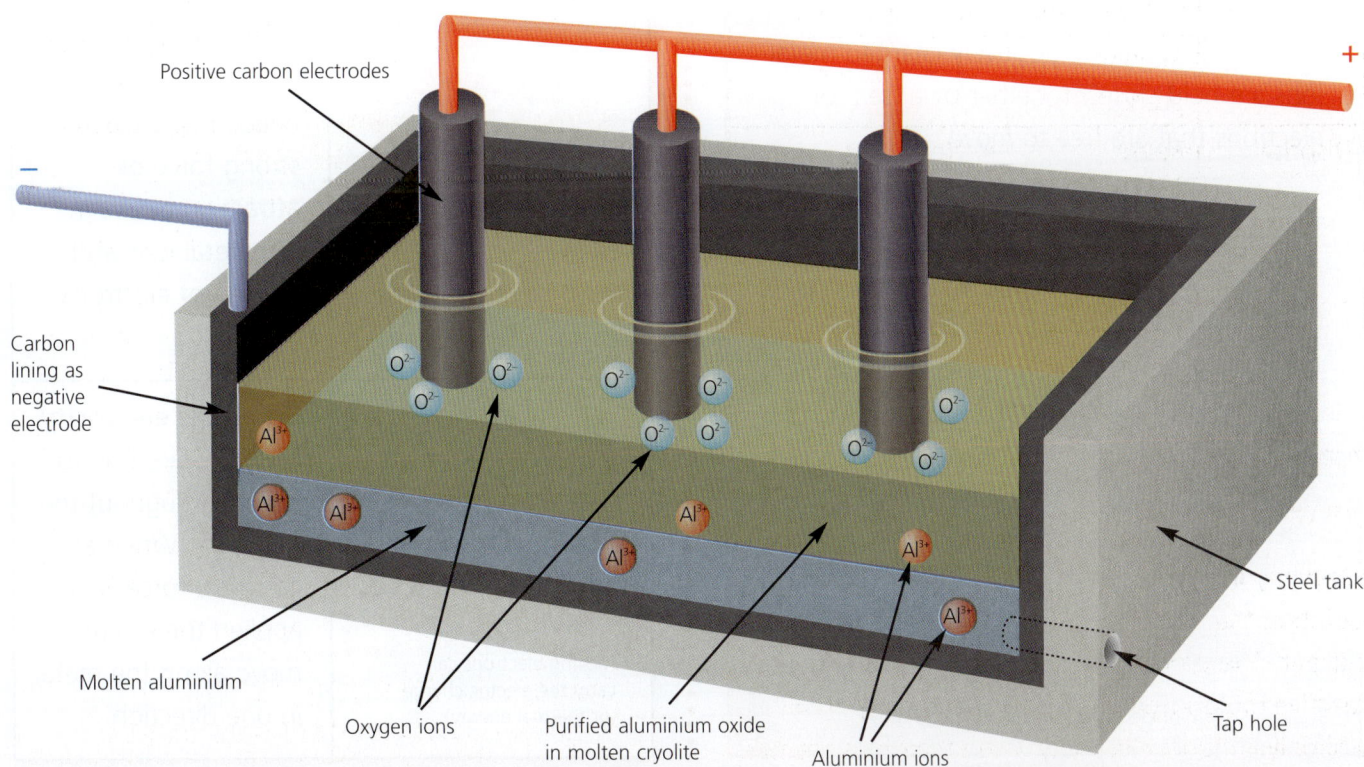

Positive carbon electrodes

Carbon lining as negative electrode

Molten aluminium

Oxygen ions

Purified aluminium oxide in molten cryolite

Aluminium ions

Steel tank

Tap hole

O^{2-} Al^{3+}

Chemicals of the Natural Environment

Properties of Metals

Generally, metals are strong and malleable, have high melting points and can conduct electricity. Their properties determine how each particular metal can be used. For example…

Metal	Property	Use
Titanium	• Very strong • Lightweight • Resistant to corrosion	• Replacement hip joints • Bicycles • Submarines
Aluminium	• Malleable • Lightweight • Resistant to corrosion	• Drink cans • Window frames
Iron	• High melting point • Strong	• Saucepans • Cars
Copper	• Conducts electricity • Conducts heat	• Cables, e.g. kettle cable • Electromagnets • Electrical switches

HT In a metal crystal the positively charged metal ions are held closely together by a 'sea' of electrons that are free to move.

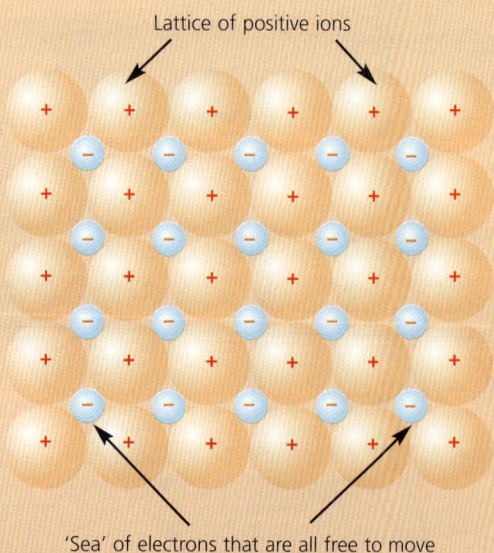

Lattice of positive ions

'Sea' of electrons that are all free to move

The properties of a metal can be explained by its structure. The force of attraction that keeps the structure together is known as the **metallic bond**. The metallic bond can be used to explain the properties of metals.

Structure	Property and Explanation
The ions are arranged in a lattice form	**Very strong** Metal ions are closely packed in a lattice structure.
Force applied Rows of ions slide over each other. Result: The metal is 'bendy' and can be dented	**Malleable** External forces cause layers of metal ions to move by sliding over other layers.
	High melting point A lot of energy is needed to break the strong force of attraction between the metal ions and the sea of electrons.
Moving electrons can carry the electric charge (or thermal energy)	**Conducts electricity** Electrons are free to move throughout the structure. When an electrical force is applied the electrons move along the metal in one direction.

Chemical Synthesis

Chemical synthesis provides the chemicals needed for food processing, health care, and many other products. This module looks at...

- chemicals, and why we need them
- relative formula mass
- calculating the mass of products and reactants
- how titrations are used
- measuring the rate of a reaction.

Chemicals

Chemicals are all around us and we depend on them daily. **Chemical synthesis** is the process by which raw materials are made into useful products such as...

- food additives
- fertilizers
- dyestuffs
- pigments
- pharmaceuticals
- cosmetics
- paints.

The chemical industry makes **bulk chemicals** such as sulfuric acid and ammonia on a very large scale (millions of tonnes per year). **Fine chemicals** such as drugs and pesticides are made on a much smaller scale.

The range of chemicals made in industry and laboratories in the UK is illustrated in the pie chart below.

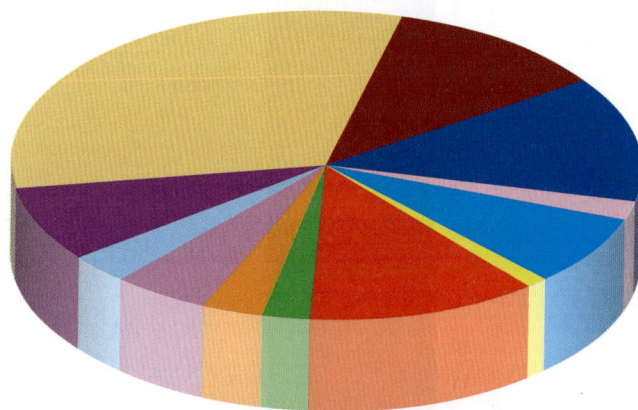

Key:

- Pharmaceuticals 31.5%
- Paint, varnishes and printing inks 8%
- Agrochemicals 3%
- Industrial glass 5%
- Dyes and pigments 3%
- Basic inorganics 2.5%
- Basic organics 12%
- Fertilizers 1%
- Plastic and synthetic rubber 7.5%
- Synthetic fibres 2%
- Other specialities 13%
- Soaps, toiletries and cleaning preparations 11.5%

Many of the raw materials are hazardous, therefore, it is important to recognise the standard hazard symbols and understand the necessary precautions that need to be taken (see p.33).

Chemical Synthesis

The pH Scale

The pH scale is a measure of the acidity or alkalinity of an aqueous solution, across a 14-point scale.

Acids are substances that have a pH less than 7.

Bases are the oxides and hydroxides of metals. Those which are soluble are called **alkalis** and they have a pH greater than 7.

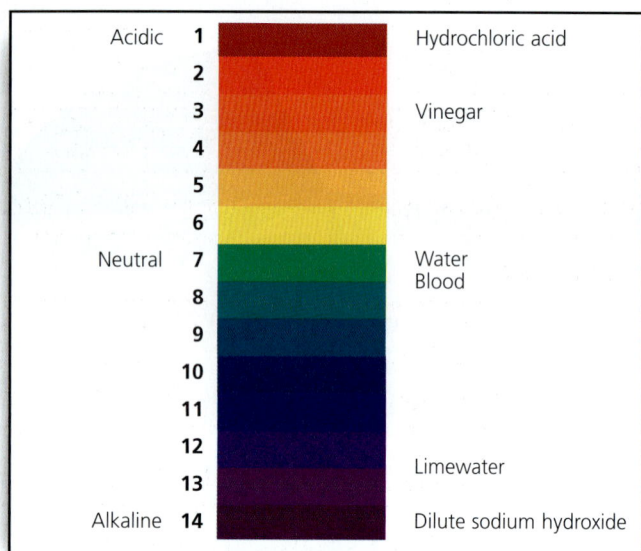

Acidic	1	Hydrochloric acid
	2	
	3	Vinegar
	4	
	5	
	6	
Neutral	7	Water Blood
	8	
	9	
	10	
	11	
	12	Limewater
	13	
Alkaline	14	Dilute sodium hydroxide

The pH of a substance is measured using an indicator, such as universal indicator solution, or a pH meter.

Universal Indicator Solution

Acidic compounds produce aqueous **hydrogen ions**, $H^+(aq)$, when they dissolve in water.

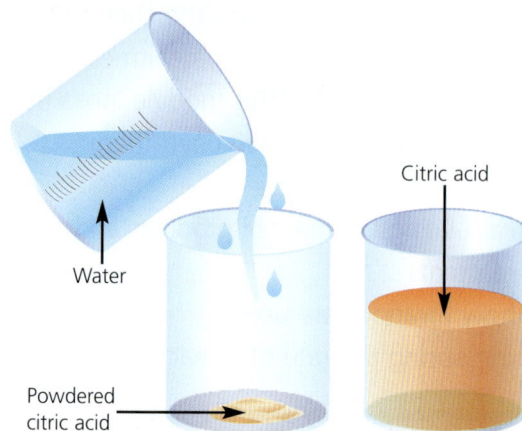

Water

Citric acid

Powdered citric acid

Common Acids	Formulae to Remember	State at Room Temp.
Citric acid	–	Solid
Tartaric acid	–	Solid
Nitric acid	HNO_3	Liquid
Sulfuric acid	H_2SO_4	Liquid
Ethanoic acid	–	Liquid
Hydrogen chloride (hydrochloric acid)	HCl	Gas

Alkali compounds produce aqueous **hydroxide ions**, $OH^-_{(aq)}$, when they dissolve in water.

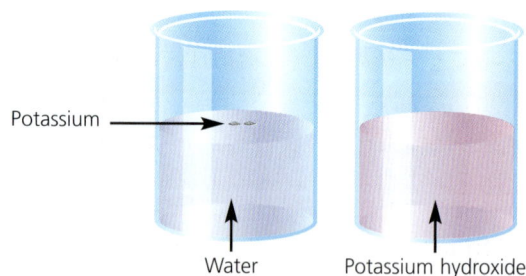

Potassium

Water

Potassium hydroxide

Common Alkalis	Formulae to Remember
Sodium hydroxide	NaOH
Potassium hydroxide	KOH
Magnesium hydroxide	$Mg(OH)_2$
Calcium hydroxide	$Ca(OH)_2$

Neutralisation

When an acid and a base are mixed together in the correct amounts they 'cancel' each other out. This reaction is called **neutralisation** because the solution which remains has a neutral pH of 7.

Example

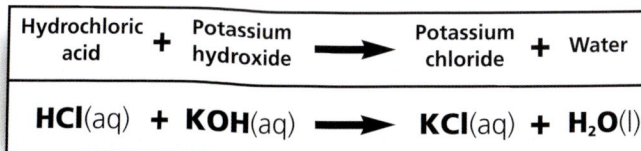

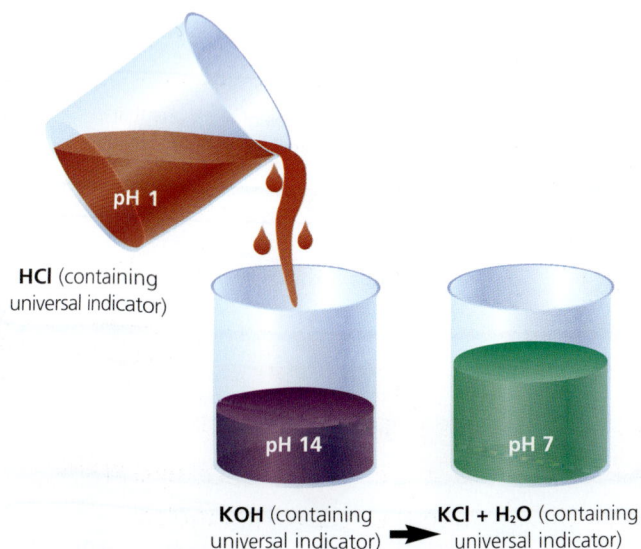

HCl (containing universal indicator)

KOH (containing universal indicator) → KCl + H₂O (containing universal indicator)

N.B. A balanced equation for a chemical reaction shows the relative numbers of atoms and molecules of reactants and products taking part in the reaction.

During neutralisation, the hydrogen ions from the acid react with the hydroxide ions from the alkali to make water. The simplest way of writing a neutralisation equation is…

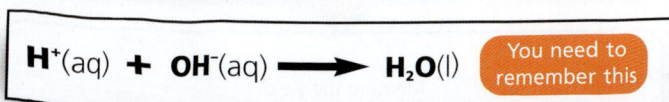

$$H^+(aq) + OH^-(aq) \longrightarrow H_2O(l)$$

You need to remember this

The salt produced during neutralisation depends on the metal in the base and the acid used. Hydrochloric acid produces chloride salts, sulfuric acid produces sulfate salts, and nitric acid produces nitrate salts.

Hydrochloric Acid

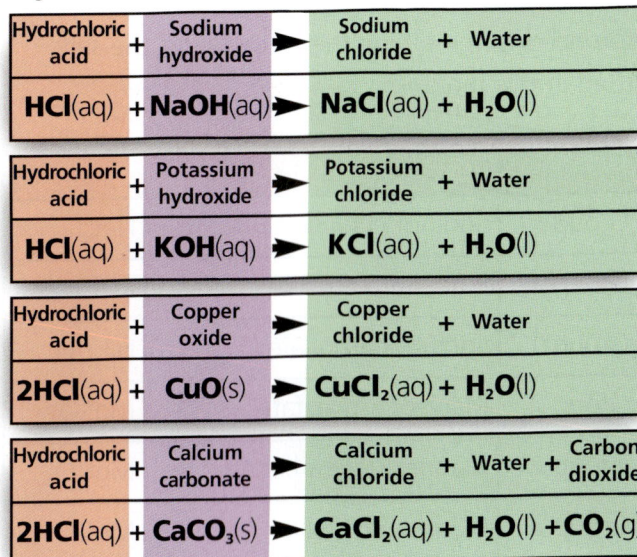

Sulfuric Acid

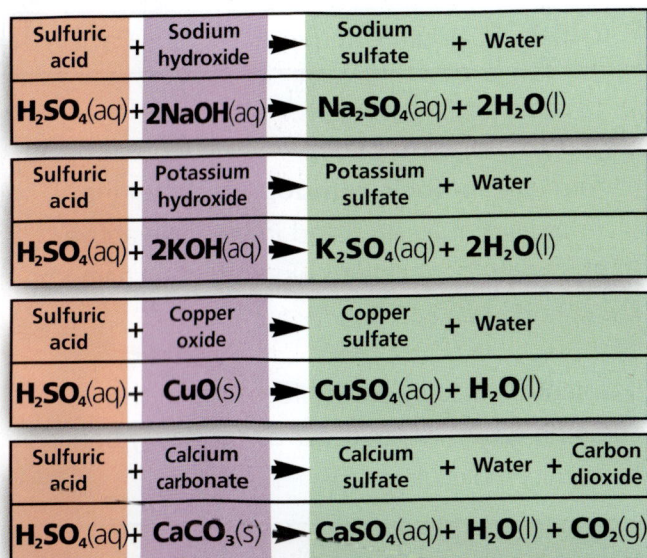

Nitric Acid

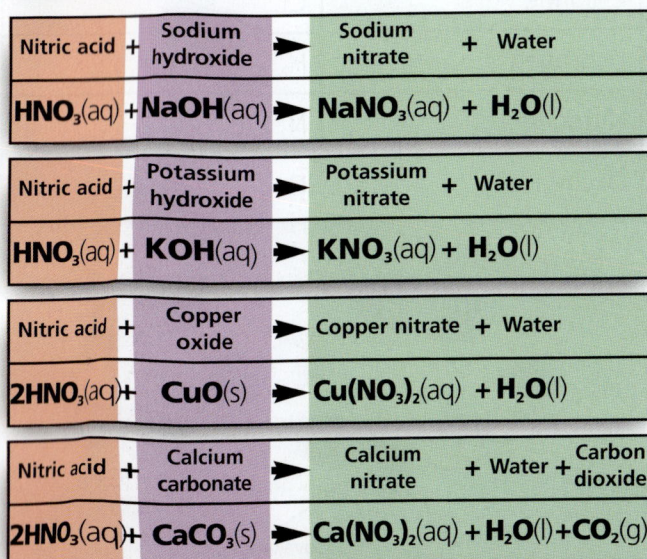

Chemical Synthesis

Writing Formulae

You need to remember the formulae of the salts listed in this table.

Group	Salt	Formula
Group 1	Sodium chloride	NaCl
Group 1	Potassium chloride	KCl
Group 1	Sodium carbonate	Na_2CO_3
Group 2	Magnesium sulfate	$MgSO_4$
Group 2	Magnesium carbonate	$MgCO_3$
Group 2	Magnesium oxide	MgO
Group 2	Calcium carbonate	$CaCO_3$
Group 2	Calcium chloride	$CaCl_2$

HT You should already know how to write formulae for **ionic compounds**. Given the formula of the salts listed in the table above, you need to be able to work out the charge on each ion in a compound.

It is important to know the formulae of the common gases, which occur as covalently bonded (diatomic) molecules.

Gas	Formula
Chlorine	Cl_2
Hydrogen	H_2
Nitrogen	N_2
Oxygen	O_2

Oxygen

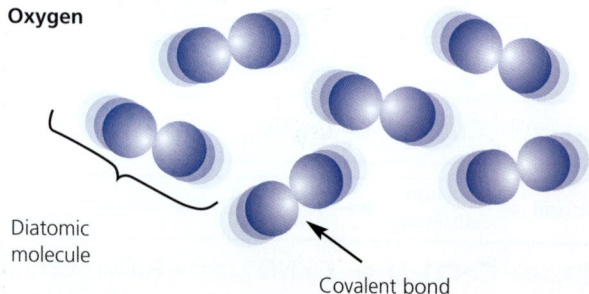

Diatomic molecule

Covalent bond

Chemical Synthesis

Whenever chemical synthesis takes place, the starting materials (reactants) react to produce new substances (products). The greater the amount of reactants used, the greater the amount of product formed. The **percentage yield** can be calculated by comparing the actual amount of product made (actual yield) with the amount of product you would expect to get if the reaction goes to completion (theoretical yield).

$$\text{Percentage yield} = \frac{\text{Actual yield}}{\text{Theoretical yield}} \times 100$$

There are a number of different stages to any chemical synthesis of an inorganic compound. Look at the flow chart below.

1. Establish the reaction or series of reactions that are needed in order to produce the product.

2. Carry out a risk assessment.

HT 3. Calculate the quantities of reactants to use.

4. Carry out the reaction under suitable conditions, e.g. temperature, concentration and presence of catalyst.

5. Separate the product from the reaction mixture.

6. Purify the product to ensure it is not contaminated by other products or reactants.

7. Measure the yield.

8. Check the purity.

Chemical Synthesis (cont.)

Example

The following steps show how to make **magnesium sulfate**.

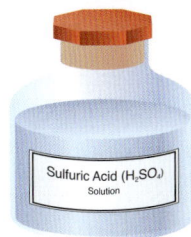

1. $Mg(g) + H_2SO_4(aq) \longrightarrow MgSO_4(aq) + H_2(g)$
2. Wear safety glasses and use dilute sulfuric acid.

> **HT** 3. To calculate the quantities of reactants you need to use, see example on p.55.

4. Measure out the sulfuric acid, and add magnesium until no more hydrogen is formed. This indicates that the reaction is complete.

5. Filter to remove any excess magnesium that has not reacted.

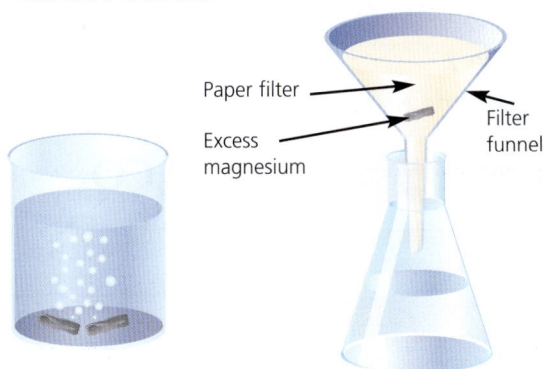

Paper filter
Filter funnel
Excess magnesium

6. Remove the water by gently heating the solution. It will evaporate slowly to form crystals that will cling to the end of a cold glass rod. Leave them to cool and crystallise. Filter to separate the crystals from any solution left behind.

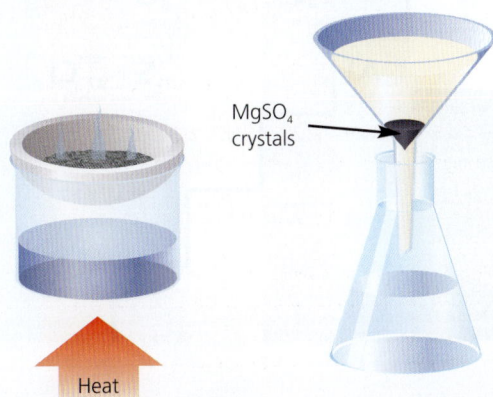

$MgSO_4$ crystals

Heat

7. Wash crystals and dry in a desiccator or oven. Weigh the mass and calculate the percentage yield (see p.52).

Distilled water

Actual yield = 8g

Theoretical yield = 10g

Percentage yield = $\dfrac{8}{10}$ x 100 = **80%**

8. Check the purity by measuring the melting point.

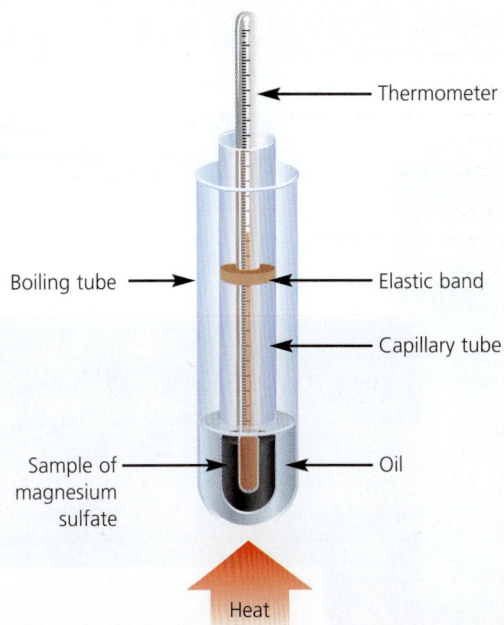

Thermometer

Boiling tube

Elastic band

Capillary tube

Sample of magnesium sulfate

Oil

Heat

Chemical Synthesis

Quantity of Products

In order to work out how much of each reactant is required to make a known amount of product, you must understand…

- how to calculate its relative atomic mass
- how to calculate its relative formula mass
- that a balanced equation shows the number of atoms or molecules taking part in the reaction
- how to work out the ratio of the mass of reactants to the mass of products
- how to apply the ratio to the question.

Relative Atomic Mass, A_r

To compare the mass of one atom to the mass of other atoms, we use the **relative atomic mass, A_r** (see p.44).

We can obtain this by looking at the Periodic Table below.

Examples
A_r of Mg = 24
A_r of Cu = 63.5
A_r of C = 12
A_r of K = 39

Relative Formula Mass, M_r

The **relative formula mass, M_r**, of a compound is the relative atomic masses of all its elements added together. To calculate M_r we need to know the formula of the compound and the A_r of each of the atoms involved.

Example 1
Calculate the M_r of water, H_2O.

The formula	H_2O
Substitute the A_rs	$(2 \times 1) + 16$
The M_r	$2 + 16 = \mathbf{18}$

Since water has an M_r of 18, it is 18 times heavier than a hydrogen atom ($M_r = 1$), or one and a half times heavier than a carbon atom ($M_r = 12$), or two thirds as heavy as an aluminium atom ($M_r = 27$).

Example 2
Calculate the M_r of potassium carbonate, K_2CO_3.

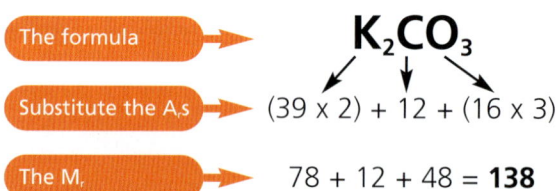

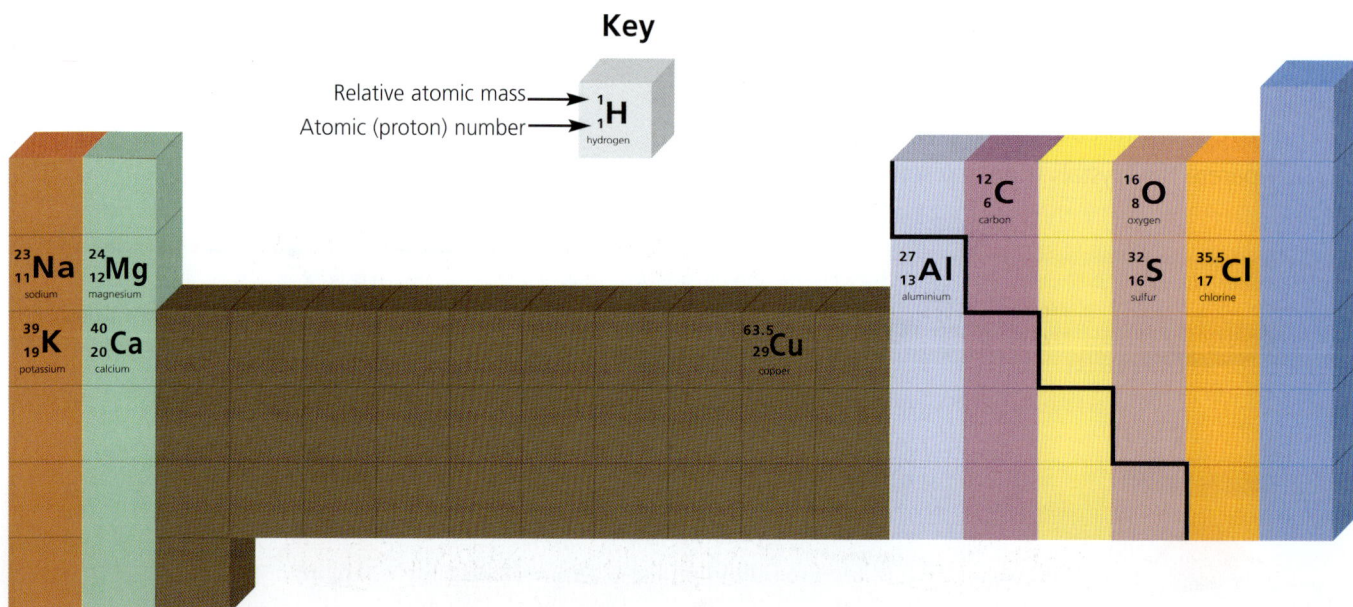

The formula	K_2CO_3
Substitute the A_rs	$(39 \times 2) + 12 + (16 \times 3)$
The M_r	$78 + 12 + 48 = \mathbf{138}$

Key

Relative atomic mass →
Atomic (proton) number →
^1_1H
hydrogen

| $^{23}_{11}Na$ sodium | $^{24}_{12}Mg$ magnesium | | | $^{12}_6C$ carbon | $^{16}_8O$ oxygen |
| $^{39}_{19}K$ potassium | $^{40}_{20}Ca$ calcium | $^{63.5}_{29}Cu$ copper | $^{27}_{13}Al$ aluminium | $^{32}_{16}S$ sulfur | $^{35.5}_{17}Cl$ chlorine |

Chemical Synthesis

Calculating a Product's Mass

Example

Calculate how much calcium oxide can be produced from 50kg of calcium carbonate. (Relative atomic masses: Ca = 40, C = 12, O = 16).

> Write down the equation

$$CaCO_3 \rightarrow CaO + CO_2$$

> Work out the M_r of each substance

$$40 + 12 + (3 \times 16) \rightarrow (40 + 16) + [12 + (2 \times 16)]$$

> Check that the total mass of reactants equals the total mass of the products. If they are not the same, check your work

$$100 \rightarrow 56 + 44 \quad ✔$$

> Since the question only mentions calcium oxide and calcium carbonate, you can now ignore the carbon dioxide. You just need the ratio of mass of reactant to mass of product.

$$100 : 56$$

If 100kg of $CaCO_3$ produces 56kg of CaO, then 1kg of $CaCO_3$ produces $\frac{56}{100}$ kg of CaO, and 50kg of $CaCO_3$ produces $\frac{56}{100} \times 50$ = **28kg** of CaO.

Calculating a Reactant's Mass

Example

Calculate how much aluminium oxide is needed to produce 540 tonnes of aluminium. (Relative atomic masses: Al = 27, O = 16).

> Write down the equation

$$2Al_2O_3 \rightarrow 4Al + 3O_2$$

> Work out the M_r of each substance

$$2[(2 \times 27) + (3 \times 16)] \rightarrow (4 \times 27) + [3 \times (2 \times 16)]$$

> Check that the total mass of reactants equals the total mass of the products

$$204 \rightarrow 108 + 96 \quad ✔$$

> Since the question only mentions aluminium oxide and aluminium, you can now ignore the oxygen. You just need the ratio of mass of reactant to mass of product.

$$204 : 108$$

If 204 tonnes of Al_2O_3 produces 108 tonnes of Al, then $\frac{204}{108}$ tonnes is needed to produce 1 tonne of Al, and $\frac{204}{108} \times 540$ tonnes is needed to produce 540 tonnes of Al, i.e. 1020 tonnes of Al_2O_3 is needed.

Chemical Synthesis

Titration

Titration can be used to calculate the concentration of an acid, such as citric acid, by finding out how much alkali is needed to neutralise it.

1 Fill a burette with the alkali sodium hydroxide (the concentration of the alkali must be known) and take an initial reading of the volume.

2 Accurately weigh out a 4g sample of solid citric acid and dissolve it in 100cm^3 of distilled water.

3 Use a pipette to measure 25cm^3 of the aqueous citric acid and put it into a conical flask.

Add a few drops of the indicator, phenolphthalein, to the conical flask. The indicator will stay colourless.

Place the flask on a white tile under the burette.

4 Add the alkali from the burette to the acid in the flask drop by drop.

- Swirl the flask to ensure it mixes well. Near the end of the reaction, the indicator will start to turn pink.
- Keep swirling and adding the alkali until the indicator is completely pink, showing that the citric acid has been neutralised.
- Record the volume of alkali added by subtracting the amount in the burette at the end from the starting value.

Repeat the whole procedure until you get two results that are the same.

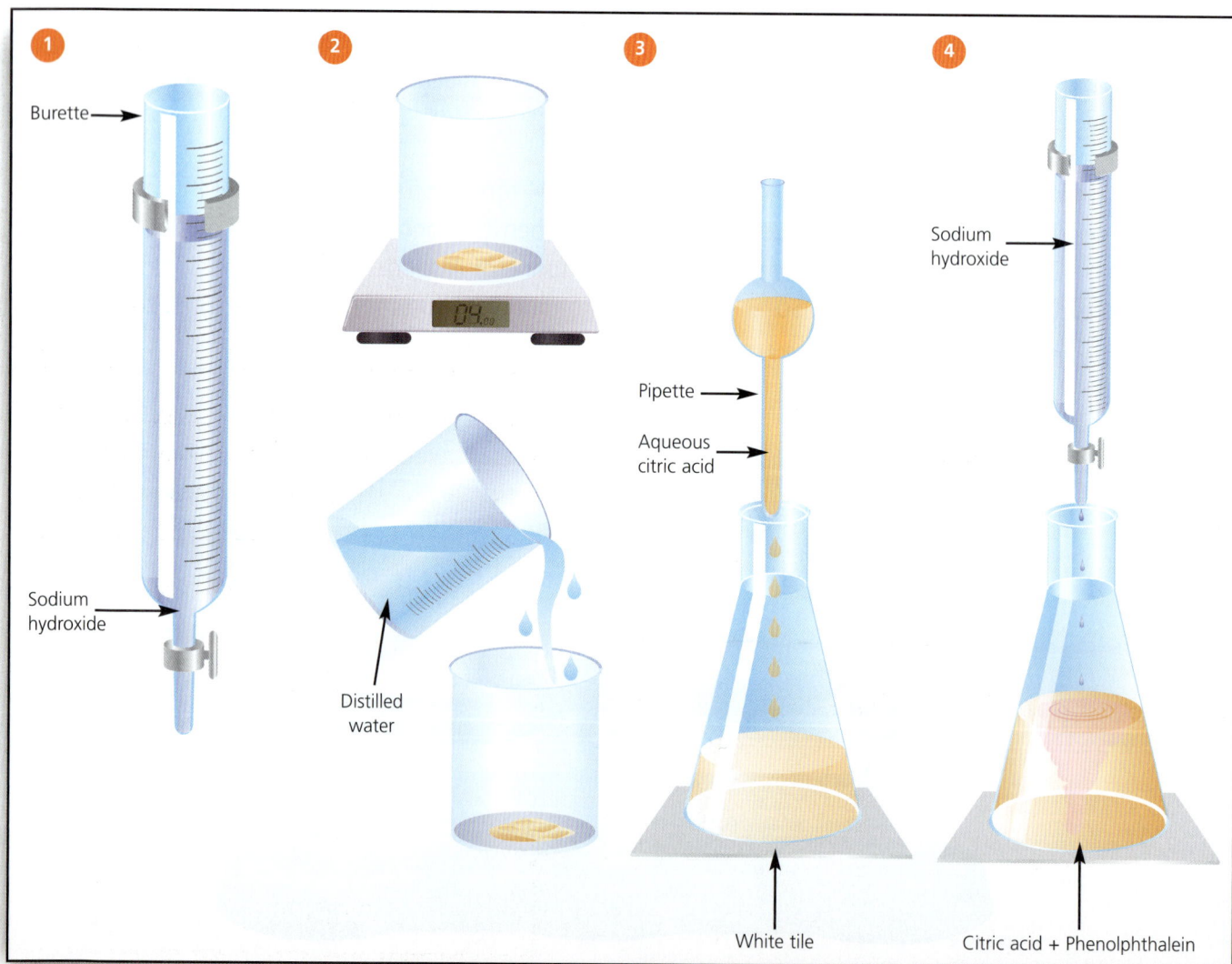

1

Burette

Sodium hydroxide

2

04 mg

Distilled water

3

Pipette

Aqueous citric acid

4

Sodium hydroxide

White tile

Citric acid + Phenolphthalein

Chemical Synthesis

Interpreting Results

Example

Calculate the purity of citric acid used when…

- concentration of sodium hydroxide (NaOH) = 40g/dm^3
- volume of sodium hydroxide = 8cm^3
- mass of citric acid = 4g
- volume of citric acid solution = 25cm^3

First, using the formula below, calculate the concentration of citric acid by substituting the values.

$$\text{Concentration of acid} = 3 \times \frac{\text{Volume of Conc. NaOH}}{\text{Volume citric acid}}$$

1 molecule of citric acid reacts with 3 molecules of sodium hydroxide

You must work in dm^3 when doing the calculations. To convert cm^3 to dm^3, divide by 1000.

$$= 3 \times \frac{\left(\frac{8}{1000} \times 40\right)}{\left(\frac{25}{1000}\right)}$$

$$= \mathbf{38.4g/dm^3}$$

Then, work out the actual mass of citric acid in the sample:

$$\text{Mass} = \text{Concentration} \times \text{Volume}$$

$$= 38.4g/dm^3 \times \left(\frac{25cm^3}{1000}\right)$$

$$= \mathbf{0.96g}$$

If the mass of citric acid dissolved in 25cm^3 is 0.96g, the mass of citric acid dissolved in 100cm^3 of water will be 4 x 0.96 = 3.84g

$$\% \text{ of Purity} = \frac{\text{Calculated mass}}{\text{Mass weighed out at start}} \times 100$$

$$= \frac{3.84}{4.0} \times 100$$

$$= \mathbf{96\%}$$

Rates of Reactions

The rate of a **chemical reaction** is the amount of reaction that takes place in a given unit of time. Chemical reactions only occur when the reacting particles collide with each other with sufficient energy to react.

These reactions can proceed at different speeds, e.g. rusting is a slow reaction whereas burning is a fast reaction.

Measuring the Rate of Reaction

The rate of a chemical reaction can be found in three different ways:

1 Weighing the reaction mixture.

If one of the products is a gas, you could weigh the reaction mixture at timed intervals. The mass of the mixture will decrease.

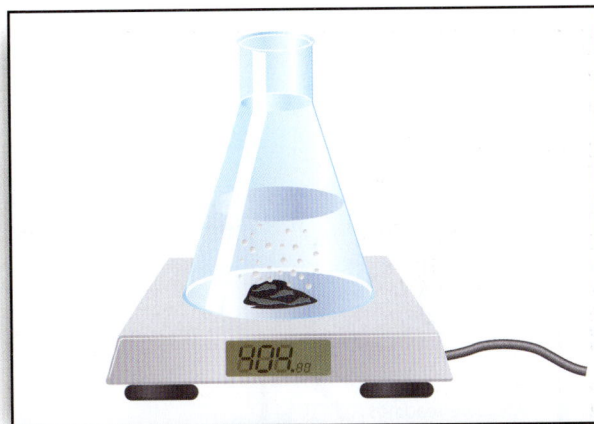

2 Measuring the volume of gas produced.

You could use a gas syringe to measure the total volume of gas produced at timed intervals.

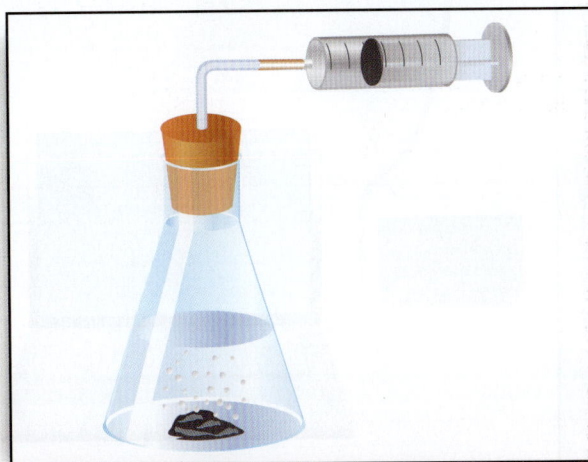

Chemical Synthesis

3 **Observing the formation of a precipitate.**

This can be done by either watching a cross (on a tile underneath the jar to see when it is no longer visible), to measure the formation of a precipitate, or by monitoring a colour change using a light sensor. The light sensor will lead to more reliable and accurate results as there is a definite end point. There are also more data points collected, especially if it is interfaced with a computer.

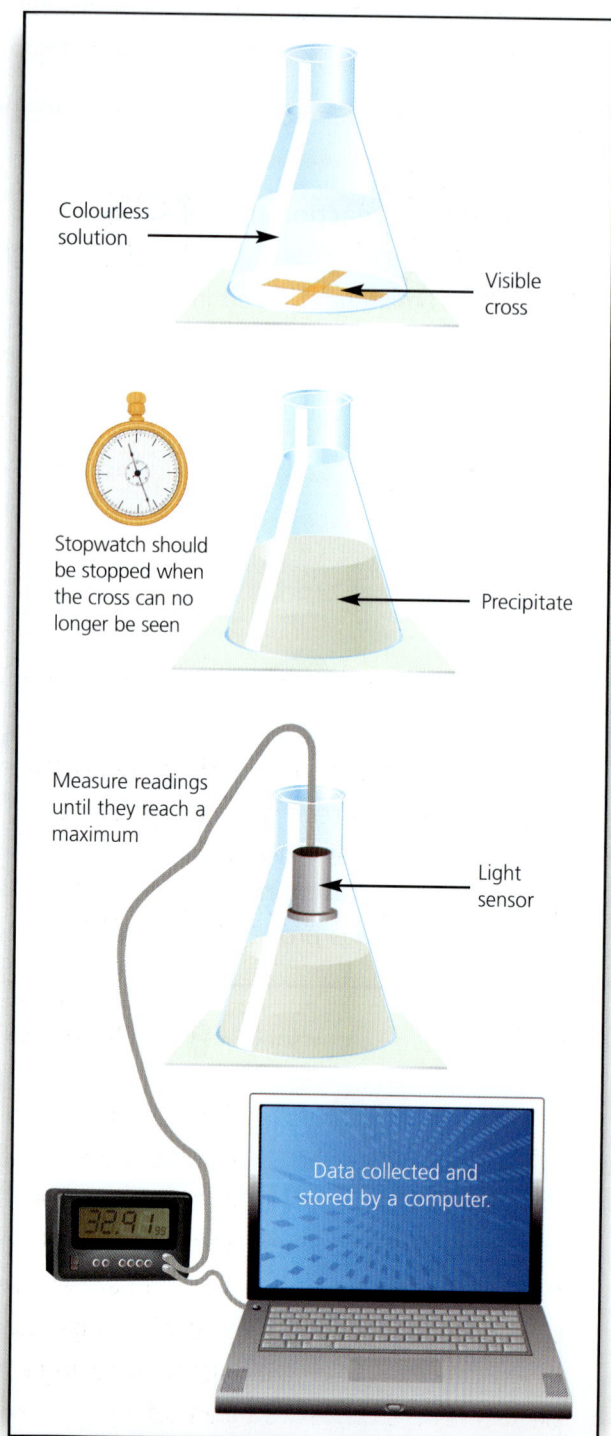

Colourless solution

Visible cross

Stopwatch should be stopped when the cross can no longer be seen

Precipitate

Measure readings until they reach a maximum

Light sensor

Data collected and stored by a computer.

Analysing the Rate of Reaction

Graphs can be plotted to show the progress of a chemical reaction – there are three things to remember:

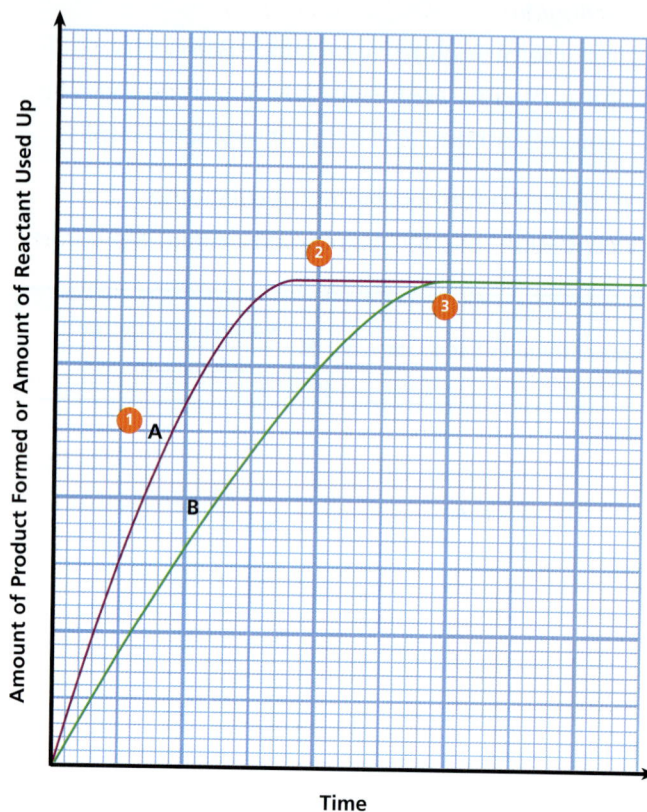

Amount of Product Formed or Amount of Reactant Used Up

Time

1 The steeper the line, the faster the reaction.

2 When one of the reactants is used up the reaction stops (line becomes flat).

3 The same amount of product is formed from the same amount of reactants, irrespective of rate.

Reaction A is faster than reaction B. This could be because…

- the surface area of the solid reactants in reaction A is greater than in reaction B (i.e. smaller particles are used)
- the temperature of reaction A is greater than reaction B
- the concentration of the solution in reaction A is greater than in reaction B
- a catalyst is used in reaction A but not in reaction B.

Chemical Synthesis

Changing the Rate of the Reaction

There are four important factors which affect the rate of reaction – temperature, concentration of dissolved reactants, surface area and the use of a catalyst.

1 Temperature of the Reactants

In a cold reaction mixture, the particles move quite slowly. They will collide less often, with less energy, so fewer collisions will be successful.

In a hot reaction mixture, the particles move more quickly. They will collide more often, with greater energy, so many more collisions will be successful.

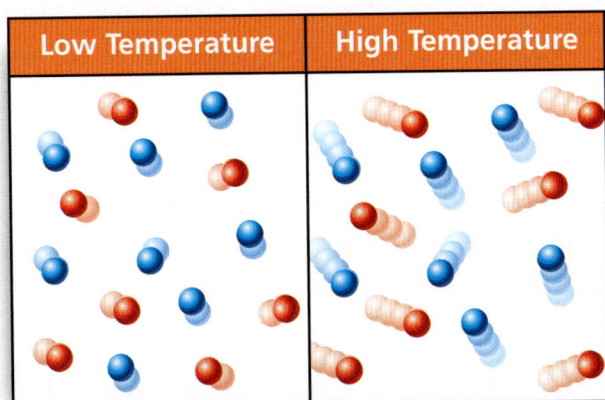

Low Temperature	High Temperature

2 Concentration of the Dissolved Reactants

In a low concentration reaction, the particles are spread out. The particles will collide with each other less often resulting in fewer successful collisions.

In a high concentration reaction, the particles are crowded close together. The particles will collide with each other more often, resulting in many more successful collisions.

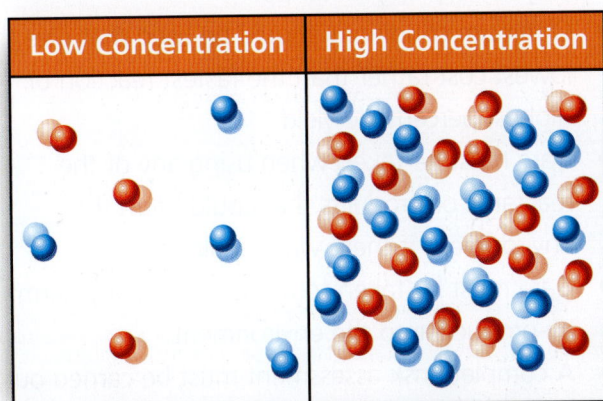

Low Concentration	High Concentration

3 Surface Area of Solid Reactants

Large particles (e.g. of powdered solids) have a small surface area in relation to their volume, meaning fewer particles are exposed and available for collisions. This means fewer collisions and a slower reaction.

Small particles (e.g. of powdered solids) have a large surface area in relation to their volume, so more particles are exposed and available for collisions. This means more collisions and a faster reaction.

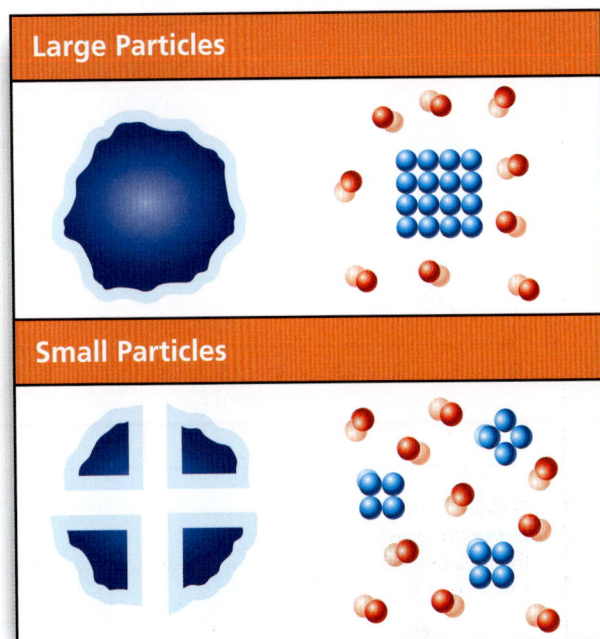

Large Particles

Small Particles

4 Using a Catalyst

A catalyst is a substance which increases the rate of a chemical reaction, without being changed during the process.

If we consider the decomposition of hydrogen peroxide...

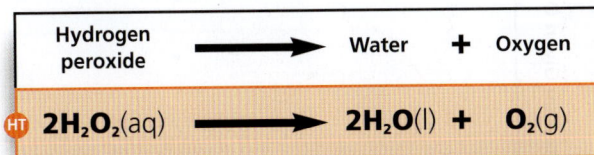

Hydrogen peroxide	$\longrightarrow$	Water	+	Oxygen

HT $2H_2O_2(aq) \longrightarrow 2H_2O(l) + O_2(g)$

We can measure the rate of this reaction by measuring the amount of oxygen given off at one-minute intervals. This reaction happens very slowly unless we add a catalyst of manganese (IV) oxide. With a catalyst, plenty of fizzing can be seen as the oxygen is given off.

Chemical Synthesis

Without a Catalyst

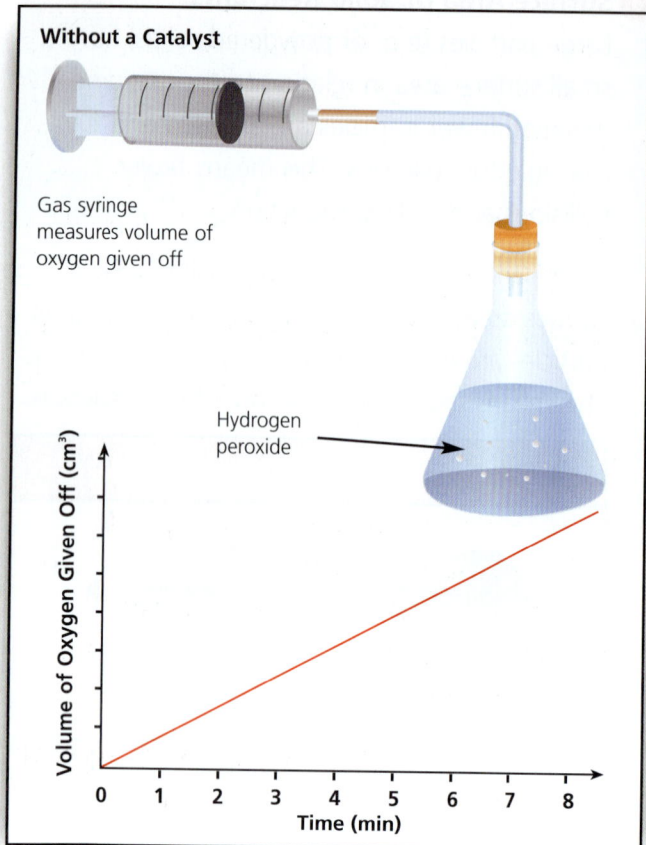

Gas syringe measures volume of oxygen given off

Hydrogen peroxide

Volume of Oxygen Given Off (cm³) vs Time (min)

With a Catalyst

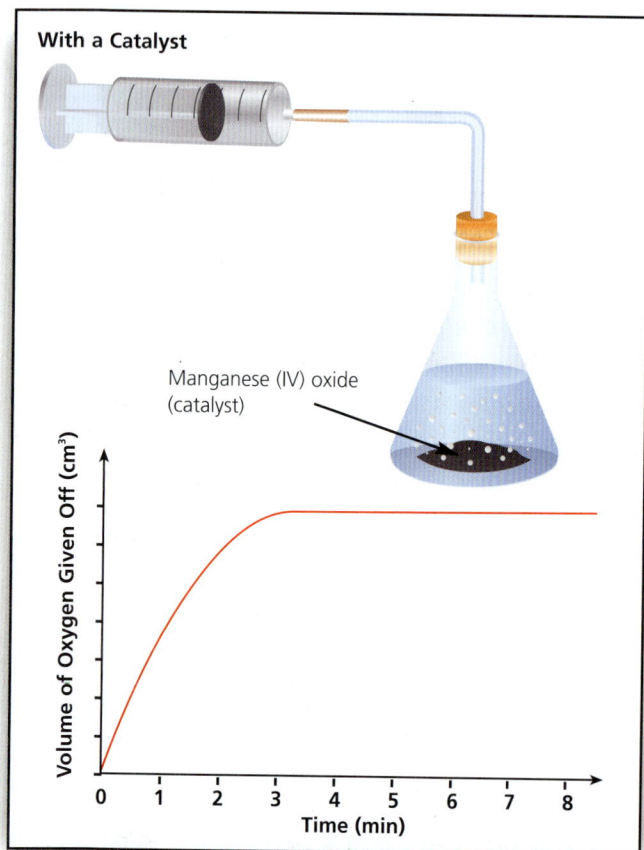

Manganese (IV) oxide (catalyst)

Volume of Oxygen Given Off (cm³) vs Time (min)

The same amount of gas is given off, but it takes a far shorter time when a catalyst is present.

Catalysts work by lowering the amount of energy needed for a successful collision. They are specific to a particular reaction and are not used up during the reaction. Consequently, only small amounts are needed.

HT Collision Theory

Chemical reactions only occur when particles collide with each other with sufficient energy. Increasing temperature causes an increase in the kinetic energy of the particles, i.e. they move a lot faster. This results in more energetic collisions happening more frequently. The minimum energy required for a reaction will, therefore, be achieved more often, resulting in a greater rate of reaction.

An increase in concentration or surface area results in more frequent collisions and, therefore, more collisions which are sufficiently energetic for a reaction to occur.

Controlling a Chemical Reaction

When carrying out a chemical synthesis on an industrial scale there are also economic, safety and environmental factors to consider:

- The rate of manufacture must be high enough to produce a sufficient daily yield of product.
- Percentage yield must be high enough to produce a sufficient daily yield of product.
- A low percentage yield is acceptable providing the reaction can be repeated many times with recycled starting materials.
- Optimum conditions should be used that give the lowest cost rather than the fastest reaction or highest percentage yield.
- Care must be taken when using any of the reactants or products that could harm the environment if there was a leak.
- Care must be taken to avoid putting any harmful by-products into the environment.
- A complete risk assessment must be carried out, and the necessary precautions taken.

Further Chemistry

Module C7

Further chemistry provides an opportunity to study selected chemistry topics in depth. This module looks at…
- the properties of different compounds
- how chemical reactions work
- analytical procedures
- the chemical industry today.

HT You must be able to write balanced symbol equations for the combustion of alkanes, for example…

$$CH_4(g) + 2O_2(g) \longrightarrow CO_2(g) + 2H_2O(g)$$

$$2C_4H_{10}(g) + 13O_2(g) \longrightarrow 8CO_2(g) + 10H_2O(g)$$

Hydrocarbons

Hydrocarbons are made up only of carbon and hydrogen atoms.

The 'spine' of a hydrocarbon is made up of a chain of carbon atoms. There is a group of hydrocarbons called the **alkanes**.

In an alkane the carbon atoms are joined together by single carbon–carbon bonds. So, all the carbon atoms are linked to four carbon or hydrogen atoms by single bonds.

This means that all their bonds are single and the hydrocarbon is **saturated**.

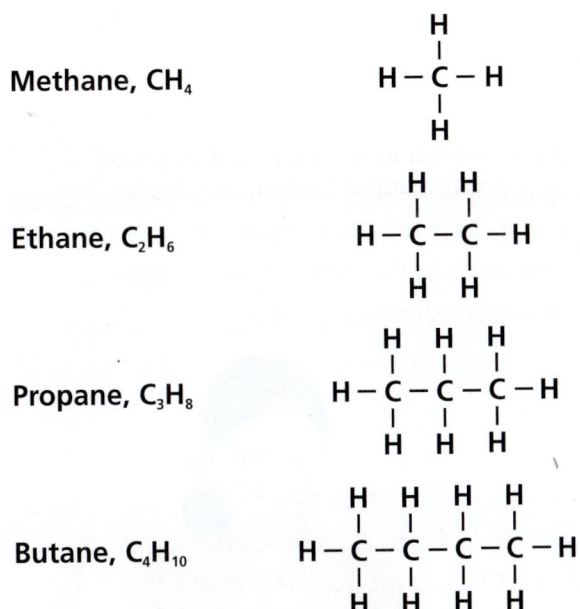

Methane, CH_4

Ethane, C_2H_6

Propane, C_3H_8

Butane, C_4H_{10}

Alkanes do not react with aqueous reagents, however, they do burn well in plenty of air to produce carbon dioxide and water.

Alcohols

Alcohols form a **homologous series** with the **functional group** –OH. The presence of the –OH gives alcohols their characteristic properties. The general formula for alcohols is $C_nH_{2n+1}OH$, where n is the number of carbon atoms.

The two simplest alcohols are **methanol** and **ethanol**:

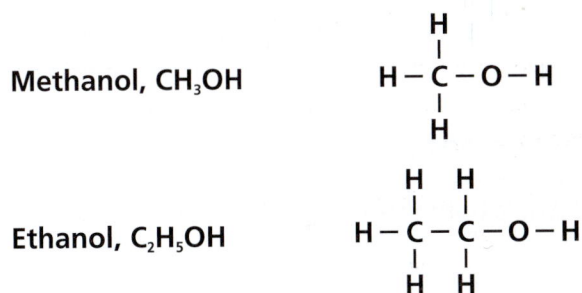

Methanol, CH_3OH

Ethanol, C_2H_5OH

Ethanol can be used as a solvent, a fuel or a component in alcoholic drinks.

Methanol is an important chemical feedstock (i.e. a raw material used for an industrial process.) Methanol can be used in the manufacture of fuels, adhesives, foams, cosmetics and solvents.

Further Chemistry

Physical Properties of Alcohols

Alcohols contain a hydrocarbon chain and an –OH group, so we can compare their physical properties to those of the alkanes and water.

	Boiling Point (°C)	Melting Point (°C)	Density (g/cm³)
Alcohol, e.g. Ethanol	78	-117	0.79
Water	100	0	1.0
Alkane, e.g. Ethane	-89	-183	0.546

From the table, it can be seen that…
- the hydrocarbon chain behaves like the alkane, i.e. it is less dense than water because the long hydrocarbon chains do not mix with water
- the –OH group behaves like water, which explains the higher than expected boiling point.

Chemical Reactions of Alcohols

Alcohols burn in air to produce carbon dioxide and water.

They produce these substances because of the presence of the hydrocarbon chain.

HT The following equation shows what happens when an alcohol burns in air:

$$C_2H_5OH(l) + 3O_2(g) \rightarrow 3H_2O(g) + 2CO_2(g)$$

Alcohols react with sodium to produce a salt and hydrogen gas. It is the presence of the functional group –OH that allows this reaction to occur as in the example below. (Sodium ethoxide is a white, solid ionic salt.)

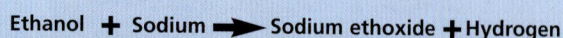

$$\text{Ethanol} + \text{Sodium} \rightarrow \text{Sodium ethoxide} + \text{Hydrogen}$$

$$2C_2H_5OH(l) + 2Na(s) \rightarrow 2C_2H_5O^-Na^+(s) + H_2(g)$$

HT Water, alcohols and alkanes react differently with sodium:
- Sodium floats on **water**, melts, rushes around on the surface and rapidly gives off hydrogen.
- Sodium sinks in **alcohol**, does not melt and steadily gives off hydrogen.
- There is no reaction between sodium and an **alkane**.

Carboxylic Acids

Carboxylic acids form a **homologous series** with the **functional group** –COOH. The presence of the –COOH gives carboxylic acids their characteristic properties.

The two simplest carboxylic acids are **methanoic acid** and **ethanoic acid**:

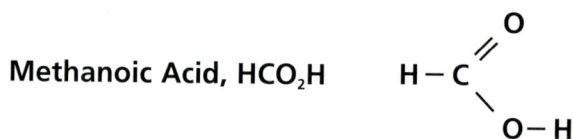

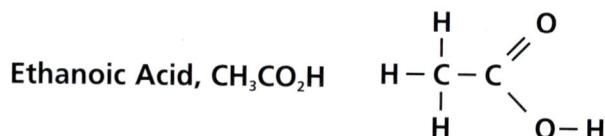

Methanoic Acid, HCO_2H

Ethanoic Acid, CH_3CO_2H

Vinegar is a dilute solution of ethanoic acid.

Carboxylic acids are found in many substances and some have unpleasant smells and tastes. For example, they are responsible for…
- the aroma of a sweaty training shoe
- the taste of rancid butter.

Chemical Reactions of Carboxylic Acids

Carboxylic acids are weak acids. Like all acids, they can react with metals, alkalis and carbonates to produce carboxylic acid salts. Some examples are shown below:

Reaction of a carboxylic acid with a **metal**:

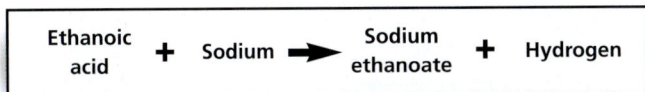

Ethanoic acid	+	Sodium	→	Sodium ethanoate	+	Hydrogen

Reaction of a carboxylic acid with an **alkali**:

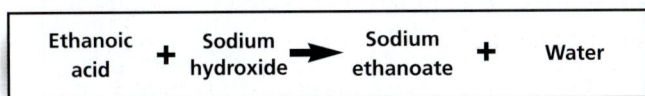

Ethanoic acid	+	Sodium hydroxide	→	Sodium ethanoate	+	Water

Reaction of a carboxylic acid with a **carbonate**:

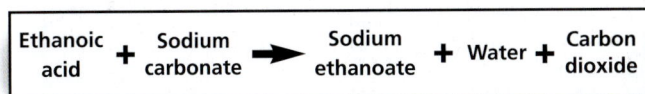

Ethanoic acid	+	Sodium carbonate	→	Sodium ethanoate	+	Water	+	Carbon dioxide

Fats

Fats and oils are naturally occurring esters. Living organisms make them to use as an energy store.

Fats are the esters of…
- **glycerol** which is an alcohol with three –OH groups
- **fatty** acids which are carboxylic acids with very long hydrocarbon chains.

Saturated Fats

Animal fats, such as lard and fatty meat, are mostly **saturated molecules**. This means they have single carbon–carbon bonds and the molecules are unreactive.

For example, glycerol is a saturated fat.

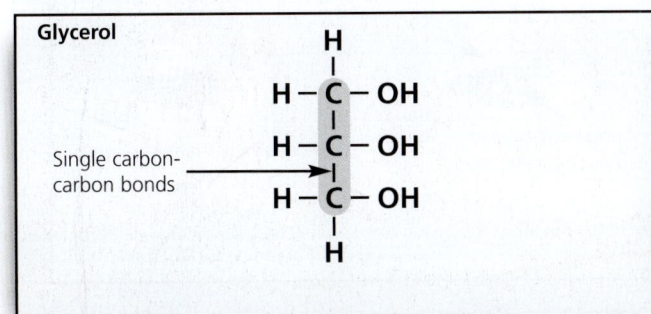

Glycerol — Single carbon-carbon bonds

Unsaturated Fats

Vegetable oils, such as olive oil and sunflower oil, are mostly **unsaturated molecules**. This means that they contain some double carbon–carbon bonds ($C=C$). The presence of the $C=C$ bonds means that the molecules are reactive.

For example, vegetable oils (hydrogenated fats) are unsaturated fats.

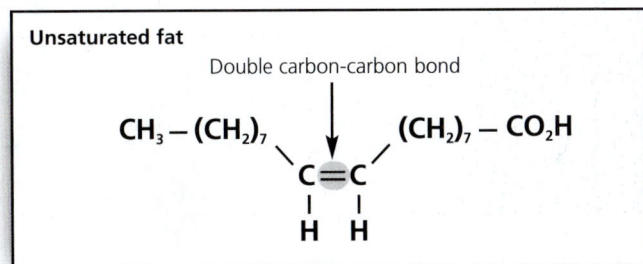

Unsaturated fat — Double carbon-carbon bond
$$CH_3 - (CH_2)_7 \quad C=C \quad (CH_2)_7 - CO_2H$$

Esters

Carboxylic acids react with alcohols to form **esters**, as in the following example:

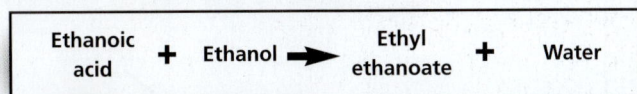

Ethanoic acid	+	Ethanol	→	Ethyl ethanoate	+	Water

This reaction is carried out in the presence of a **catalyst**, i.e. concentrated sulfuric acid.

Esters have distinctive smells that are responsible for the smells and flavours of fruits. Due to their sweet smell, they are often used in the manufacture of perfumes, fragrances and food products (for artificial flavours such as raspberry, pear and cherry).

Esters are also found in products such as solvents in **adhesives** and **plasticizers** because they contain hydrocarbon chains.

Further Chemistry

HT Preparing Esters

An ester can be prepared by the following method.

1 Ethanol and excess ethanoic acid are heated under **reflux** in the presence of concentrated sulfuric acid.

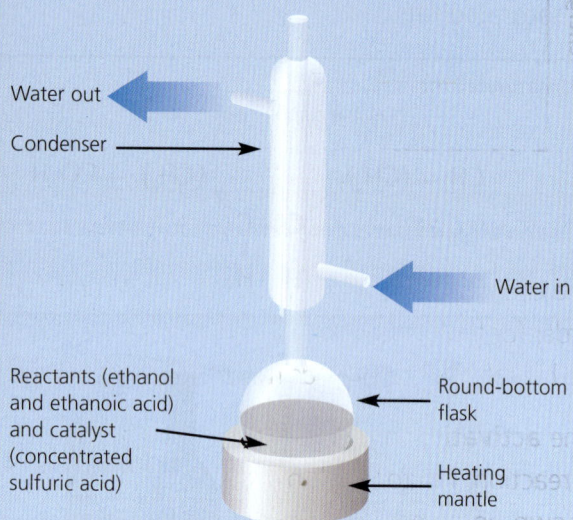

Water out

Condenser

Water in

Reactants (ethanol and ethanoic acid) and catalyst (concentrated sulfuric acid)

Round-bottom flask

Heating mantle

2 The ester is removed by **distillation**. (Ethyl ethanoate boils at 77°C.)

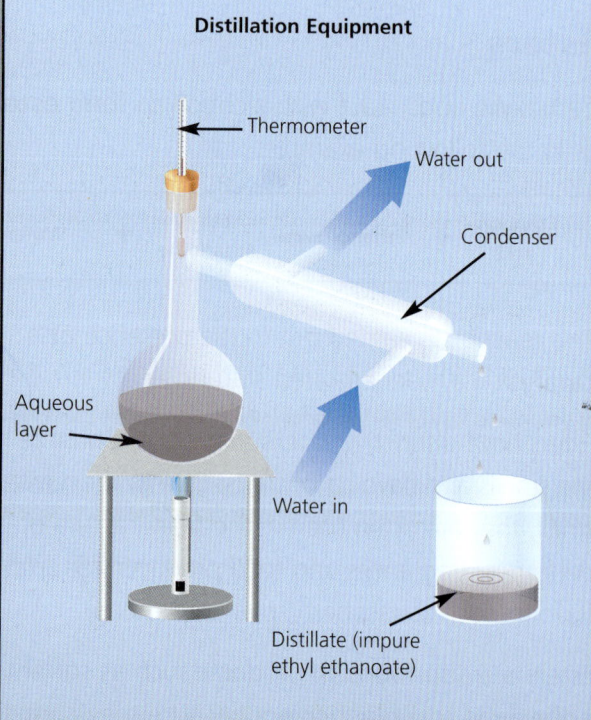

Distillation Equipment

Thermometer

Water out

Condenser

Aqueous layer

Water in

Distillate (impure ethyl ethanoate)

3 The distillate is transferred to a separating funnel where it is purified. A solution of sodium carbonate is added, and the mixture is shaken up. This mixture will react with any remaining acid and extract it into the aqueous phase. The aqueous phase is then run off leaving the ester in the funnel.

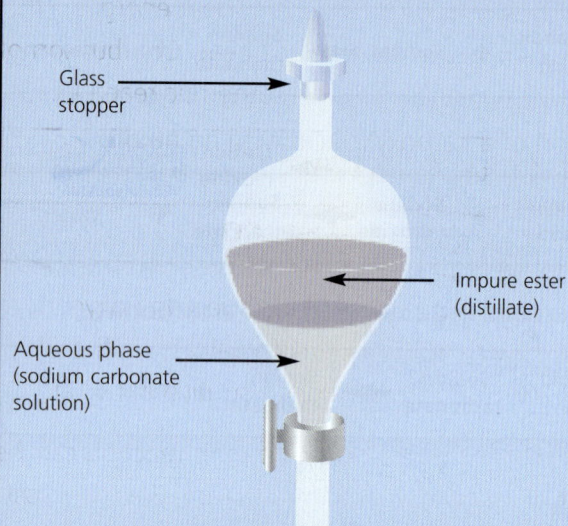

Glass stopper

Impure ester (distillate)

Aqueous phase (sodium carbonate solution)

4 The product is transferred to a conical flask and anhydrous calcium chloride is added to remove any remaining water molecules. The calcium chloride is removed later by filtration.

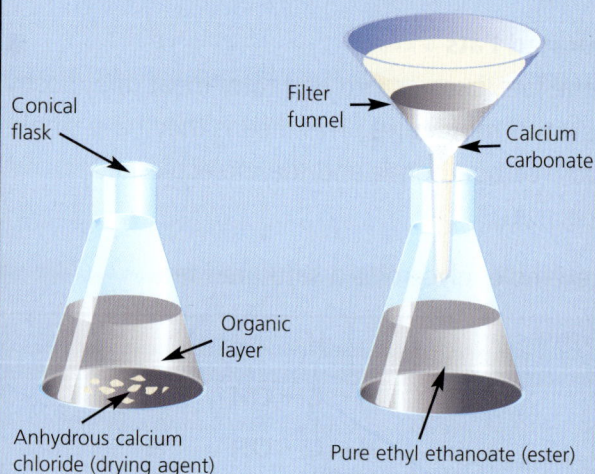

Conical flask

Filter funnel

Calcium carbonate

Organic layer

Anhydrous calcium chloride (drying agent)

Pure ethyl ethanoate (ester)

Further Chemistry

Energy Changes

When chemical reactions occur, energy is transferred to or from the surroundings. Therefore, many chemical reactions are accompanied by a **temperature change**.

Exothermic Reactions

Exothermic reactions are accompanied by a **temperature rise**. They transfer heat energy to the surroundings, i.e. they give out heat. Combustion of carbon is an example of an exothermic reaction.

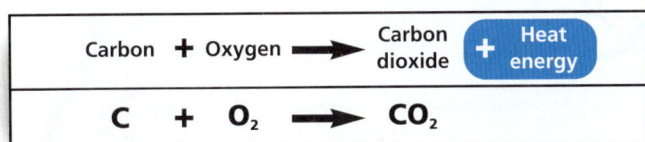

Carbon	+ Oxygen	→	Carbon dioxide	+	Heat energy
C	+ O_2	→	CO_2		

It is not only reactions between fuels and oxygen that are exothermic. Neutralising alkalis with acids and many oxidation reactions also give out heat.

The energy change in an exothermic reaction can be shown using an energy level diagram. Energy is lost during the reaction, so the products have less energy than the reactants.

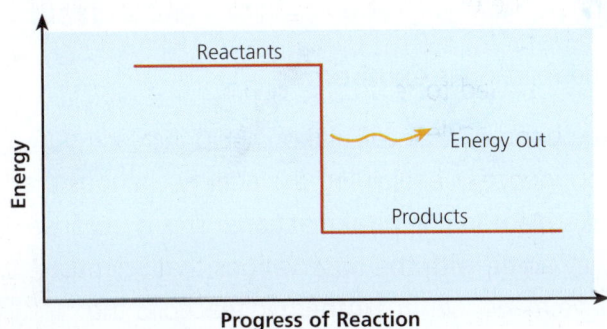

Endothermic Reactions

Endothermic reactions are accompanied by a **fall in temperature**. Heat is transferred from the surroundings, i.e. they take in heat. Dissolving ammonium nitrate crystals in water is an example of an endothermic reaction.

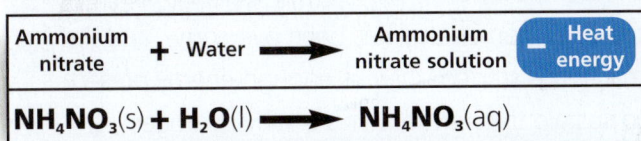

Ammonium nitrate	+ Water	→	Ammonium nitrate solution	−	Heat energy
$NH_4NO_3(s)$	+ $H_2O(l)$	→	$NH_4NO_3(aq)$		

Thermal decomposition is also an example of an endothermic reaction.

The energy change in an endothermic reaction can be shown using an energy level diagram. Energy is taken in during the reaction, so the products have more energy than the reactants.

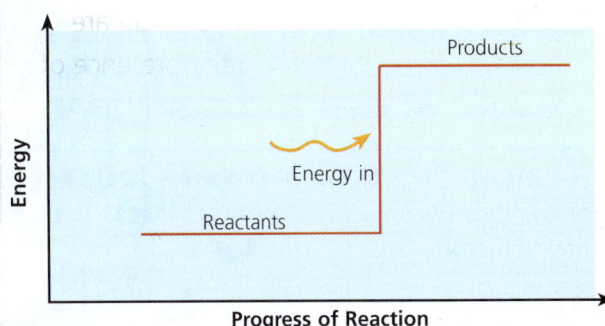

Making and Breaking Bonds

In a chemical reaction, new substances are produced. In order for this to happen, the bonds in the reactants must be broken and new bonds made to form the products.

The **activation energy** is the energy needed to start a reaction, i.e. to break old bonds. This can also be shown on an energy level diagram.

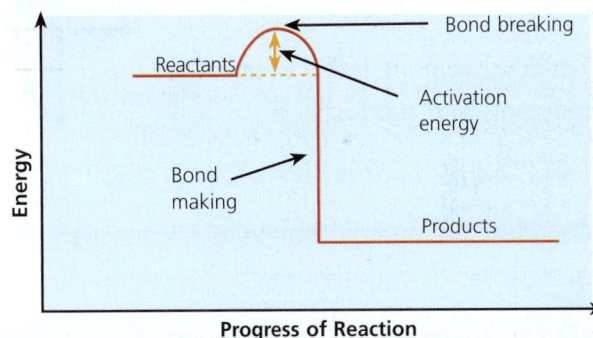

Breaking a chemical bond requires a lot of energy – this is an **endothermic** process. When a new chemical bond is formed, energy is given out – this is an **exothermic** process.

If more energy is required to break old bonds than is released when the new bonds are formed, the reaction is **endothermic**.

ENERGY	→	REACTANTS	→	PRODUCTS	→	ENERGY

If more energy is released when the new bonds are formed than is needed to break the old bonds, the reaction is **exothermic**.

ENERGY	→	REACTANTS	→	PRODUCTS	→	ENERGY

Further Chemistry

Energy Calculations and Supplied Bond Energies

Example 1

Hydrogen is burned in oxygen to produce water:

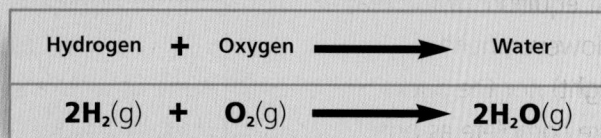

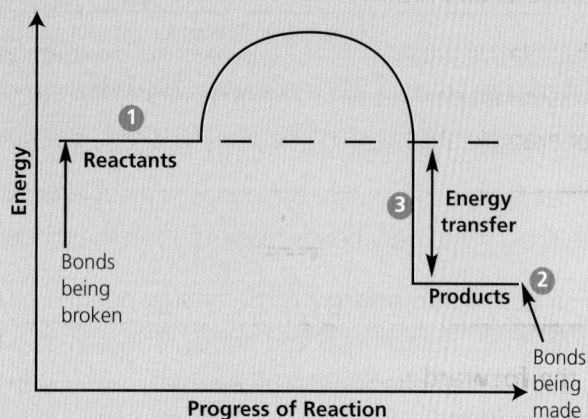

Hydrogen	+	Oxygen	$\longrightarrow$	Water
$2H_2(g)$	+	$O_2(g)$	$\longrightarrow$	$2H_2O(g)$

The following are bond energies for the reactants and products:

H-H is 436kJ; O=O is 496kJ; O-H is 463kJ

Calculate the energy change. Is this reaction exothermic or endothermic?

1 The energy used to break bonds is…
   2 x H-H + O=O = (2 x 436) + 496
   = **1368kJ**

2 The energy used to make bonds is…
   (water is made up of 2 x O-H bonds)
   2 x H-O-H = 2 x (2 x 463)
   = **1852kJ**

3 The energy change (ΔH) = 1368 – 1852
   = **-484kJ**

The reaction is **exothermic** because the energy from making the bonds in the product is more than the energy needed to break the bonds in the reactants.

Example 2

Hydrogen and halogens react together to form hydrogen halides. For example, the formation of hydrogen chloride is shown below.

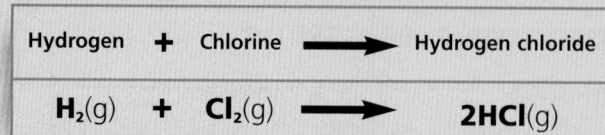

Hydrogen	+	Chlorine	$\longrightarrow$	Hydrogen chloride
$H_2(g)$	+	$Cl_2(g)$	$\longrightarrow$	$2HCl(g)$

The following are bond energies for the reactants and products:

H-H is 436kJ; Cl-Cl is 243kJ; H-Cl is 432kJ.

Calculate the energy changes in this reaction.

1 The energy used to break bonds is…
   H-H   = 436
   Cl-Cl = 243
   Total = **679 kJ**

2 The energy used to make bonds is…
   2 x H-Cl = 2 x 432
   = **864 kJ**

3 The energy change is = 679 – 864 = **-185kJ**

The reaction is **exothermic**.

The bond energy calculations help increase our confidence in explaining the energy changes that take place in chemical reactions. This is because they agree with the observations that scientists have made, i.e. in exothermic reactions the temperature goes up and energy is given out.

Research scientists find the use of this data very important. For example, when looking for non-polluting fuels, scientists need to know how much energy is given out during the reaction. Example 1 shows that burning hydrogen in oxygen is a very exothermic reaction that only produces water. Once the activation energy has been overcome, and the reaction is started, there is enough energy present to sustain the reaction. This is why hydrogen-fuelled cars may be used more in the future.

Reversible Reactions

Some chemical reactions are reversible, i.e. the products can react together to produce the original reactants.

$$A + B \rightleftharpoons C + D$$

This means that…

- A and B can react together to produce C and D
- C and D can react together to produce A and B.

For example, solid ammonium chloride decomposes when heated to produce ammonia and hydrogen chloride gas, both of which are colourless. Hydrogen chloride gas and ammonia react to produce white clouds of ammonium chloride.

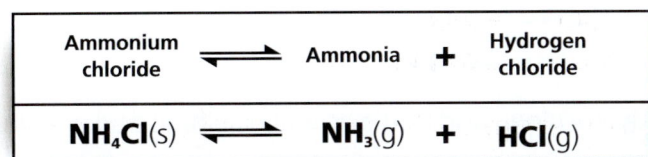

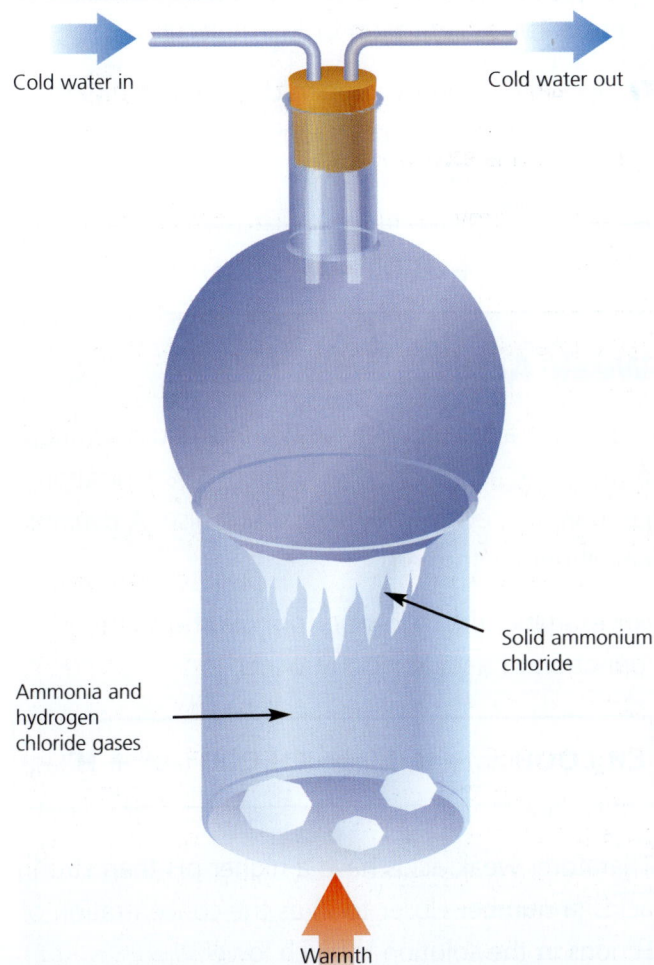

Ammonium chloride	$\rightleftharpoons$	Ammonia	+	Hydrogen chloride
$NH_4Cl(s)$	$\rightleftharpoons$	$NH_3(g)$	+	$HCl(g)$

Cold water in
Cold water out

Solid ammonium chloride

Ammonia and hydrogen chloride gases

Warmth

Equilibrium

A reversible reaction will reach a state of **equilibrium** if it is in a **closed system** (a system where no reactants are added and no products are taken away).

At equilibrium the reaction appears to have stopped. However, neither the forward reaction (from left to right) nor the backward reaction (from right to left) are complete as both reactants and products are present at the same time. The concentration of the reactants and products does not change.

The relative amounts of all the reacting substances at equilibrium depend on the conditions of the reaction. For example, the following diagram represents a reaction:

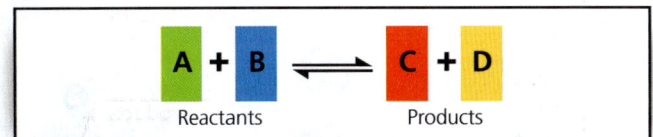

A + B $\rightleftharpoons$ C + D
Reactants   Products

If the **forward reaction** (the reaction that produces the products C and D) is **endothermic** then…

- If the temperature is increased, the yield of products is increased.

- If the temperature is decreased, the yield of products is decreased.

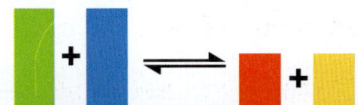

If the **forward reaction** is **exothermic** then…

- If the temperature is increased, the yield of products is decreased.

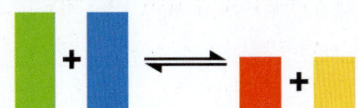

- If the temperature is decreased, the yield of products is increased.

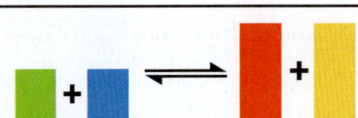

Although a reversible reaction might not go to completion, it could still be used efficiently in an industrial process, e.g. the Haber process for the industrial manufacture of ammonia.

Further Chemistry

Achieved Equilibrium

Once equilibrium is achieved, the concentration of the reactants and products does not change. The equilibrium can be approached from either direction, i.e. the 'reactant' side or the 'product' side.

Chemical equilibriums are **dynamic**. Both the forward and the backward reactions are still occurring, but at the same rate. Therefore, there is no overall change in concentration of the substances.

The diagrams below show what happens to iodine particles when you shake a solution of iodine in an organic solvent with aqueous potassium iodide.

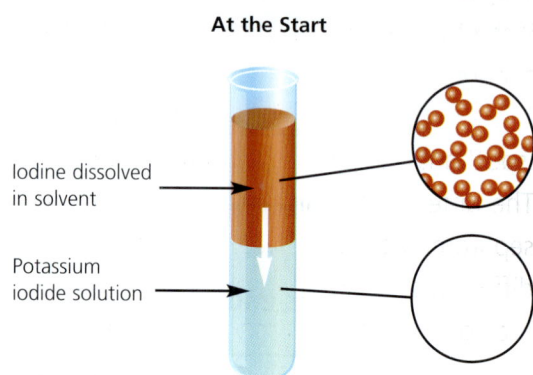

At the Start

Iodine dissolved in solvent

Potassium iodide solution

Dynamic Equilibrium
(Particles move between the solvent and solution)

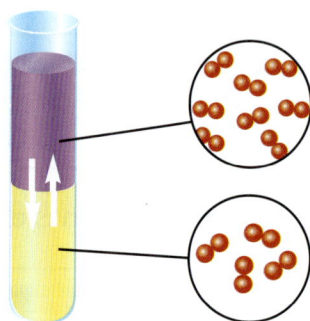

At Equilibrium
(Particles continue to move, but equilibrium is maintained)

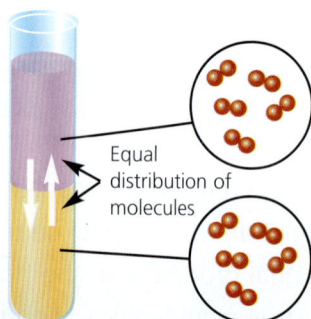

Equal distribution of molecules

Many everyday products use equilibria.

Dynamic equilibrium may be used to explain the difference between a strong acid and a weak acid.

Strong Acids

Hydrochloric acid, nitric acid and sulfuric acid are all examples of strong acids. When the acid is formed, there is 100% ionisation of the molecules.

For example, when hydrogen chloride gas dissolves in water, all the molecules ionise to give hydrogen ions and chloride ions.

$$HCl(g) \; + \; H_2O(l) \longrightarrow H^+(aq) \; + \; Cl^-(aq)$$

Weak Acids

Carboxylic acids are weak acids. In a dilute solution of ethanoic acid there is only about 1% ionisation, i.e. only 1 in every 100 molecules ionise. A dynamic equilibrium is formed.

For example, the following formula shows the ionisation of a weak acid in water.

$$CH_3COOH(aq) + H_2O(l) \rightleftharpoons CH_3COO^-(aq) \; + \; H^+(aq)$$

Therefore, weak acids have a higher pH than strong acids (a number closer to 7) as the concentration of H^+ ions in the solution is much lower.

Further Chemistry

Analysis

There are two types of analytical procedures:
- **Qualitative** methods.
- **Quantitative** methods.

Qualitative analysis is any method used to identify the **chemicals** in a substance. For example, using an indicator to find out if acids are present or using thin layer chromatography.

Quantitative analysis is any method used to determine the **amount** of chemical in a substance. For example, carrying out an acid–base titration to find out how much acid is present.

Many of the analytical methods you have learned are based on samples in solutions.

When collecting data, it is very important that the samples are representative of the **bulk** of the material under test.

This is achieved by collecting multiple samples at random. After a sample has been collected, it should be stored in a sterile container to prevent change or deterioration.

The container should be sealed, labelled and stored in a safe place.

There are **standard procedures** for the collection, storage and preparation of samples for analysis.

Using a system of common practices and procedures, such as ensuring that samples are not contaminated, can increase reliability since there is less room for human error. Different people can also repeat a test on the same sample and produce the same result.

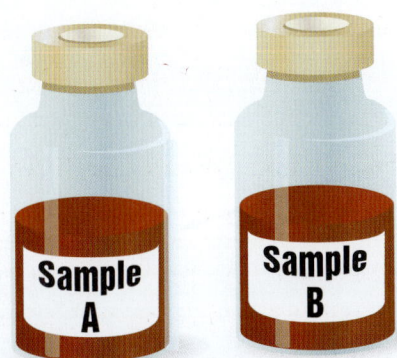

Chromatography

Chromatography is a technique used to find out what unknown mixtures are made up of. Substances are separated by the movement of a mobile phase through a stationary phase.

Paper Chromatography

1. If the substance to be analysed is a solid, dissolve it in a suitable solvent (the solvent used will depend on the solubility of the substance.
2. Place a spot of the resulting solution onto a sheet of chromatography paper on the pencil line, and allow it to dry.
3. Place the bottom edge of the paper into a suitable solvent.
4. The solvent rises up the paper, dissolving the 'spot' and carrying it, in solution, up the paper.
5. The different chemicals in the mixture become separated because their molecules have different sizes and properties. The molecules that bind strongly to the paper, travel a shorter distance than the molecules that bind weakly to the paper.

The chromatogram can then be compared to standard chromatograms (**standard reference materials**) of known substances to identify the different chemicals.

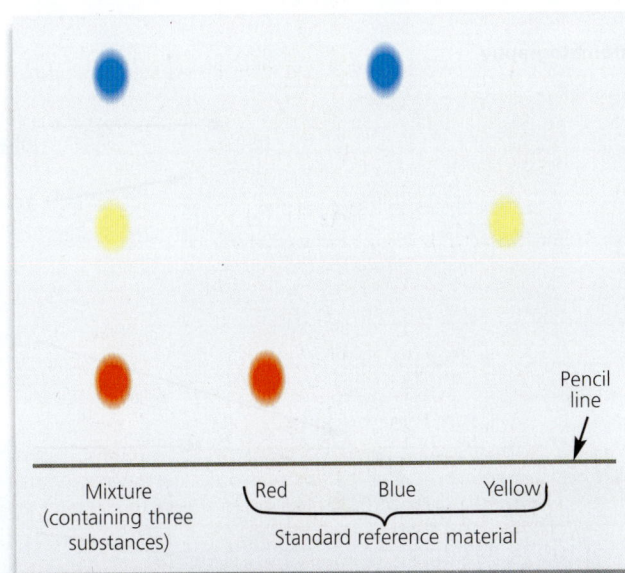

Further Chemistry

Chromatography (cont.)

The solvent that is used to move the solution is called the **mobile** phase.

A range of aqueous and non-aqueous solvents may be used. Aqueous solvents are water based, whereas non-aqueous solvents are made from organic liquids such as alkanes.

The medium that it moves through is called the **stationary** phase. In this case the paper is the stationary phase.

A chromatogram is formed when the chemicals come out of solution and bind to the paper, i.e. they move between the mobile phase and the stationary phase.

For each component of the sample, a dynamic equilibrium is set up between the stationary and mobile phase.

Different molecules in the sample mixture travel different distances according to how strongly they are attracted to the molecules in the stationary phase, in relation to their attraction to the solvent molecules.

Therefore, the overall separation depends on the distribution of the compounds in the sample between the mobile and stationary phases.

Some chromatograms have to be developed to show the presence of colourless substances **using locating agents**.

Thin Layer Chromatography (TLC)

TLC is similar to paper chromatography. However, the stationary phase is a thin layer of absorbent material (e.g. silica gel, alumina or cellulose) supported on a flat, unreactive surface (e.g. a glass, metal or plastic plate).

There are several advantages of thin layer chromatography over paper chromatography. The advantages include…
* faster runs
* more even movement of the mobile phase through the stationary phase
* a choice of different absorbencies for the stationary phase (which can increase the attraction between molecules in the mixture and the stationary phase).

As a result, thin layer chromatography usually produces better separations for a wider range of substances.

Some chromatograms have to be developed to show the presence of colourless substances:
* Colourless spots can sometimes be viewed under ultraviolet (UV) light and then marked on the plate.
* The chromatogram can be viewed by being sprayed with a chemical that reacts with the spots to cause coloration.

Chromatography

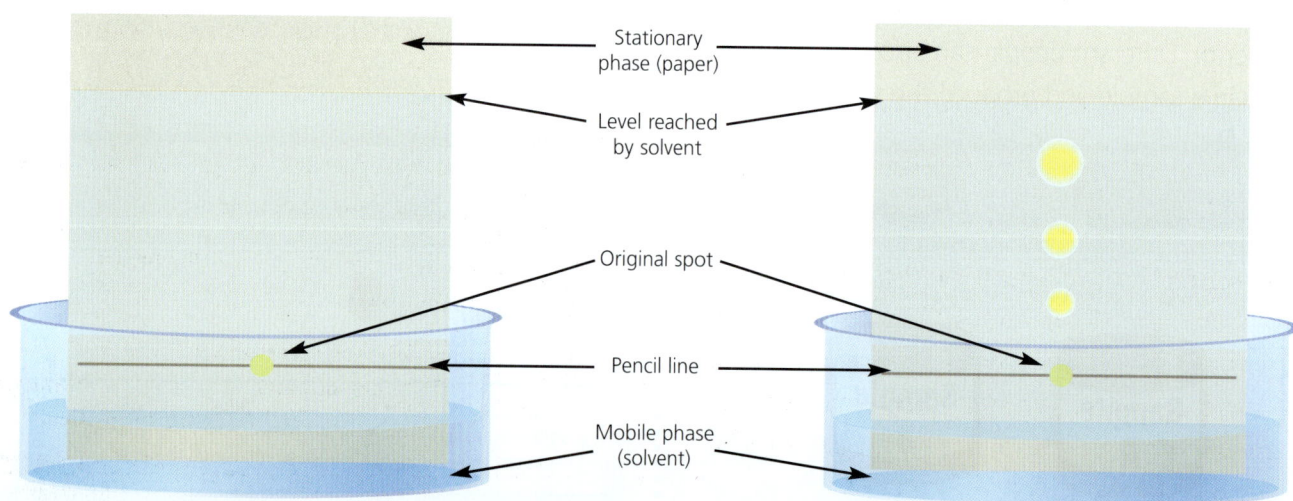

Labels: Stationary phase (paper); Level reached by solvent; Original spot; Pencil line; Mobile phase (solvent)

R$_f$ Value

In paper and thin layer chromatography, the movement of a substance relative to the movement of the solvent front is known as the **R$_f$ value**:

$$R_f \text{ value} = \frac{\text{Distance travelled by substance}}{\text{Distance travelled by solvent}}$$

Calculating the R$_f$ value can aid in the identification of unknown substances.

Example

The diagram below shows the distance travelled by a substance and the distance travelled by the solvent. Calculate the R$_f$ value.

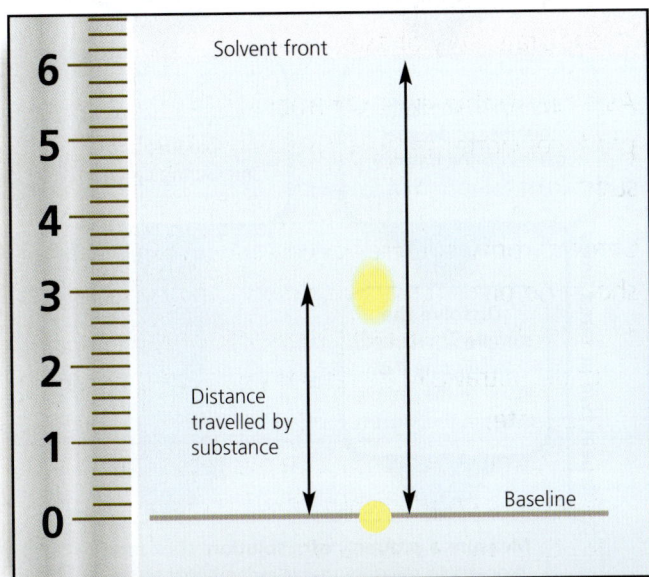

$$R_f = \frac{\text{Distance travelled by substance}}{\text{Distance travelled by solvent}}$$

$$= \frac{3cm}{6cm}$$

$$= 0.5cm$$

Gas–Liquid Chromatography

In gas–liquid chromatography, or simply gas chromatography (GC), the mobile phase is a carrier gas, usually an inert gas such as helium or nitrogen. The stationary phase is a microscopic layer of liquid on an unreactive solid support. The liquid is inside glass or metal tubing, called a **column**.

A sample of the substance to be analysed is injected into one end of the heated column where it vaporises. The carrier gas then carries it up the column where separation takes place.

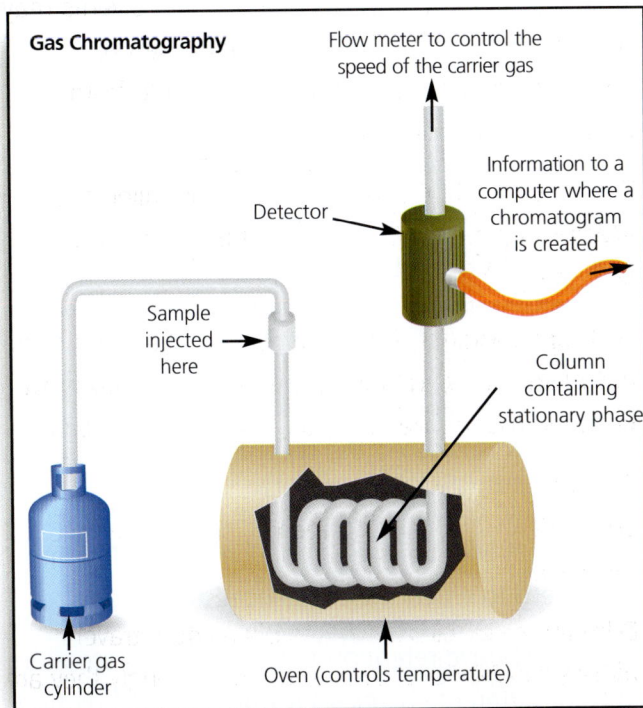

GC has a greater separating power than TLC or paper chromatography, and can separate complex mixtures. It can produce quantitative data from very small samples of liquids, gases and volatile solids.

The size of each peak in the chromatogram, produced by GC, shows the relative amount of each chemical in the sample. For example, the chromatogram below shows six different compounds present in a sample.

It can be seen that Compound A is present in the largest amount and Compound D in the smallest amount.

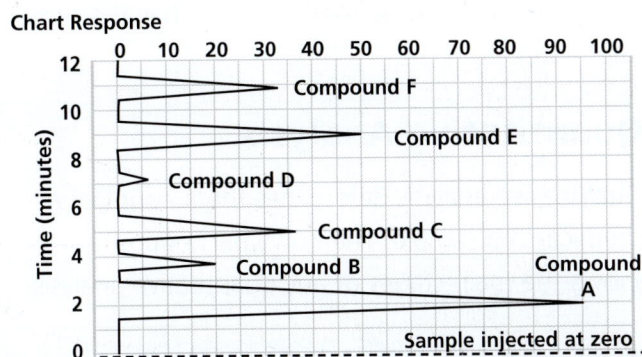

Further Chemistry

Gas–Liquid Chromatography (cont.)

GC is able to separate the components in a mixture because of their different solubilities in the stationary or mobile phases.

Practical uses of GC include...

- detecting banned substances in blood and urine samples (e.g. random sampling of athletes)
- analysing the exact characteristics of oil or pesticide spills and matching them to samples from suspected sources, to identify sources of pollution.

The time taken for each substance to pass through the chromatographic system depends on its solubility. This is called the **retention time**.

In gas–liquid chromatography, the retention time is the time taken from the sample being injected into the system to when the substance is detected.

Tables of relative retention times show the retention times of different chemicals relative to the retention time of a specific compound.

Example

Methanol has a retention time of 2.24 minutes. Using the data below, which compound could be methanol?

Compound	Retention Time (minutes)
A	2.08
B	2.24
C	3.01

Compound B could be methanol as it has the same retention time.

Quantitative Analysis

Quantitative analysis determines the amount of a chemical in a sample. The flow chart opposite shows the main stages of any quantitative analysis.

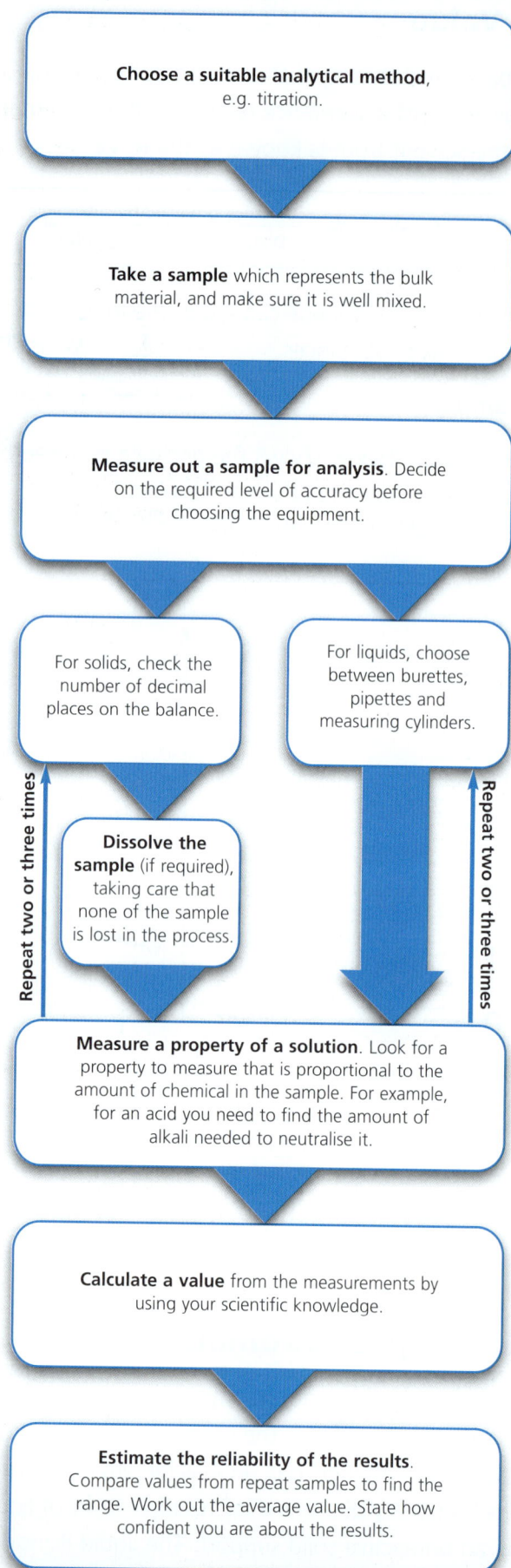

Choose a suitable analytical method, e.g. titration.

Take a sample which represents the bulk material, and make sure it is well mixed.

Measure out a sample for analysis. Decide on the required level of accuracy before choosing the equipment.

For solids, check the number of decimal places on the balance.

For liquids, choose between burettes, pipettes and measuring cylinders.

Repeat two or three times

Dissolve the sample (if required), taking care that none of the sample is lost in the process.

Repeat two or three times

Measure a property of a solution. Look for a property to measure that is proportional to the amount of chemical in the sample. For example, for an acid you need to find the amount of alkali needed to neutralise it.

Calculate a value from the measurements by using your scientific knowledge.

Estimate the reliability of the results. Compare values from repeat samples to find the range. Work out the average value. State how confident you are about the results.

Calculating Concentration and Mass

Many methods of quantitative analysis use solutions. The **concentration** of a solution is the quantity of solid dissolved in the liquid. The concentration of a solution is measured in g/dm^3.

> **HT** The formula below is used to calculate concentration:
>
> $$\text{Concentration (g/dm}^3\text{)} = \frac{\text{Mass (g)}}{\text{Volume (dm}^3\text{)}}$$
>
> **Example 1**
> 3.6g copper sulfate is dissolved in $80cm^3$ water. What is the concentration of the solution?
>
> $$\text{Concentration} = \frac{\text{Mass}}{\text{Volume}}$$
>
> *Divide by 1000 to convert cm³ to dm³* $\rightarrow$
> $$= \frac{3.6g}{\left(\frac{80cm^3}{1000}\right)} = \textbf{45g/dm}^3$$
>
> **Example 2**
> Calculate the concentration of the solution when 105g sodium chloride is dissolved in 3 litres of water.
>
> $$\text{Concentration} = \frac{\text{Mass}}{\text{Volume}}$$
>
> *1 litre is the same as 1dm³* $\rightarrow$
> $$= \frac{105g}{3dm^3} = \textbf{35g/dm}^3$$
>
> **Example 3**
> $100cm^3$ copper sulfate is prepared at a concentration of $52g/dm^3$. Calculate the mass.
>
> Rearrange the formula…
>
> $$\text{Mass} = \text{Concentration} \times \text{Volume}$$
>
> $$\text{Mass} = 52g/dm^3 \times \frac{100}{1000} dm^3$$
>
> $$= \textbf{5.2g}$$
>
> **Example 4**
> Calculate the mass of solute if the concentration of a solution is $42g/dm^3$ and the volume is $2dm^3$.
>
> $$\text{Mass} = \text{Concentration} \times \text{Volume}$$
>
> $$\text{Mass} = 42g/dm^3 \times 2dm^3 = \textbf{84g}$$

Standard Solutions

The concentrations of **standard solutions** are known accurately. Therefore, these solutions can be used to measure the concentration of other solutions. A standard procedure is used to make up the solution.

For example, the following method is used to make up a standard solution of copper sulfate:

1. Weigh out 5g copper sulfate in a beaker.
2. Transfer the solid copper sulfate into a volumetric flask using a short-stem funnel. Wash the funnel and beaker with distilled water. Pour the washings into the volumetric flask (this will ensure that all of the solid has been transferred).
3. Add distilled water to the flask until it is about three-quarters full. Place the stopper in the top and gently shake until all the solid is dissolved.
4. Place the flask on a level surface and fill it up with water until the level of solution reaches the $100cm^3$ mark.

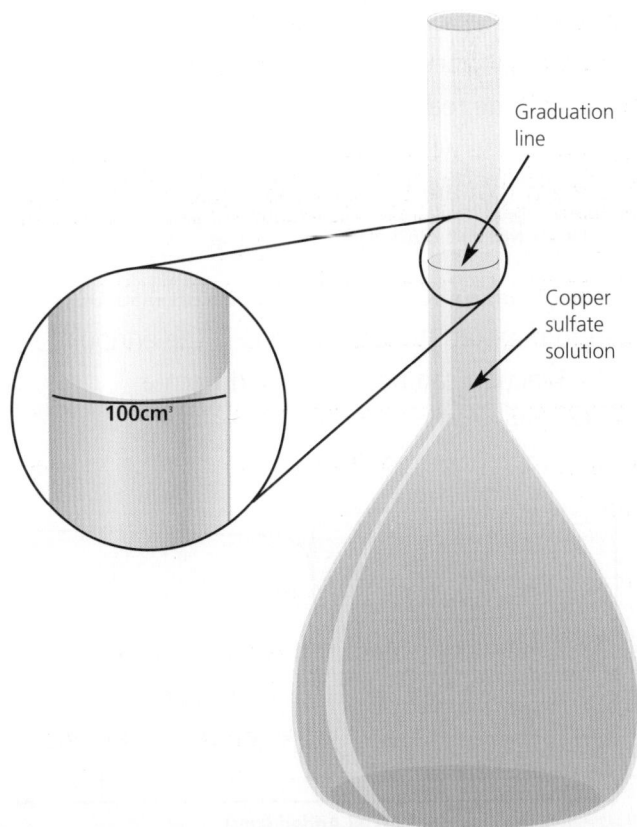

Graduation line

Copper sulfate solution

$100cm^3$

Further Chemistry

Quantitative Analysis by Titration

Acid–alkali titration is a very important method of quantitative analysis. You must be able to apply the procedure outlined below to different situations:

1. Fill a burette with the alkali (the concentration of the alkali must be known) and take an initial reading of the volume.

2. Accurately weigh out a 4g sample of solid acid and dissolve it in $100cm^3$ of distilled water.

3. Use a pipette to measure $25cm^3$ of the aqueous acid and put it into a conical flask. Add a few drops of an indicator (e.g. phenolphthalein) to the conical flask. (The indicator will show its acidic colour.) Place the flask on a white tile under the burette.

4. Add the alkali from the burette to the acid in the flask drop by drop. Swirl the flask to ensure it mixes well. Near the end of the reaction, the indicator will start to turn the alkali colour, e.g. pink for phenolphthalein. Keep swirling and adding the alkali until the indicator is completely pink, showing that the acid has been neutralised.

5. Record the volume of the alkali added by subtracting the amount in the burette at the end of the reaction from the starting value.

6. Repeat the whole procedure until you get two results that are the same, or repeat three times and take the average.

As well as an indicator, a pH probe can also be used to measure the change in pH. The endpoint of the reaction can be determined from a pH/volume graph.

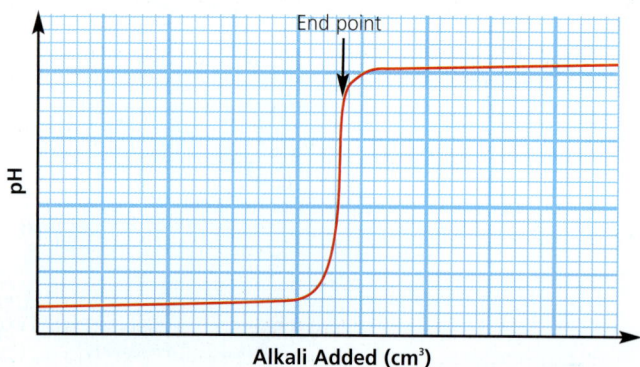

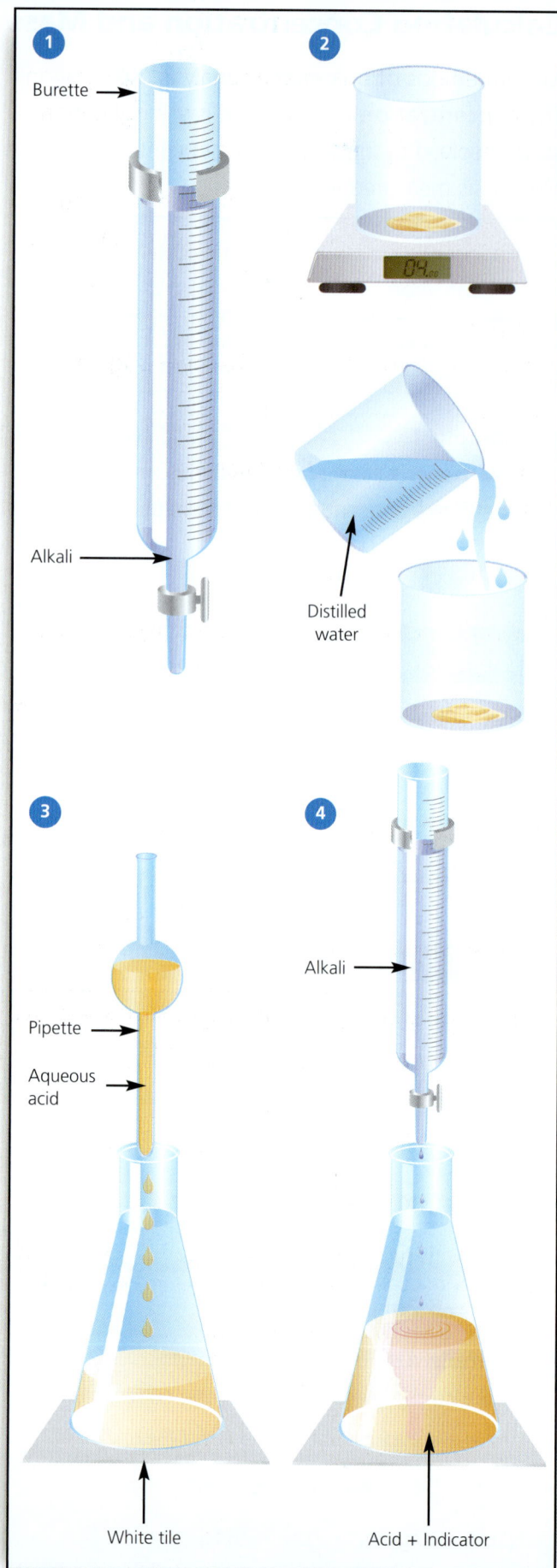

Interpreting Results

When asked to interpret the results of a titration experiment you may be given all the information required to carry out the calculation.

You will be given the titration formula and you need to be able to substitute the correct numbers and work out the final answer.

Example

Concentration of sodium hydroxide = 30g/dm³

Volume of sodium hydroxide = 25cm³

Volume of hydrochloric acid added:
Experiment 1: 10.0cm³
Experiment 2: 9.9cm³
Experiment 3: 10.1cm³

a) Work out the average volume of hydrochloric acid used in the three experiments.

$$\text{Average volume} = \frac{10.0cm^3 + 9.9cm^3 + 10.1cm^3}{3}$$

$$= \textbf{10cm}^3$$

b) Using the given formula, calculate the concentration of hydrochloric acid.

N.B. One molecule of hydrochloric acid reacts with one molecule of sodium hydroxide.

| Concentration of acid | = | Volume x Concentration NaOH (g) / Volume HCl |

$$\text{Concentration} = \frac{\left(\frac{25cm^3}{1000}\right) \times 30g/dm^3}{\left(\frac{10cm^3}{1000}\right)}$$

You must work in dm³ when doing concentration calculations. To convert cm³ to dm³, divide by 1000.

$$= \frac{0.75g/dm^3}{0.01g/dm^3}$$

$$= \textbf{75g/dm}^3$$

You must be able to interpret the results of a titration using a balanced equation and the relative formula masses (see p.54). Use the steps in the worked example below.

Example

A titration is carried out and 35cm³ sulfuric acid of concentration 60g/dm³ neutralises 25cm³ of sodium hydroxide. Calculate the concentration of sodium hydroxide.

1 Work out the relative formula mass of the acid and alkali.

$$H_2SO_4 = 2 + 32 + (4 \times 16) = 98$$

$$NaOH = 23 + 16 + 1 = 40$$

2 Write down the equation.

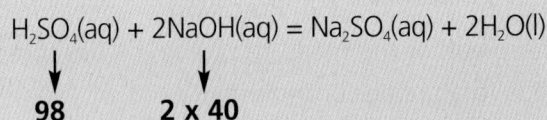

$$H_2SO_4(aq) + 2NaOH(aq) = Na_2SO_4(aq) + 2H_2O(l)$$

$$98 \qquad 2 \times 40$$

This means that 98g of sulfuric acid reacts with 80g of sodium hydroxide.

3 Work out the mass of sulfuric acid used in the titration.

$$\text{Mass} = \text{Concentration} \times \text{Volume}$$

$$= 60g/dm^3 \times \left(\frac{35cm^3}{1000}\right)$$

$$= \textbf{2.1g}$$

4 Work out the mass of sodium hydroxide used in the reaction.

If 98g of sulfuric acid reacts with 80g of sodium hydroxide, then 2.1g reacts with $\frac{2.1}{98} \times 80g$ = 1.7g sodium hydroxide.

5 Work out the concentration of sodium hydroxide.

$$\text{Concentration} = \frac{\text{Mass}}{\text{Volume}}$$

$$= \frac{1.7}{\left(\frac{25cm^3}{1000}\right)}$$

$$= \textbf{68g/dm}^3$$

Further Chemistry

Estimating the Reliability of Results

The validity of an experiment can depend on the accuracy of the results.

Inaccurate results can be the result of errors of measurements or mistakes. Mistakes are errors that are introduced when the person undertaking the experiment does something incorrectly, for example…
- misreading a scale
- forgetting to fill a burette up to the correct level
- taking a thermometer out of the solution to read the scale.

There are two general sources of measured uncertainty: **systematic** errors and **random** errors.

Accuracy describes how close a result is to the true value or 'actual' value. **Precision** is a measure of the spread of the measured values. A big spread leads to a greater uncertainty.

The degree of uncertainty is often assessed by working out the average results and stating the range.

Example

In an experiment the following repeat measurements of a concentration were taken: $72.0g/dm^3$, $72.4g/dm^3$, $71.9g/dm^3$, $72.1g/dm^3$, $71.8g/dm^3$

Calculate the average result and degree of uncertainty.

The average result:

$$\frac{72.0 + 72.4 + 71.9 + 72.1 + 71.8}{5}$$

$$= \textbf{72.04g/dm}^3$$

The range is from $71.8g/dm^3$ to $72.4g/dm^3$

This gives an overall uncertainty of $0.6g/dm^3$

Percentage error $= \dfrac{0.6g/dm^3}{72.04g/dm^3} \times 100$

$$= \textbf{0.83\%}$$

Certainty is $100 - 0.83 = \textbf{99.17\%}$

This result may be quoted as 99.17+/- 0.83% certain.

Systematic Errors

Systematic errors mean that repeat measurements are consistently too high or low. This could result from an incorrectly calibrated flask.

For example, a burette reading could be plus or minus $0.5cm^3$. In the diagram below the burette reading is $0.05cm^3$ out due to poor calibration. This means that when the meniscus is on the line, the actual volume is $25.05cm^3$.

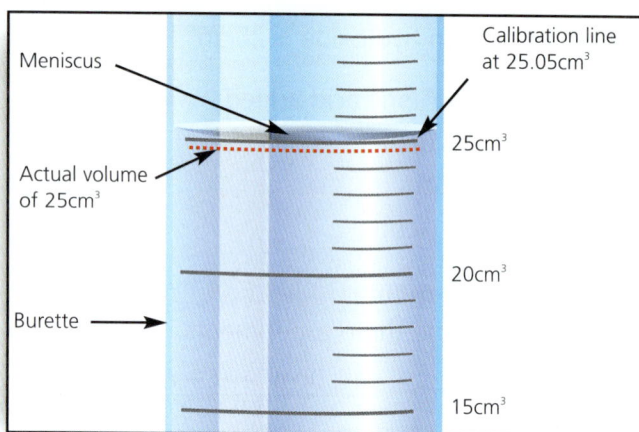

If the burette is used at a different temperature from the temperature it was calibrated at, then a systematic error might be introduced.

Random Errors

Random errors mean that repeat measurements give different values. For example, repeat measurements can introduce random errors because the meniscus is not on the calibration line.

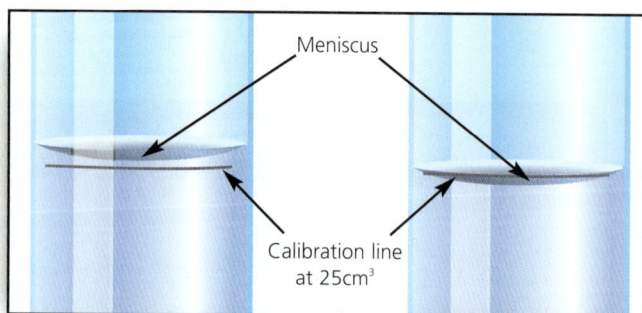

The endpoint of a titration can be determined by using a pH meter or light sensor. It can also be detected using the naked eye, but this method may introduce random errors.

Further Chemistry

The Chemical Industry

The chemical industry synthesizes chemicals on different scales according to their value.

Bulk chemicals are made on a large scale, for example...

- ammonia
- sulfuric acid
- sodium hydroxide
- phosphoric acid.

Fine chemicals are made on a small scale, for example...

- drugs
- food additives
- fragrances.

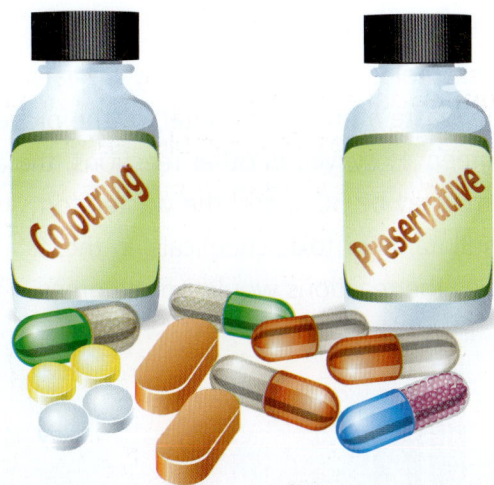

New chemical products or processes are the result of an extensive programme of research and development, for example, researching catalysts for new processes.

Products have to be thoroughly tested to ensure that they are effective and safe to use.

Health and Safety

Governments have a duty to protect people and the environment from any dangers that could occur as a result of procedures involving chemicals.

They impose strict regulations in order to control...

- chemical processes
- the storage of chemicals
- the transportation of chemicals
- the research and development of chemicals.

In the UK, the Health and Safety Executive (HSE) is responsible for the regulation of risks to health and safety arising from the extraction, manufacture and use of chemicals. For example, all hazardous chemicals need to be labelled with the standard hazard symbols.

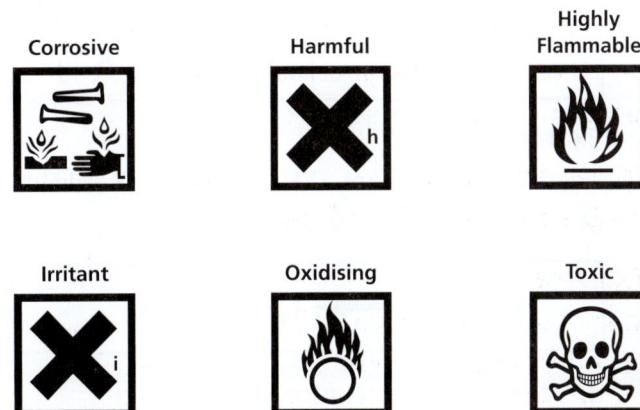

Corrosive

Harmful

Highly Flammable

Irritant

Oxidising

Toxic

More recently, legislation has been passed to encourage companies to reduce the amount of pollution they produce.

Working in the Chemical Industry

In your exam, you need to be able to interpret information about the work done by people who make chemicals. In general terms, you may need to know that chemists are required to...

- follow standard procedures, for example, when making up a solution (see p. 73)
- carry out a titration (see p. 74)
- scale up production
- interpret results
- carry out quality assurance.

Further Chemistry

Green Chemistry

The production of useful chemicals involves several stages, including…

- preparation of feedstocks
- synthesis
- separation of products
- handling of by-products and waste
- monitoring purity.

Green chemistry is based on a number of principles, which if followed lead to more **sustainable** processes. They have been summed up as follows:

1 Atom Economy

The final product should aim to contain all the atoms used in the process, thereby reducing waste products and increasing the yield.

$$\text{Atom economy} = \frac{\text{Mass of atoms in the product}}{\text{Mass of atoms in the reactants}} \times 100$$

Example

Heating cyclohexanol, $C_6H_{11}OH$, in the presence of a catalyst produces cyclohexene, C_6H_{11}.

$$C_6H_{11}OH \longrightarrow C_6H_{10} + H_2O$$

a) What is the percentage yield if 10.0g cyclohexanol gives 7.5g of cyclohexene?

Calculate the relative formula masses:
$$(12 \times 6) + (1 \times 12) + 16 = (12 \times 6) + (1 \times 10)$$
$$72 + 12 + 16 = 72 + 10$$
$$100 = 82$$

We know from the equation that 100g of cyclohexanol produces 82g of cyclohexene.

So, theoretical yield from 10g $= \dfrac{10}{100} \times 82$

$$= 8.2g$$

$$\text{Percentage yield} = \frac{\text{Actual yield}}{\text{Theoretical yield}} \times 100$$

Percentage yield $= \dfrac{7.5}{8.2} \times 100$

$$= \mathbf{91.5\%}$$

N.B. This is a good yield for a preparation, but there is still some waste.

b) Calculate the atom economy, assuming that all the catalyst is re-used.

Total number of atoms in reactant
$= 6C, 12H, 1O\ (A_r = 100)$

Total number of **green atoms** in product
$= 6C, 10H\ (A_r = 82)$

Total number of **brown atoms** ending as waste
$= 2H, 1O\ (A_r = 18)$

Atom economy $= \dfrac{82}{100} \times 100$

$$= \mathbf{82\%}$$

In this example, the atom economy is relatively high, and the waste atoms form water, so the process is quite green. However, in other reactions, the atom economy may be 50% and the waste atoms may form pollutants or toxic chemicals. In these examples the reactions would not be green.

② Use of Renewable Feedstocks

Whenever possible, a renewable raw material should be used. Crude oil (non-renewable) is currently the main source of chemical feedstocks.

Several companies are developing new materials from plants, but plants take up a lot of land. Fertilizers can be used to increase productivity but they use up a lot of energy during manufacture.

③ Energy Inputs or Outputs

The energy needed to carry out a reaction should be minimised in order to reduce the environmental and economic impact. Where possible, the processes should be carried out at ambient temperature and pressure. Using catalysts make reactions more efficient and can significantly reduce the amount of energy needed in the process.

④ Health and Safety Risks

Substances used in a chemical process should be chosen to minimise the risk of chemical accidents, including explosions and fires.

Methods need to be developed to detect harmful products before they are made.

⑤ Prevention

If waste is not made, then it will not have to be cleaned up.

⑥ Environmental Impact

The environmental impact can be reduced by using alternatives to hazardous chemicals.

Efficient chemical products could be designed that pose minimal harm to people or the environment. They should be able to be broken down into non-toxic substances that do not stay in the environment.

⑦ Social and Economic Benefits

Social benefits include cleaner air quality and generally less creation of pollution. This will lead to cleaner buildings in towns and improved water quality in rivers and lakes.

Economic benefits include reduced energy costs, as many industrial processes will be operated at lower temperatures and pressures.

Sustainable Development

The chemical industry carries out research and development to ensure that its processes are **sustainable**, i.e. they meet the needs of present generations without compromising future generations.

Sustainability of any chemical process depends on the principles of Green chemistry.

In recent years, there has been a lot of research and development into **catalysts**. A large reaction can be created using only a small amount of energy and, as the catalyst remains unchanged, it can be used over and over again. This makes the process more sustainable.

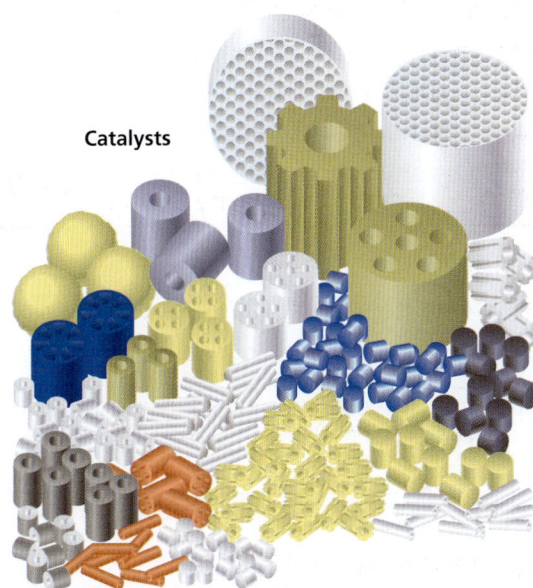

Catalysts

Catalysts reduce the **activation energy** needed for a reaction – this makes the reaction go faster. This can be illustrated using an energy level diagram.

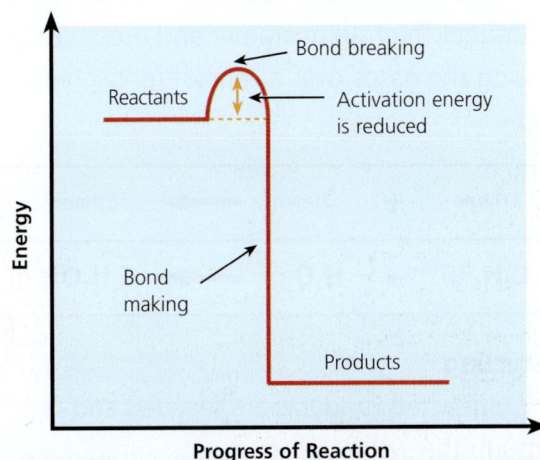

Progress of Reaction

Further Chemistry

The Production of Ethanol

Ethanol can be produced by three methods:

- Synthesis.
- Fermentation.
- Biotechnology.

Method 1: Synthesis

Raw materials: crude oil and steam.
Product: produces up to 96% pure ethanol on an industrial scale and is used as a feedstock, solvent or fuel.

1 **Preparation of Feedstock**

Crude oil undergoes fractional distillation. The fractions containing the long-chained hydrocarbons are collected. The alkanes are then heated until they vaporise. The molecules are cracked by passing the vapour over a catalyst at…

- high temperature (300°C)
- 60–70 atmospheres pressure.

After purification by further fractional distillation, the ethene molecules produced in the cracking process are used for feedstock.

The remaining 4% water is removed by zeolites, which absorb the water molecules to produce pure ethanol. This method replaced the old dehydration method, which used more energy and produced carcinogenic by-products.

2 **Synthesis of Ethanol**

Ethene is continuously reacted with steam at a moderately high temperature and pressure by passing the gases over a catalyst (phosphoric acid).

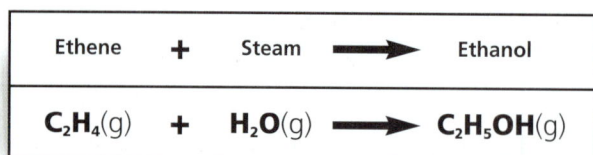

Ethene	+	Steam	$\longrightarrow$	Ethanol
$C_2H_4(g)$	+	$H_2O(g)$	$\longrightarrow$	$C_2H_5OH(g)$

3 **Recycling**

Any unreacted products are recycled and fed through the system again.

Method 2: Fermentation

Raw materials: natural sugars, yeast and water.
Product: wine (produces up to approx. 15% alcohol by volume).

Water and yeast are mixed with the natural sugars contained in fruits at just above room temperature. Enzymes (biological catalysts), found in the yeast, react with the sugars to form ethanol and carbon dioxide. The carbon dioxide is allowed to escape from the reaction vessel, but air is prevented from entering it.

Water **+** Sugars **+** Yeast $\longrightarrow$ Ethanol **+** Carbon dioxide
$C_6H_{12}O_6(aq) \longrightarrow 2C_2H_5OH(g) + 2CO_2(aq)$

Temperature and **pH** are important factors to consider when determining optimum conditions for the fermentation process. Enzymes use a 'lock and key mechanism', which means that a specific reactant fits into a specific enzyme. If the temperature of the reaction rises too much, the enzyme is **denatured** (the shape is irreversibly changed) and the reactant can no longer fit into the enzyme.

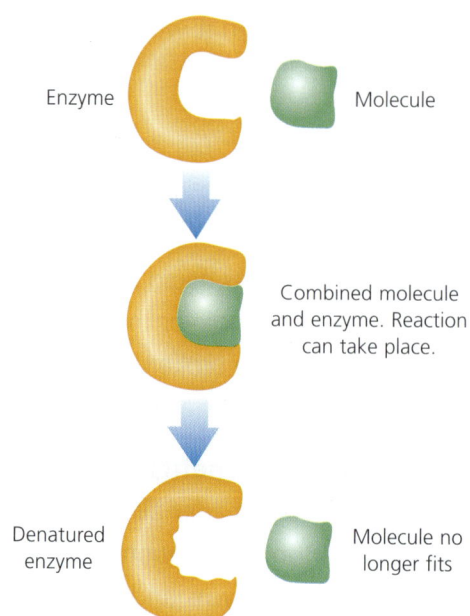

Enzyme — Molecule

Combined molecule and enzyme. Reaction can take place.

Denatured enzyme — Molecule no longer fits

If the pH of the mixture changes too much the enzyme may also become denatured due to attractions of excess H^+ or OH^- ions.

When ethanol solution is manufactured by fermentation the concentration is limited. The main limiting factors are…

- the amount of sugar in the mixture (the reaction will stop once the sugar is all used up)
- the enzymes in the yeast (if the concentration of ethanol rises above approx. 15%, the enzymes will die of alcohol poisoning and the reaction will stop).

When the fermentation reaction is over, the concentration of the ethanol may be **increased** by distilling the mixture. This distillation process produces spirits such as whisky and brandy. In some distilleries the whisky is distilled twice.

Method 3: By Biotechnology

Raw materials: waste biomass and genetically engineered *E.coli* bacteria.
Product: ethanol with a 90–95% efficiency.

The biotechnology method uses genetically modified *E.coli* bacteria that have had new genes introduced. The new genes allow the bacteria to digest all the sugars in the biomass and convert them into ethanol.

This means that a wider range of biomass, such as wood waste, corn stalks and rice hulls, can be converted to ethanol, rather than remaining as waste. This method still needs a variety of organic substrates for bacterial metabolism and growth.

The optimum temperature for this reaction is 25–37°C. The optimum pH level needs to remain fairly constant otherwise the enzyme will be **denatured**.

Interpreting the Processes

In your exam, you will need to be able to interpret information about the three processes used to produce ethanol, and evaluate their sustainability.

For example, you may be supplied with the following information and be asked a question, such as 'Is fermentation or biotechnology the most sustainable method of producing ethanol? Explain your answer'.

Ethanol is an important raw material found in fuels, paints, cosmetics and polymers. Ethanol can be produced by three different methods; the advantages and disadvantages are listed below:

Synthetic Method

- High energy usage.
- Toxic by-products produced.
- A purification stage is needed.
- Uses non-renewable raw materials.
- Ethene is converted to ethanol using steam and a catalyst.

Fermentation Method

- Uses renewable raw materials, e.g. sugar cane.
- Carbon-neutral process.
- Some household waste can be used to produce ethanol.
- Large areas of land are needed to grow specific crops as the raw materials.
- Only part of the plant material is used; the rest can be used to make animal feedstocks.
- Sugars are converted into ethanol and carbon dioxide.

Biotechnology Method

- Raw materials are waste biomass and not specifically grown for ethanol production.
- Genetically engineered *E.coli* bacteria are used to convert plant sugars into ethanol.
- Carbon-neutral process.

Ideas in Context

The Exam Paper

One of the aims of OCR Twenty First Century Chemistry is to develop your knowledge and understanding of key scientific explanations and ideas, so that you can evaluate information about important science-based issues and make informed personal decisions when required.

In addition to your practical investigation and case study, you will have to sit three exams.

The first two papers will focus on the scientific explanations and ideas covered in Modules 1–3 and Modules 4–6 respectively (covered on pages 4–60 of this revision guide).

The third paper will cover Module 7, Further Chemistry, and also your understanding of Ideas in Context. The Idea in Context question(s) will be based on current science-based issues (which you may well be aware of from Coverage in the media).

To answer these questions, you will have to recall scientific facts and draw upon your knowledge of how science works, i.e. the practices and procedures involved in collecting scientific evidence, and its impact on society.

This section of the revision guide looks in more detail at the Ideas in Context section of the Unit 3 exam. It looks at the type of questions that may come up, the format that they are likely to take, and what skills you will need to use to answer them.

You will sit either the Foundation or Higher Tier paper. This will be decided with your teacher during the build up to the exams.

Ideas in Context

Question Format

The Ideas in Context question will be based on a topic covered in Modules 1–6. Each year, the topic featured in the exam is chosen at random. You will not be asked a question relating to any topics that are not covered on the specification.

The pre-release material will be sent to your school before the exam. This material is presented as facts and information about a science-based issue connected to the chosen topic. This could be written information, data (i.e. tables and graphs), or a combination of both.

You will be able to read through the pre-release material in class and look up any technical terms or phrases that you do not understand. You are not expected to do further research, but you should revise any of the relevant scientific explanations or ideas.

In the exam you will be given a fresh copy of the pre-release material and a series of questions relating to the information.

You will **not** be able to take the original articles or any notes into the exam with you.

The questions can take a variety of formats, from multiple-choice and matching questions to data analysis and questions that require a written response. The questions will be designed to test your…

- understanding of the information
- understanding of related scientific information
- understanding of the practices and procedures used in scientific investigations
- ability to identify the benefits and drawbacks of the science and technology involved
- ability to identify the different arguments surrounding the issue (i.e. for and against)
- ability to evaluate the impact of the technology involved on the environment and society.

Ideas in Context

Exam and Revision Tips

- Try to watch the news and read newspapers and publications like *New Scientist* and *Flipside* whenever you can. This will alert you to any topical science-based issues that might come up in the exam. You should be able to find these in your school library or resource centre. You can also find websites for these publications with up-to-date information.

- Make sure that you read the information carefully before attempting to answer any of the questions. Underline key words as this might help you to focus on the content.

- The answers to many of the questions will be in the information, so keep referring back to it.

- The total marks available for each question are shown in the right-hand margin. The marks allocated and the space provided should give you a clue as to the length of answer required and how much information you need to give. For example, if a question is worth two marks, the examiner is likely to be looking for two key points in your answer.

- If you are asked to make a calculation, always show your working. Marks are often given if you use the correct method, even if the final answer is incorrect.

- If you are giving measurements, make sure you remember to include the units of measure and use the correct abbreviation.

- For some questions, an extra mark might be awarded for the quality of written communication of your answer. If this is the case, it will say so clearly by the relevant question and a pencil icon (✎) will be shown. This means that you should…
  - write in clear sentences
  - order your sentences in a logical way
  - pay special attention to your spelling, punctuation and grammar
  - use the correct scientific words.

The next few pages include an exam-style question, with model answers and handy hints on how to approach the different parts of the question.

Make sure you read all the information below carefully before you attempt to answer the questions.

1

Answer all questions.

1. This newspaper article is about a food scare that occurred in February 2005.

Carcinogenic dye causes food scare

More than 400 well-known processed foods have been removed from sale because they are contaminated with an illegal red dye which can cause cancer.

The bright red dye has been used to colour a batch of chilli powder used as an ingredient in a brand of Worcester sauce. The sauce in turn was sold on to hundreds of food companies for manufacture into famous brands of food and supermarket ready meals.

Some flavours of crisps were removed from supermarket shelves.

This table shows how the crisis developed.

28 January 2005	Sudan 1 contamination of chilli powder is discovered by a laboratory in Italy.
1 February 2005	Sudan 1 is found in a brand of Worcester sauce. Environmental health officers are notified.
7 February 2005	Further tests finally confirm presence of the dye.
10 February 2005	The Food Standards Agency (FSA) demands a list of companies supplied the Worcester Sauce for use in other products.
14 February 2005	The list of 200 companies is received by the FSA. The FSA begins ringing the companies.
15 February 2005	The FSA begins telling the companies and supermarkets that they are planning a recall.
18 February 2005	Britain's largest food recall is launched, with more that 400 products withdrawn from supermarket shelves.

Sudan 1 has been shown to cause liver cancer in animal tests. It has not been shown to cause cancer in humans. Sudan 1 is not permitted as a dye for foods in the EU but is used as a colour for boot polish, industrial solvents and petrol.

"At the levels present the risk is likely to be very small but it is sensible to avoid eating any more. There is no risk of immediate ill-health," said the chief executive of the FSA.

A further difficulty is that by the time the contaminated chilli has been used in other ingredients such as Worcester sauce it is present only in parts per billion making it virtually undetectable.

Specimen paper: Chemistry A

Reproduced from an OCR specimen exam paper

Ideas in Context

2

1   (a) Sudan 1 was added to make the chilli powder bright red.

      (i) Suggest why the manufacturers wanted the chilli powder to be bright red.

Because chillies are red OR to look attractive OR to attract buyers.

.... [1]   **1**

      (ii) Why was it not a good idea to add Sudan 1 to chilli powder?

2 → It has been found to cause liver cancer (in animal tests).

.... [1]

3 → (iii) Sudan 1 has a variety of uses that are not connected with food.
Describe one of these uses.

A colouring for boot polish OR industrial solvents OR petrol

.... [1]

4 → (b) How long did it take from the discovery of Sudan 1 in a brand of Worcester sauce to the
recall of contaminated food from UK supermarkets?

.... 17 days [1]   **5**

Specimen paper: Chemistry A

1 Look at the marks for each question (given on the right-hand side of the question paper) – this will give you a clue as to how much information you need to give. This question is worth one mark, so although there are several points that would be correct, you only need to give one.

2 Your answer does not have to be word perfect; there are several different wordings that are acceptable as an answer here, e.g. it is a carcinogenic / it causes cancer. The most important thing is that your answer clearly states that Sudan 1 has a connection with causing cancer.

3 Make sure that you read the question carefully. There are several uses that could be given here, but the question only requires one use, so do not waste your time giving more than one use.

4 This question is testing your understanding of the information given. By referring back to the text you should be able to work out the answer.

5 For this question, the answer of 18 days would also be accepted.

3

(c) Over 400 food products were removed from supermarket shelves.

Describe how the Sudan 1 contamination got into so many food products.

✎ One mark will be for a clear ordered answer.

Sudan 1 was added to chilli powder. The chilli powder was used to make

Worcester sauce and this sauce was used as an ingredient in a wide variety

of food products.

[3 + 1]

(d) The chief executive of the FSA says that the risk from eating these foods contaminated with Sudan 1 is very small.

Suggest why the risk is small.

The amount of Sudan 1 in food products is very small and it has not been

shown to cause cancer in humans. [2]

(e) Scientists test a brand of meat pie for the presence of Sudan 1.

They test samples from two different supermarkets.

Results of their tests are shown in the table.

	Sudan 1 content in ppm							
sample	1	2	3	4	5	6	range	average
supermarket **A**	16	13	19	15	12	14	12 to 16	14
supermarket **B**	12	10	13	14	12	11	_____	_____

Specimen paper: Chemistry A

6 This question is worth four marks. The pencil symbol ✎ means you will gain an extra mark if your answer is ordered into clear, logical statements. Make sure that your spelling, punctuation and grammar are all correct.

7 Again, make sure that you look at the mark scheme. This question is worth two marks so you need to supply at least two points to gain full marks. You will receive one mark for commenting on the amount of Sudan 1 in food products, and one mark for saying that there has been no link with Sudan 1 causing cancer in humans.

Ideas in Context

(i) The scientists test several samples from each supermarket.
     Suggest why.

8 →

To increase reliability OR to get a mean / average OR to identify / discard outliers OR because the content in a sample varies OR to avoid a one-off error.   [3]

(ii) The scientists work out the range and average for the samples from supermarket **A**. They ignore the value for sample 3.

9 →

     Suggest why.

It is an outlier.

[1]

(iii) Work out the range and best estimate for the samples from supermarket **B**.

← 10

Range = ..10..

to ..14.. ppm

Best estimate = ..12.. ppm

[2]

[Total: 16]

Specimen paper: Chemistry A

---

8 This sample answer gives all five options that would be accepted as an answer. You only need to supply three of the options as indicated by the mark scheme.

9 This question requires you to recall information from your science knowledge, i.e. being able to recognise an outlier. This is why it is important for you to revise thoroughly before the exam.

Even if you cannot remember the technical term, you can still gain a mark if you can explain why the value would be ignored. For example, the answer 'it is far different from all of the other results' would also be accepted.

10 This question is a bit harder than the rest, because the answer is not in the text; you need to calculate the range and average values. But do not be put off – it just requires a bit of careful thinking and using your knowledge.

Acid – an aqueous compound with a pH value less than 7.

Activation energy – the minimum amount of energy required to cause a reaction.

Alkali – a substance that has a pH value higher than 7.

Aqueous solution – a solution made when a solute dissolves in water.

Atmosphere – the layer of gas surrounding the Earth.

Atom – the smallest part of an element which can enter into a chemical reaction.

Brown atom – a reacting atom that ends up in a waste product.

Bulk chemicals – chemicals made on a large scale.

Catalyst – a substance that is used to speed up a chemical reaction without being chemically altered itself.

Chromatography – a technique used to separate different compounds in a mixture according to how well they dissolve a particular solvent.

Combustion – a chemical reaction which occurs when fuels burn, releasing heat.

Compound – a substance in which the atoms of two or more elements are chemically joined, either by ionic or covalent bonds.

Crystallisation – the formation of solid crystals from a solution.

Denatured – the state of an enzyme that has been destroyed by heat or pH and can no longer work.

Diabetes – a condition caused by the pancreas not producing and releasing enough insulin, causing the concentration of glucose in the blood to rise to very high levels.

Diffusion – the net movement of particles from a high concentration to a low concentration.

Distillate – the product of distillation.

Distillation – the process of separating a liquid from a mixture by boiling the mixture to evaporate the liquid, and then condensing the vapours.

Electrolysis – the process by which an electric current causes a solution, containing ions, to undergo chemical decomposition.

Electron – a negatively charged particle that orbits the nucleus.

Element – a substance that consists of one type of atom.

Endothermic – a chemical reaction that takes in heat from its surroundings so that the products have more energy than the reactants.

Enzyme – a protein molecule and biological catalyst found in living organisms that helps chemical reactions to take place (usually by increasing the rate of reaction).

Evaporate – to change a liquid into a gas by heating.

Exothermic reaction – a chemical reaction that gives out energy (heat) to its surroundings so that the products have less energy than the reactants.

Filtrate – the liquid produced during filtration.

Filtration – a method for separating solids from liquids by passing a mixture through a porous material.

Fine chemicals – chemicals made on a small scale.

Formulation – mixing ingredients according to a fixed formula.

Fossil fuel – fuels formed in the ground, over millions of years, from the remains of dead plants or animals.

Fuel – a substance that releases energy when burned in the presence of oxygen.

Global warming – the increase in the average temperature on Earth due to a rise in the level of greenhouse gases in the atmosphere.

Green atom – a reacting atom that ends up in a useful product.

Green chemistry – the production of chemistry based on principles that can lead to a more sustainable process.

Greenhouse gas – gases in the Earth's atmosphere that absorb radiation and stops it from leaving the Earth's atmosphere.

Group – a vertical column of elements in the periodic table.

Hydrocarbon – a compound made of carbon and hydrogen atoms only.

Hydrosphere – contains all the water on Earth including rivers, oceans, lakes, etc.

Glossary

Insoluble residue – anything left behind by a reaction or other process which will not dissolve in a solvent.

Insoluble substance – a substance that is unable to dissolve in a solvent.

Ion – a positively or negatively charged particle formed when an atom, or group of atoms, loses or gains electrons.

Isotopes – atoms of the same element but with different numbers of neutrons.

Life Cycle Assessment – an assessment of a product from manufacture to disposal.

Lithosphere – the rigid outer layer of the Earth made up of the crust and the part of the mantle just below it.

Neutralisation – the reaction between an acid and a base which forms products that are pH neutral.

Neutron – a particle found in the nucleus of an atom that has no electric charge.

Nitrogen cycle – the constant recycling of nitrogen through natural processes in life, death and decay.

Non-aqueous solution – a solution formed when a solute is dissolved in a solvent other than water.

Non-biodegradable – a substance that does not decompose naturally by the action of microorganisms.

Non-renewable resources – resources (especially energy sources) that cannot be replaced in a lifetime.

Period – a horizontal row of elements in the periodic table.

Photosynthesis – the chemical process that takes place in green plants where water combines with carbon dioxide to produce glucose using light energy.

Pollutant – a chemical that can harm the environment and health.

Polymer – long-chain hydrocarbon molecule built up from small units called monomers.

Precipitate – an insoluble solid formed during a reaction involving solutions.

Precipitation – the process of forming a precipitate by mixing solutions.

Proton – a positively charged particle found in the nucleus of an atom.

Random errors – repeat measurements that give different values.

Recycling – to re-use materials that would otherwise be considered as waste.

Reflux – a process of continuous heating without the loss of volatile substances.

Relative atomic mass (A_r) – the average mass of an atom of an element compared with a twelfth of the mass of a carbon atom.

Relative formula mass (M_r) – the sum of the atomic masses of all the atoms in a molecule.

Residue – the substance that remains after a chemical reaction or a process (e.g. filtration).

R_f value – the movement of a substance relative to the movement of the solvent front.

Salt – the product of a chemical reaction between a base and an acid.

Soluble – a property that means a substance can dissolve in a solvent.

Solution – the mixture formed when a solute dissolves in a solvent.

Solvent – a liquid that can dissolve another substance to produce a solution.

Standard reference material – a material that has known properties and can be used as a control.

Sustainable – capable of being continued with minimal long-term effect on the environment; resources that can be replaced or maintained.

Systematic errors – repeated measurements that are consistently too high or too low.

Titration – an accurate technique which can be used to find the volume of liquid needed to neutralise an acid or decolourise DCPIP.

Universal indictor – a mixture of pH indicators, which produces a range of colours according to pH and can, therefore, be used to measure the pH of a solution.

Yield – the amount of product obtained, e.g. from a crop or a chemical reaction.

Notes

Acknowledgements

Every effort has been made to contact the holders of copyright material, but if any have been inadvertently overlooked, the publisher will be pleased to make the necessary arrangements at the first opportunity.

The author and publisher would like to thank everyone who has contributed to this book:

p.8   ©iStockphoto.com / Rich Harris
         ©iStockphoto.com
         ©iStockphoto.com
p.10   ©iStockphoto.com / Patrick Hermans
p.18   ©iStockphoto.com
p.27   ©iStockphoto.com
p.49   ©iStockphoto.com / Peter Galbraith
p.58   ©iStockphoto.com
p.61   ©iStockphoto.com / Todd Harrison
p.82   ©iStockphoto.com / Paul I Jsendoorn
p.84   ©iStockphoto.com

Data on p.9 provided by Pfizer
Data on p.16 provided by *Disposable Nappies: a case study in waste prevention*, ©Women's Environmental Network, April 2003; www.wen.org.uk

ISBN: 1-978-1-905896-87-5

Published by Letts and Lonsdale

Author: Dorothy Warren

Project Editor: Charlotte Christensen

Cover and concept design: Sarah Duxbury

Designer: Ian Wrigley

Artwork: Letts and Lonsdale

Letts and Lonsdale make every effort to ensure that all paper used in our books is made from wood pulp obtained from well-managed forests, controlled sources and recycled wood or fibre.

Author Information

Dr Dorothy Warren, is a member of the Royal Society of Chemistry, a former science teacher, and a Secondary Science Consultant with the Quality and Improvement Service for North Yorkshire County Council. Having been involved in the pilot scheme for OCR Twenty First Century Science, she has an excellent understanding of the new specifications, which she has helped to implement in local schools.

Index

Periodic Table

Key

relative atomic mass
atomic symbol
name
atomic (proton) number

| 1 | H | hydrogen | 1 |

Group 1	Group 2											Group 3	Group 4	Group 5	Group 6	Group 7	Group 0
																	4 **He** helium 2
7 **Li** lithium 3	9 **Be** beryllium 4											11 **B** boron 5	12 **C** carbon 6	14 **N** nitrogen 7	16 **O** oxygen 8	19 **F** fluorine 9	20 **Ne** neon 10
23 **Na** sodium 11	24 **Mg** magnesium 12											27 **Al** aluminium 13	28 **Si** silicon 14	31 **P** phosphorus 15	32 **S** sulfur 16	35.5 **Cl** chlorine 17	40 **Ar** argon 18
39 **K** potassium 19	40 **Ca** calcium 20	45 **Sc** scandium 21	48 **Ti** titanium 22	51 **V** vanadium 23	52 **Cr** chromium 24	55 **Mn** manganese 25	56 **Fe** iron 26	59 **Co** cobalt 27	59 **Ni** nickel 28	63.5 **Cu** copper 29	65 **Zn** zinc 30	70 **Ga** gallium 31	73 **Ge** germanium 32	75 **As** arsenic 33	79 **Se** selenium 34	80 **Br** bromine 35	84 **Kr** krypton 36
85 **Rb** rubidium 37	88 **Sr** strontium 38	89 **Y** yttrium 39	91 **Zr** zirconium 40	93 **Nb** niobium 41	96 **Mo** molybdenum 42	[98] **Tc** technetium 43	101 **Ru** ruthenium 44	103 **Rh** rhodium 45	106 **Pd** palladium 46	108 **Ag** silver 47	112 **Cd** cadmium 48	115 **In** indium 49	119 **Sn** tin 50	122 **Sb** antimony 51	128 **Te** tellurium 52	127 **I** iodine 53	131 **Xe** xenon 54
133 **Cs** caesium 55	137 **Ba** barium 56	139 **La*** lanthanum 57	178 **Hf** hafnium 72	181 **Ta** tantalum 73	184 **W** tungsten 74	186 **Re** rhenium 75	190 **Os** osmium 76	192 **Ir** iridium 77	195 **Pt** platinum 78	197 **Au** gold 79	201 **Hg** mercury 80	204 **Tl** thallium 81	207 **Pb** lead 82	209 **Bi** bismuth 83	[209] **Po** polonium 84	[210] **At** astatine 85	[222] **Rn** radon 86
[223] **Fr** francium 87	[226] **Ra** radium 88	[227] **Ac*** actinium 89	[261] **Rf** rutherfordium 104	[262] **Db** dubnium 105	[266] **Sg** seaborgium 106	[264] **Bh** bohrium 107	[277] **Hs** hassium 108	[268] **Mt** meitnerium 109	[271] **Ds** darmstadtium 110	[272] **Rg** roentgenium 111							

Elements with atomic numbers 112–116 have been reported but not fully authenticated

*The Lanthanoids (atomic numbers 58–71) and the Actinoids (atomic numbers 90–103) have been omitted.

The relative atomic masses of copper and chlorine have not been rounded to the nearest whole number.